Margo Kingston was born in Maryborough, Queensland, in 1959, and grew up in the North Queensland sugar city of Mackay. After graduating from the University of Queensland with an arts/law degree, she practised as a solicitor in Brisbane and lectured in commercial law in Rockhampton before joining *The Courier-Mail* as a journalist. Fairfax recruited her for *The Times on Sunday* within a year, and she has since worked for *The Age, The Canberra Times* and 'A Current Affair'. She is a political writer in the Canberra bureau of *The Sydney Morning Herald*.

To my father, John Alcorn, engineer.

Off the Rails
THE PAULINE HANSON TRIP

MARGO KINGSTON

ALLEN & UNWIN

This project has been assisted by the Commonwealth Government through the Australia Council, its arts funding and advisory body.

First published in 1999 by
Allen & Unwin
9 Atchison Street
St Leonards NSW 1590
Australia
Phone: (61 2) 8425 0100
Fax: (61 2) 9906 2218
E-mail: frontdesk@allen-unwin.com.au
Web: http://www.allen-unwin.com.au

National Library of Australia
Cataloguing-in-Publication entry:

Kingston, Margo.
    Off the rails: the Pauline Hanson trip.

    ISBN 1 86508 159 0.

1. Hanson, Pauline (Pauline Lee)—Relations with
journalists. 2. Pauline Hanson's One Nation—Press
coverage. 3. Politicians—Press coverage—Australia.
4. Journalism—Political aspects—Australia. 5. Press and
politics—Australia. I. Title.

070.4088329

Set in 11.5/15 pt Centennial Light by Bookhouse Digital, Sydney
Printed by Griffin Press, Adelaide
10 9 8 7 6 5 4 3 2 1

CONTENTS

ILLUSTRATIONS

COLOUR PHOTOGRAPHS

ACKNOWLEDGMENTS

Phillip Adams suggested I write this book, and Catharine Lumby dismissed my anxieties and dragged me to her agent, Gaby Naher. Sophie Cunningham took on the job of convincing booksellers to put a book about Pauline Hanson on their shelves. *The Sydney Morning Herald* editor Paul McGeough and Canberra bureau chief Michelle Grattan gave me the time and space to write and Gabrielle Hooton did the research with aplomb. Renée Leon helped me believe I could do it. Renée, Gai Stern, Jennifer St Clair, Susan Brennan, Jana Wendt and Mathew Horan read the manuscript in its various guises and tossed up ideas. On the campaign, Paul McGeough delivered cast-iron backing in the clinches and Susan Brennan kept me intellectually honest. Helen McCabe kept me sane, and after the campaign spent hours talking through our experiences and critiquing my writing efforts. Without her, this book would not have been written. Julie Lambert polished my prose and pushed me through the pain barrier when I wanted to give up.

INTRODUCTION

Falling for Pauline Hanson

The 1996 election campaign left me with a sense of discontent beyond the regular price of idealism in politics. Something was very wrong with the political–media compact, and the bottom line for journalists was disempowerment. I certainly had no wish to repeat that experience, though until I went off the beaten track with Pauline Hanson in 1998 I had no concept of quite how personally and professionally challenging the alternative could be.

A modern election campaign is a cocoon. The political minders book hotels for the travelling media and supply the transport. Each day produces a meticulously staged 'picture opportunity' for television demonstrating the day's campaign theme. There might be one chance a day to question the leader if you are lucky. An election campaign is a time when politicians 'look after' the media, and we are assisted in every sense—bar that of doing the job which earns us our privileged position in a democracy, that of asking questions politicians don't want to answer.

In the age of the sound bite and the makeover, political parties are obsessed with scripting and styling. 'Advancers' descend on a site four days and then 24 hours before the leaders arrive, neutralising potential 'problems', mapping every step of the leader's route, and briefing those chosen to meet the boss. The campaign—supposedly the showcase of democracy in action—has lost even the pretence that the leaders are connecting with voters.

By the 1996 campaign, known to journalists as 'the magical mystery tour', this blatantly undemocratic process had begun to atrophy. The leaders were so desperate not to face protesters or voters with inconvenient questions that the daily schedules would be slipped under our hotel room doors on the same morning. Reporters following Liberal Party leader John Howard didn't even know the topic of the policy announcement of the day until it was upon them, and were given policy documents only minutes before a doorstop.

The travelling media, invariably from the Canberra press gallery, were frustrated to find ourselves sidelined by the political leaders' rapturous use of talkback radio. The hosts rarely knew the inside story, often didn't ask the questions the leader wanted to avoid, and were sometimes partisan. Naturally, the leaders began choosing their favourites. For me, one of the defining moments came during a rare Howard press conference for the travelling media. The ABC's Catherine Job—in desperation at the joint Labor/Liberal election lie, that there was no big budget deficit so the big spending promises were kosher—raised her voice and demanded a non-tricky response. 'Whose side are you on?' Howard replied, and the moment was gone. Passion, a driving force of the best political reporting, was passé.

To be a political journalist is necessarily to understand the art of the deal. But any honest look at disillusion in the Australian political landscape has to face up to the media's complicity—inadvertent and otherwise—in the gamesmanship of the electoral process. The leaders and the journalists are actors in a play, bound by intricate codes of etiquette and self-interest. We pick their spin, they pick ours, and both sides look only at each other, as journalists present our theatre reviews to an ever more disconnected public. Little wonder that the public has come to distrust us, the media, as much as politicians.

The election play has become so ritualised that most senior political journalists no longer travel with the leaders, instead ensconcing themselves in head offices, issuing orders to reporters on the road, and packaging election news from the vision and sound sent in. The end product is detached, cynical, looking for the gaffe (the unintended departure from the script) and so distanced from real people and what they care about as to feed into growing public alienation from politics. With the voters locked out of the process, the politician–media pact is beginning to destroy the comfortable certainties of both the political seducers who want votes and the media seducers who want attention to sell advertising.

Pauline Hanson's political birth in 1996 saw voters in revolt. She was a nobody Liberal candidate in an unwinnable seat until the issue of race, John Howard's Achilles heel, flared way off script. Two Queensland National Party candidates talked about 'de-wogging ceremonies' and 'slitty-eyed ideologues'. Howard, quietly fanning resentment against 'minorities' while pretending he wasn't, said the outbursts were National Party leader Tim Fischer's problem. Then the national media picked up an anti-Aboriginal letter Hanson wrote to her local paper. Howard, having successfully papered over his bad record on race, had no choice but to expel Hanson to stop Paul Keating seizing on his failure to do so.

Hanson was thrust onto the election campaign stage by the media to test Howard on race. He pushed her off with full media support. But voters threw her back on as an independent in March 1996, handing her the formerly safe Labor seat of Oxley with the biggest swing in the nation.

Pauline Hanson was a shunned, solitary figure around federal parliament until 5.15 p.m. on 10 September 1996. I was at work in the Canberra bureau of *The Sydney Morning Herald* in Parliament House when a whiny voice on the closed circuit House of Representatives channel caught my attention: Hanson had begun her maiden speech. The bureau members gathered around, mesmerised by her style and grotesque beliefs. It was like an alien had entered the citadel.

Hanson described an Australia under threat from within and without. Her solution was an end to multiculturalism, withdrawal from the United Nations, immediate cessation of foreign aid, and the reintroduction of national service. 'I believe we are in danger of being swamped by Asians,' Hanson said. ATSIC was a 'failed, hypocritical and discriminatory organisation' and the UN was an ATSIC on a grander scale. Her debt to the 1950s rhetoric of Yellow Peril and the simplistic appeal to isolationism was all too clear, too surreal.

As the bureau chief of staff, responsible for selling stories to Sydney, I suggested we ignore her speech. She was just an independent saying ridiculous things, after all. But our bureau chief, Geoff Kitney, said we had to run it. We decided to combine her remarks with the maiden speech of Greens Senator Bob Brown, delivered the same day. And that, we hoped, would be the end of her.

But Hanson proved a hit with the punters on talkback radio and on television. Only one Sydney commercial talkback host, Mark Day, took a strong stand against her views, and his ratings fell as a result. In 1997, Hanson used her momentum to form her own party, Pauline Hanson's One Nation, the first Australian political party to include the leader's name in its title. Her party formation meetings were accompanied by strident, sometimes-violent protests and the occasional black ban by venue owners wary of appearing to align themselves with her racist message.

Midway through 1997, to my surprise, One Nation decided to line up with me. On 4 June, I had appeared on ABC TV's 'First Wednesday' program and made various vitriolic remarks about the dangers of losing diversity in Australia's media. The Liberals wanted to change the law to enable Kerry Packer, Australia's richest businessman, to keep the Nine Network and take over Fairfax, the owner of *The Sydney Morning Herald*, without competition from foreigners. That would mean a further crunching of media ownership from four to three main players. With the ABC under consistent funding and political attack, the Australian media would be dominated by Packer and Rupert Murdoch, effectively signing away the imperative in a democracy of an independent free press.

I was particularly vehement about the dangers of a Packer-run *Herald*.

'Over time, the cream of Fairfax would be cleared out—and the Fairfax culture, the only commercial media culture that backs its journalists over management interference. Once that culture goes it's the end of free speech in this country,' I said. 'That's why Fairfax journalists unanimously have vowed to fight to the end. We're not just trying to protect our jobs. We're trying to protect the meaning of good journalism in a democracy.'

Those remarks brought a flood of congratulatory letters from One Nation supporters and a call from the proudly redneck National Party member for the North Queensland seat of Kennedy, Bob Katter, praising my 'courage'. One Nation's Internet propagandist Scott Balson called to say he was lobbying Hanson to speak out on behalf of Fairfax. Hanson's adviser David Oldfield rang, the first time we had spoken, to run a draft press release by me.

Hanson's 26 June press release on cross-media ownership aligned the free speech arguments for an independent Fairfax with the trouble at her public meetings. It was truly unnerving that the National Party and One Nation—whose constituencies would never see the small 'l' liberal Sydney and Melbourne-based Fairfax papers—joined the Democrats in their total opposition to Packer owning Fairfax and their support for a diversely owned free press. With an unregulated industry, only competition between media groups keeps them honest. Yet despite the institutional democratic responsibilities of the media, both major parties in government had no qualms about a crunching of media ownership. Only the minor parties—the relatively powerless ones—gave a damn.

Around the same time, I received a disturbing letter from a listener to Phillip Adams' Radio National 'Late Night Live' program, on which I talk politics once a week. Ms Susan Leembruggen, of Branxton in New South Wales, wrote:

> 'You have lamented the so-called Pauline Hanson phenomenon, saying that Queenslanders are mostly good, tolerant people—amongst other such patronising comments. Both you and Phillip expressed your contempt and dismay over the consequent rising tide of social discontent—inter alia racism and its perceived concomitant, unemployment. On Monday night you spoke with passion and conviction about media ownership and the importance of maintaining the Fairfax newspaper as the last chance for some kind of impartial freedom of speech.'

Yet what was the point of a free press, she asked, when the media 'had not addressed the real issues of the day—anxiety about unemployment and the disenfranchisement of large sectors of society through diminution of standards of living?

'This media neglect is a significant factor in the rise of Hansonism,' she wrote. 'Instead of academic arguments about Aussie "tolerance and fair play" [remember 'tolerance' really means apathy, not acceptance] and the sense of abhorrence which goes with racism, you could more productively question the status quo in this country that gives rise to division and bigotry.'

In short, Hansonism was partly the media's fault for failing to act as the interface between the people and the powerful, and for turning our backs on the public to become just another part of a complacent establishment. I was loathe to ponder that one, and resumed my avoidance of covering or thinking about One Nation.

From mid-1997 I reported on the Government's response to the High Court's Wik decision recognising residual native title rights on pastoral leases. It was a bitter, intensely emotional and draining debate that had split the nation by the end of 1997, when John Howard first threatened to call a double dissolution race election to resolve the matter. Bipartisan commitment to reconciliation collapsed. Hanson demanded the abolition of native title without compensation and backed Howard's refusal to apologise on behalf of the nation to the stolen generations of Aborigines. Howard in turn refused to condemn Hanson's cultural agenda, raising serious international concerns about whether Australia was in retreat from multiculturalism, a non-discriminatory immigration policy, and the Aboriginal land rights so belatedly won in the High Court.

When the stakes are high the politicians get heavy, and John Howard personally lobbied my editor-in-chief and editor, alleging pro-black bias by myself in particular and the paper in general. Some Liberals called the *Herald* the 'Aboriginal Morning Herald', in protest at the number of black faces and stories in the paper. I argued that the Wik debate was similar to the movement for black civil rights in the United States— and that our coverage must be factual but uncompromising when a blatant injustice was perpetrated on a minority with no clout but the justice of their cause.

In April 1998, the Senate knocked back for a second time John Howard's Wik ten-point plan as racially discriminatory. Howard now had his trigger for a double dissolution race election and he maintained his threat to pull it, despite the horrific divisiveness it would cause.

In May, the Queensland Coalition Government called a State election.

Wik had become a city versus country flashpoint, and the Queensland National Party had no answer to Hanson's populist, impossible and racist pledge to abolish Aborigines' property rights on pastoral leases without compensation. In early June, a Newspoll in *The Australian* newspaper, conducted midway through the Queensland State election campaign, showed a startling resurgence in support for One Nation, which had been languishing in the polls since the screening of a bizarre video Hanson had made for supporters in case she was murdered. The surge, partly driven by the Wik impasse, came amid uproar at the decision of the Queensland Government to give One Nation its preferences. John Howard said he was 'not uncomfortable' with the decision, and told his federal colleagues that the Liberals would also not put One Nation last at the federal election.

From that moment, *The Sydney Morning Herald* changed its focus on Hansonism, moving from seeing it as a sick joke, waiting for the laughter to die down (while paradoxically urging Howard to remove the threat by condemning her views) to treating it as a serious political phenomenon.

Flush with her Newspoll revival, Hanson delivered her 'Queensland election speech' in Parliament, falsely accusing the Coalition and Labor of conspiring to set up separate Aboriginal States. 'Queenslanders will be the first Australians in living memory to have the chance to elect a real alternative to the multicultural and politically correct Labor and Coalition parties [whose] policy fulfils the agenda of overseas interests, not ours. The winds of change blow ever stronger as the day of the ballot box draws ever nearer.'

The next morning, Hanson wandered around the press gallery in triumphal fashion, leper-turned-woman in peak media demand. In a chance meeting in the corridor, she said: 'So how are you going with your work? I hope you're still safe from Packer.' It was my first experience of Hanson's capacity to unbalance her critics. The second was soon to come.

I went to her office to seek an interview and found Hanson alone reading a newspaper. She said One Nation MPs would back a minority National Party government in Queensland in return for looser gun laws and pressure to abolish native title, the first statement of her plans post Queensland election. As I rose to leave, she said, 'Margo, I know you think differently to me. But I like you, you're direct, you say it to my face. All I want is a fair go.'

The Sydney Morning Herald led page one with the interview, headlined 'Enter the Powerbroker'. Some readers complained that we should maintain a policy of ignoring her, and some in the press gallery were also critical. There was strong non-tabloid opinion that the treatment promoted her by taking her too seriously. We argued that she now had to be taken seriously—her poll results were showing she could be an influential, explosive political player.

The *Herald* sent me to follow Hanson for the last week of the Queensland election campaign. I had always covered Queensland elections past because I am a Queenslander, having grown up under Sir Joh Bjelke-Petersen. But this time the editor, John Lyons, had vetoed my going, fearing my pro-Aboriginal stance on Wik would preclude access to the conservative side of politics. Now it seemed I had, for reasons none of us could fathom, 'access' to Pauline Hanson, the most extreme of the conservatives on Wik.

I was keen to go. There was a real chance that my home town, Maryborough, where my grandfather had been independent Labor mayor during World War II, could fall to One Nation. Maryborough was a working-class Labor town always facing hard times, so to swing behind One Nation meant something fundamental must be going on. If I couldn't understand and empathise with it, I felt, I would have lost touch with my roots. I also felt that since One Nation was now a serious force in politics it was important that 'Southerners' understood it and to whom it appealed, so they could seriously address the causes of the Hanson phenomenon. Our readers needed the facts—her political style on the road, her rhetoric, and voter reaction.

Some days *The Sydney Morning Herald* photographer Andrew Meares and I were the only reporters following Hanson, despite the fact that she was engulfing Queensland politics. Those who stayed away, and their audience, missed an amazing phenomenon. Hanson's raw political charisma on the ground was startling, but the sight of whole townships in inland North Queensland gathering for a handshake or an autograph meant she was threatening to become a cult figure with even religious overtones. Then there was the shock of Hanson snaring respectability—true-blue Australian business icon RM Williams asked her to his property for a private meeting, and Toowoomba's millionaire businessman Clive Berghofer escorted her round his shopping centre. He said her policies weren't important. 'Every bloody politician needs a bit of a shakeup. We've got to bring a few of them down to earth.'

My stories described these events and ran slabs of her grammatically tortured, earthy rhetoric so that her voice could be exactly relayed to readers. The Sydney *Daily Telegraph*'s chief political reporter, Malcolm

Farr, also left the Canberra press gallery to see Hanson on the road, and was similarly flabbergasted. His paper splashed with a picture of Hanson holding a baby and the headline 'Queen of the Mall'. 'Not since Bob Hawke was at his most magnetic has a party leader been able to draw the punters to almost universal approval,' he wrote.

On Election Day the *Herald* led the paper with the headline 'A poll to shake the nation'. I wrote: 'Pauline Hanson is no longer the stumbling, gauche, ordinary woman at whom educated and politically aware Australians can afford to sneer...The themes resonating with her people are an anarchistic desire to punish the big parties for their sins, and an energy for political activism generated by the fact that Hanson is speaking their language and expressing their instincts. In an era of the political alienation of the new underclass, Hanson says that rather than wanting experts in charge, "people like people like them".'

One Nation's Queensland election result greatly exceeded poll predictions and rocked the nation. One Nation attracted a whopping 23 percent of the vote and won eleven seats with the help of National Party preferences. Labor picked up Liberal seats in Brisbane partly due to Liberal voters' disgust with their party preferencing One Nation.

One Nation's federal support ballooned instantly, and the political establishment was on fire with panic. If Howard called a double dissolution election, the prospect loomed of One Nation snatching a swag of Senate seats at the National Party's expense and gaining the Senate balance of power. In the rural New South Wales seat of Gwydir, held by deputy National Party leader and Primary Industry Minister John Anderson, private party polling showed an incredible 49 percent of voters intended to vote One Nation.

Within days John Howard rushed into action. He back-flipped on preferences, now pushing for the Liberals to put One Nation last in the impending federal election, and began talks with independent Senator Brian Harradine to reach a compromise on Wik, after having pledged never to amend his ten-point plan. He flew to the Queensland federal National Party seat of Wide Bay, where all three State seats including Maryborough had fallen to One Nation, to be met with antagonism at public meetings and a line-up of new One Nation MPs. My only relative left in Maryborough, a widowed aunt, dismissed Hanson as 'a lot of hot air', but added, 'People won't say how they voted, but I look around and think "Some of you must have voted for One Nation".'

By the time Howard announced the election, on Sunday, 30 August, Hanson's position was mixed. The Wik compromise, under which Howard had made significant concessions to Aborigines, had stymied her chance of easy Senate spots, because without a double dissolution election she needed double the votes to secure Senate seats. The Government threw promises aplenty at disaffected voters in the bush, and watered down its unpopular plan to sell the rest of Telstra. The National Party was allowing its Queensland MPs to take an overtly independent line on Wik and Telstra.

Internal ructions over One Nation's structure, directed against Hanson's joint absolute controllers of the Party—David Oldfield and David Ettridge—and some mad, nasty performances by her new Queensland MPs had also taken their toll. But on Tuesday, the first Newspoll of the campaign showed Hanson's national vote at 10 percent. If she could repeat her Queensland campaign surge, she had a strong platform.

During the Queensland election campaign, I had observed Hanson from a distance. I had not discussed racial issues with her, but it seemed possible her evident racism was based on ignorance rather than malice. I had strongly supported the compromise Wik settlement forced on Howard by her Queensland success—I thought Harradine's fear that a race election would severely set back good race relations and tear at the social fabric was well founded, and that Aborigines could not win a race election. But this was hotly contested ground—many people believed race had to be fought out sooner or later and it may as well be now, on the eve of the new millennium.

I knew there was a lot of casual racism around. I'd been stunned when, as Prime Minister, Paul Keating had told Singapore journalists that 'Australia is singularly devoid of racial problems.' That remark seemed Orwellian. The truth is that we hoped that if racism were not given a mouthpiece, it would, over time, die out. I wanted to test Hanson on race—to find out if she was consciously racist, and if it was possible to communicate on the matter.

I was also questioning the relationship between Hanson and the media, and whether the media was battling to maintain relevance to many Australians. Her success in Queensland had added weight to the argument that the constant bad publicity surrounding One Nation had fuelled her flame. I wanted to seriously engage with her politics on the ground, to see if an open dialogue was possible.

Yet any coverage of Hanson seemed to polarise the country at every level. Throughout my Queensland tour, my purely observational reporting had triggered digs from colleagues at fraternising with the enemy, and some plain disgust. 'So you've fallen for Pauline Hanson,' one senior press gallery journalist remarked. 'You'll have to be disinfected before I see you,' my partner said. My feeling of being personally on trial only intensified during the 1998 federal election campaign.

It was a mistake to believe that Australia had settled a few things about our identity, our tolerance and our place in the world. The celebrity of Pauline Hanson forced all Australians to take a hard look at what they stood for, and to accept the need to return to the debate. In the 1998 federal election campaign, *The Sydney Morning Herald* demonstrated an unrivalled commitment to serious reporting of Hansonism. That involved challenging the party, whose first contact with me had been as a blind grab for a potential ally in the free speech debate, every step of the way.

This is an in-the-moment account of a campaign that posed some dreadful professional and personal dilemmas and shook my fundamental beliefs about the journalist's role. Amid the clash of cultures and personalities, I felt I was watching a train I was on moving in slow motion toward a head-on collision no one could prevent.

Not only were Hanson and her party on trial in 1998. So, too, were the media, the established parties, the police and even the judiciary, who would be asked whether they could appreciate satire of one of the most colourful and controversial public figures the nation has produced. Pauline Hanson's 1998 election campaign trip would be like no other. No cocoon for Hanson. No cocoon for us.

PART ONE

GETTING TO KNOW HER

ONE

Thrown into it at the deep end

DAY 1

One Nation's stunning success at the Queensland State election in June 1998—the first election it had contested—transformed Hanson into a rolled gold political star. She might be an exotic product of the Deep North, but through nothing more than popularity with powerless people she had ruptured the stability of political discourse and become the most infamous Australian politician in the world. Yet entering the federal election campaign just a few months later, Hanson was in uncharted territory. She was about to find out that once you've got a part in the play, especially a part so resentfully conceded, you have to learn the rules—because now you're being watched.

When her seat of Oxley had become unwinnable after a redistribution, Hanson had flabbergasted commentators by deciding to stand for the new seat of Blair, which looked a very safe National Party seat. No one could understand why she hadn't switched to the Senate, where she was guaranteed a win in Queensland. With Hanson to be put last on all major party how-to-vote cards, she would need a staggering first preference vote of more than 40 percent to win. But at the beginning of the campaign, the experts agreed that she had a good chance in Blair, and that One Nation could hold a joint balance of power with the Democrats in the Senate. One Nation preferences would decide the election result, and the Nationals were fighting for their lives. So how would the media cover Hanson's campaign?

The Sydney Morning Herald decided that I would cover Hanson ('access' again), and that no one would cover National Party leader Tim Fischer, a decision I successfully fought on the grounds that it would be unbalanced to cover only one side of the battle for the bush. (We pulled out of covering Fischer after a few days because of cost and a lack of daily news.) *The Daily Telegraph* assigned its Canberra press gallery Wik reporter, Helen McCabe—the daughter of a South Australian sheep farmer—to cover Hanson for all News Limited papers bar *The Australian*. Helen and I, as well as ABC cameraman Marty Helmreich and soundman Dave Fraser, were the only Canberra press gallery members assigned to the Hanson trail. For all its endless pontificating on Hanson and what politicians should do about her, the press gallery—with the experience, toughness and national perspective needed to fulfil the media's institutional responsibility to scrutinise politicians of influence during election campaigns—opted out. Instead, the press gallery relied on Queensland-based reporters to feed it the news.

Helen McCabe and I thought we were lucky to be on Hanson. She wanted to break a lot of rules (or, more precisely, she had no idea what the rules were in the first place), so it was an exciting prospect journalistically. Her party didn't have the money, structure or skills to choreograph a campaign, and Hanson's political appeal was grounded in her contact with real people and their reactions to her, both positive and negative.

Hanson had become a symbolic figure in politics so quickly that many Australians didn't know who she actually was. It was as though she was the hidden underbelly of the Australian psyche, throwing up ideas and values most of us had thought buried or even gone. Now we were here to take a look.

When I'd followed Hanson during the Queensland State election campaign I hadn't questioned her on policy, instead taking the role of observer, trying to set out the Hanson phenomenon for readers and relaying as much raw material as I could squeeze in. But now she was well and truly in the game, and we knew from the Queensland election that—given a whiff of momentum—anything could happen to the One Nation vote. As the fourth major party in the game, One Nation had to be scrutinised like any other—except, of course, that it was like no other.

One Nation, despite months of early election speculation, was ill-prepared to campaign. My bags were packed, but One Nation wasn't ready, and wouldn't be until four days after John Howard called the election, when it would launch its tax policy in Queensland. I was dumb-founded, but One Nation's breach of a basic rule of election campaigns—be ready to start—would be just the beginning.

Brisbane *Courier-Mail* reporter Christine Jackman had rung Hanson on Sunday night for her campaign details. 'I don't want the media,' Hanson had said. But aren't election campaigns *for* the media, as a conduit to the public? David Oldfield's first big campaign job was to get her to change her mind.

She flew to Canberra from Ipswich on Tuesday and I wandered into her office to find a group of One Nation candidates in the reception area. A New South Wales candidate wearing an Australian flag tie asked *Herald* photographer Andrew Campbell to take a picture of himself with Hanson for his campaign poster. Andrew reluctantly agreed. We both felt strange—it is hardly the media's role to help construct party election material. It was to be the first of many such dilemmas when trying to report on a party without nous or cash.

In Brisbane on Wednesday night, *Herald* photographer Dean Sewell and I dined with Helen McCabe and her photographer, Grant Turner. 'The thing about this campaign is that if she doesn't do well, we'll be pulled off the story. It's in our interests that she does okay,' Helen remarked. 'I don't agree. If she crumbles, the story is the decline of the Hanson phenomenon—it's still a great story,' I replied.

■

The campaign began early on Thursday morning in the semi-darkness of the Nine Network's TV studio in Brisbane. Hanson was alone, having driven herself to an interview on the 'Today' show. David Oldfield, in breach of Hanson's explicit instructions, had leaked the guts of her 'Easytax' plan to Brisbane's *Courier-Mail*, giving the media and the experts time to pull it to pieces. Hanson had insisted that One Nation needed to produce alternative policies—to toss new ideas into the ring, to scramble the certainties. Now she proposed a cascading tax of 2 percent every time there was a change of ownership of a product. It was a mad scheme that had been worked on for thirteen years by a fringe group of accountants. But Hanson would not elaborate in the TV interview. We'd have to wait.

Hanson and I had got along fine during the Queensland election campaign. After the interview I began chatting to her, before realising that an 'A Current Affair' crew had a microphone under our noses. I protested at being recorded without permission and Hanson said, 'Welcome to my life'.

Helen and I couldn't believe our luck—Hanson had nothing to do for a couple of hours and she agreed to a coffee at the Nine canteen. We turned on our tape recorders, but she spoke like she was having a chat over coffee with friends. We questioned her on the three themes that would come to dominate the One Nation campaign on the road—race, her character, and the Hanson/media relationship.

We asked about her first reaction to media attention.

'Of course the first day that I was out of it and I was disendorsed [by the Liberals] it was funny, because I was disendorsed the night before and I went to the fish markets that morning and I came back and I was about to turn into my shop, and I thought "holy hell"—there was all this media in front of the shop. And I never expected anything and I just sort of—I just kept going, I didn't turn in. And I had a boot full of fish! Anyway, I got home and I phoned my campaign manager and I said, "I've got all this media at the front of my shop, what's going on?" And of course it was on the front page of the paper. They were out at the fish markets trying to chase me but I just missed them. And then it was constant, full on that day, everything that was happening. Then I realised that night when I went onto Charlie Perkins [a television debate with the Aboriginal leader] that I really didn't have any idea who he was. They said "Would you debate Charlie Perkins on these issues?" because I was talking about the inequalities in the system. Well that night, not having new facts or figures or actually knowing—it was virtually just talking to people, and you knew the perception of what was happening and what was out there, and you knew what was happening in your schools with your kids and all the rest of it. So I suppose what I want to say is, coming from not really having your facts or figures or the knowledge or the real information, now I do. I've gathered a lot of knowledge, I've gathered a lot of information, and probably you build your confidence a lot more with it.'

Wow, a politician who admitted she didn't know what she was talking about on the big policy issue that brought her to public attention. I wondered if anything would have been different if, instead of exiling her from the mainstream and leaving the far right to tutor her on race, others had taken up the race debate with her. Helen asked if she was scared when she first saw herself on television.

'No, it didn't scare me. I probably got cranky with myself that I didn't come across better, with a stronger confidence with myself. Like I said, it's built up a bit more over the time, because I haven't come from experience in the political field, I've just gone straight into it, thrown into it at the deep end with the publicity I have received.'

I asked about an incident after the Queensland State election, when she'd thrown her local newspaper, *The Queensland Times*, out of a press conference and blackballed it ever since. She'd also blackballed *The Toowoomba Chronicle* because it published pro-abortion comments she'd made at a public meeting, a no-no in ultra-conservative Toowoomba. The ABC had once been denied access for eight months—a big disadvantage for any media group. Why was she so critical of the media?

'Because I feel in a lot of cases—although I use the media, by all means, as much as the media uses me—I do not like deceit, I do not like lies. *The Queensland Times* [incident arose] when a journalist wanted to do a story with me; it was to do with how much mail [you get] and how busy your office is, and the letters and phone calls, and everything like that. So she got into the office there and she was taking notes when they were setting in the alarm systems. Well that got her attention—putting in these alarm systems. So she started asking me about the letters, ·but it was no sooner off that than she said, "We've heard that there's a price on your head." I said, "Look, I have heard that," and she said, "How do you feel about it?" I said, "I don't know if it's true or not and I'm not here to discuss that with you." And she said, "Well how do you feel about the kids"? I said, "Look, I'm not going to drag my kids into this, I want them out of it…I don't want people out there maybe taking a pot shot at my kids or anything like that." So anyway, in the conversation she got what she could out of me, and next thing there on the front page of the QT is me sitting in my chair—they just got me at the moment where I had this long, sour, unhappy look on my face—and the whole story was about my security, with a picture of my kids in the corner [a photograph on her office bookshelf]. That's one thing I stressed—I'd try and keep my kids out of it. I know that they're against me, *The Queensland Times*.' I'm telling everyone, I'm telling you, too, don't be my judge and jury. Just print the facts and just let the people judge me.'

That was exactly what I intended to do—get the facts. I had my doubts about whether she'd really learned the lesson she said she had— to get her facts straight before talking about policy—but her tax-policy performance later that day should resolve that query. We asked about her background.

'Being reared in the shop and seeing Mum and Dad work the hours they did—my father, for 25 years he had that shop [Jacks Café in Woolloongabba, South Brisbane] and he worked 106 hours a week. It was one of the best-known shops, and Dad was really well known. We grew up there, and by the time we were old enough we used to peel the onions on the weekend, or we had our jobs—mop the floor or do the spuds or make the chips or we're in there serving. So from the age of twelve, every Saturday morning for two years I worked on the counter in the shop…I left school when I was fifteen and I got a job at Drug Houses of Australia, clerical work, and you got paid $16.40 for the week. And here I was training seniors how to use the telex machine, and then I'd come home and maybe two nights a week I'd work in Dad's shop.

So I'd work from eight till five o'clock at my day job, and then I'd come home and change and I'd start in the shop, waitress on the tables from six and get to bed about twelve o'clock…I'd get $5 for the night, but then I'd walk up the stairs and there's Mum in bed waiting for the board. That was my board money—so Dad would pay me in one hand, and I'd walk up and give Mum the $5 for the board. But it made you respect money. It made you realise that you don't get anything for nothing. And I think that's what's been instilled in all of us.'

I asked whether her ingrained work ethic helped explain her resentment against single mothers getting supporting parent benefits and Aborigines getting extra help.

'There's no resentment. We're not helping them; we're not helping society. You see, what's happening is that people have come to take too much for granted. It's all in your upbringing. No one owes me a living, no one told me to have four children or bring these children into the world. They were my responsibility. That's what I'm saying—people must start being responsible for themselves and their own actions. Stop passing the buck. Look, there was a time in my life when my marriage split up and I had two kids, and my youngest one was six months old when my marriage first split up, and the other one was five. There was a time when I didn't even have enough money to put food on the table. I fed the kids, but I went without. And you got through that, and I've gone on and I've had different jobs, and I met my second husband. He was a plumber, but he never had the business. He would have always loved to but he didn't own the business when he met me, because he never had the knowledge and the experience, and he didn't have the drive. So I said, "You're never going to do anything unless you get in there and do it—right, we're going into business." He just needed that push, he needed that drive, he needed someone behind him. And we ended up running a successful plumbing business and employed three full-timers. I was there behind him, but see on the side what I did was I delved into real estate [she bought flats]. I had another two children in that second marriage, plus his stepdaughter—although we only had her every second weekend—so it wasn't unusual for me to go and drag five kids to the footy ground or drag five kids around shopping. And we had a block of land, and I went and borrowed the money and we built the house, and we went on from there. To pay off the loan I put some of my child endowment towards the loans, and I cut back on my grocery shopping and I did all of my own cooking. Because I used to rent out flats, I had to look after the tenants. And that was my sideline —any plumbing work [my husband would] do, but I'd go round and buy the carpet and at times there I lay the carpet myself. You'd be in there laying the carpets, or you'd paint the flats, or you'd be out mowing the yard dragging five kids. So I had a few flats around the place, but it was all just trying to get ahead a little bit, like everyone wants to.'

This description of her life didn't explain how she'd come to have such strong views on Aborigines, and I asked where she'd got that interest, and how she'd formed her views on the matter.

'Over the years, women used to come into the shop and we'd talk about this, the inequalities at the school and problems that were happening around. Because you'd hear of the Aboriginals maybe getting into problems in the streets, or stealing handbags, or disrupting business, or coming in and stealing things. It was just that talk was around over a period of time. But what happened was that Robert Tickner [the former Labor Government's Aboriginal Affairs minister] actually came out and said, "Don't lock up Aboriginals because it's not working." Now he made that statement because, I think, of deaths in custody, and I thought, "What a stupid statement." You can't go around committing a crime against society and not expect to get punished for it. It's not helping them, it's not helping us.'

I tried to test her on this narrow attitude to Aboriginal disadvantage to find that she turned the tables and began interviewing me.

'If I can just be devil's advocate here, the facts are that there's a great disproportion of Aborigines in custody. Aborigines are over-represented.'

'Why are they there?' she asked.

'Well, there are a lot of reasons for it, aren't there,' I replied.

'What's the main reason?'

'I think a sense of alienation from society—'

'Because they've done a crime. People know what's right and what's wrong, and you don't go out there and commit a crime against someone, you just can't get away with it. It's like you teach your kids. Your kids do something wrong, they go and hit their little sister, what do you do? You give them a smack and say, "Right, that's the punishment for doing it." I keep saying treating the Aboriginal people as disadvantaged—they're not all disadvantaged. You don't have the Lois O'Donohues, the Charlie Perkins, the Noel Pearsons or Paul Coes disadvantaged, are they?'

'No, but a lot of them were when they were—'

'Not now.'

'Lois was a stolen child.'

'Yes, I know, and look what she's done. She's gone on to put herself in that position, whereas she should be doing something for her people.'

'That's what she's tried to do, though.'

'By treating the Aboriginal people as disadvantaged, you are saying they are an inferior race, which is racist in itself. Treat these people on a needs basis. You can't tell me an Aboriginal living in the city, living the way of everyone else, is disadvantaged in another way. It's keeping these differences in policy that is going to keep resentment in the community.'

I protested. 'But for so many years State governments haven't delivered the same basic services to Aboriginal towns or communities that they have to white people. Like, you've been out to those missions; there's no sewerage.'

'Margo, have you had a good look at some of these pastoralists and these people that live in outback areas?'

My phone rang, and I left to do a radio interview after Hanson promised to wait for me. It looked like access to the leader wasn't going to be a problem, although drawing the line between professional and personal might end up being a little tricky. No wall of minders. Just her and us.

■

It felt weird following Hanson in Queensland, from which I'd been a refugee for more than ten years, driven south, like so many others, by the excesses of Sir Joh Bjelke-Peteresen and the claustrophobic cultural and political climate he had imposed for so long. In the late 1980s Sir Joh had given the federal Coalition as big a scare with his 'Joh for

Prime Minister' campaign as Hanson was doing now. Queensland, like Western Australia, is a frontier State, where atrocities against Aborigines continued long after the other States—partly the reason, I thought, for the State's antipathy to land rights. It's harder to acknowledge guilt when you have memories of complicity.

Queensland is unique in that it is the only State where more than half the population lives outside the capital city, making the regions and their conservatism much more powerful in State politics. Many Queenslanders overlay their insecurity at Southerners' superciliousness towards the Deep North with fierce parochial pride, and they revel in upsetting Southerner certainties, both in politics and in often clobbering the New South Wales Blues in the annual State of Origin rugby league clashes. It's an underdog thing—and to many regional Queenslanders, Pauline Hanson was just the person to wipe the smug smiles off Southern faces.

■

At 2 p.m. in a small auditorium opposite Hanson's electorate office in Ipswich, the media—lots of us—were the only shows. She was late, and we learnt later that there'd been a last-minute panic about how she could possibly hold up under detailed questioning. An investigative piece by *The Sydney Morning Herald*'s Marion Wilkinson a week later revealed that One Nation had tried to 'buy' an Easytax spokesman by offering its architect the number one spot on the Queensland Senate ticket. Hanson had vetoed it outright, sticking by her close friend Heather Hill, to whom she'd personally offered the spot. She was about to pay the price for her loyalty.

Pauline Hanson walked in flanked by her main men—David Oldfield and Peter James. Oldfield, variously dubbed her political adviser, strategist, speechwriter and personal Svengali, had flown up for the big day from Sydney, where he was trying to win a New South Wales Senate seat for One Nation. Before hitching his ambition to Hanson's star, he'd been a Liberal Party loser, a staffer for then New South Wales Liberal right backbencher Tony Abbott after losing a contest for a State seat in his power base, Manly. He'd met Hanson at a Canberra bar on the night she made her maiden speech, and after convincing her he was the political brain she needed, worked undercover preparing the launch of Pauline Hanson's One Nation. He resigned from Abbott's employ some months later. Oldfield was a big-city carpetbagger using the One Nation roller-coaster as a fast track to political power.

Peter James, One Nation's Queensland Director and Hanson's media adviser for the campaign, was effectively her handbag. He'd supported her back in 1996 after she'd been disendorsed by the Liberals, had mortgaged his home to bolster party funds, and had left his muffler business in the hands of his wife in order to work for her. He knew nothing about politics or the media, but remained at all times stoic and devoted to Pauline Hanson.

Hanson stood beside a table on the stage and Oldfield and James sat behind it. We tried to collect the policy documents laid out on the table, but were told not to touch till the press conference was over. We would have to rely on her explanations. She outlined in the broadest terms a revolutionary tax change, and asked for questions.

It was hard to know where to begin. What a crazy thing to do—put out so radical a policy on so sensitive a topic for voters during an election campaign. Under Easytax, all taxes, including income and company tax, would be abolished for a 2 percent tax on take-home wages, on sales, and on profits. The plan kicked off a recurring theme in One Nation's campaign: that the best thing to do with our institutions or established policy frameworks was simply to tear them down and start again. Her breathtaking rationale for Easytax: 'The usual knockers have said the system has not worked anywhere in the world, when the fact is this system has not been tried—so actually, it has not failed anywhere either.' She proposed a twelve-month consultation process before implementation.

The press conference was low key and slow paced, with reporters somewhat stunned by it all. The first question brought down Easytax. ABC TV's Lisa Millar asked about vertical integration. If a big company, probably multinational (the ones Hanson loved to hate), owned everything from the chicken to the chicken burger, wouldn't the 2 percent tax on change of ownership greatly benefit the big company to the detriment of small business, which must pay 2 percent on all its inputs? In other words, wouldn't Easytax put fish and chip shops out of business? Hanson agreed that vertical integration was bad and left it at that. (The next day, Peter James announced a review of Easytax to fix the problem.)

ABC Radio's Anne Delaney asked, 'How can you say it's a fair tax if rich and poor will all be paying the same level of tax?' Hanson replied, 'I think you couldn't get any fairer than that.'

'What's the effect of the package on the bottom line? How much less tax will you collect than is collected under the current system?' I asked. Hanson suggested $50 billion (Oldfield later unsuccessfully told Helen and I not to report this answer because 'she didn't mean it'). 'So how will you afford services to the bush, how will you afford your People's Bank with 2 percent interest rates?' The answer? Somehow, because the Government wouldn't be paying income tax for its own employees, all would be well.

Peter James intervened: 'Perhaps you need to just wait and have a look at the documentation that will be provided to you. You're now asking technical questions, you're asking details—I didn't notice that you asked Mr Howard a similar level of question. We have paperwork here, please use it, and use THAT to get your details—don't tie us down here with details.'

A murmur of disbelief. Of whom then, should 'details' be asked, if not to the Party leader? James' remarks made all the news bulletins and all the newspaper reports.

Enter David Oldfield, with a slightly less crude attempt to save Hanson's bacon. Questions about fairness were 'nauseous'; our job was to compare the benefits of the One Nation policy with those offered by the major parties, he said. So what were the comparisons? Calculate them yourself.

A swing through fairyland, a swim through blancmange—whatever it was, Peter James closed it down mid-question and started handing out documents. Roger Maynard, an Englishman reporting for Asian cable channel CNBC, raised his voice: 'Can I ask you how worried you are about your ideas being received overseas?' Oldfield closed him down. 'Excuse me...we're really dealing with Australian media, for Australian voters.' Maynard: 'It's a global village.' Hanson giggled, but Oldfield didn't. 'This is Australia, this is Australia,' he said. Hanson responded to Maynard anyway. 'Actually you might learn something, and take it back to America.'

Outside, Oldfield was on the phone to the ABC, which was trying to cancel Hanson's interview with Kerry O'Brien on 'The 7.30 Report' because John Howard was on, too. Either he, or the ABC, didn't want the pair to run into each other. That sounded like censorship to me, although Oldfield was happy either way—if not an interview, then a cancellation outrage reinforcing One Nation supporters' sense of unfair treatment. Despite her electoral success, Pauline Hanson was still a political leper. While Howard and Beazley were running into each other at radio studios and shaking hands, let there be no sight of Hanson, ever, in the main feature.

But what was the problem—that Howard would give her media space when the idea was to ignore her and deprive her of air time? That she would remind anxious Liberal voters of how accommodating Howard was to her racist views in the early days, or bring back memories of his support for the Queensland Liberals preferencing One Nation? Or was it that Hanson was the personification of something neither party wanted to address? Shunning Hanson meant shunning her voters, an act of symbolic disenfranchisement. Might it have been better to make her an ordinary player in politics rather than make her a martyr in her followers' eyes?

These strange predicaments, which the media had also faced from the beginning in 'handling' Hansonism, were partly the result of a fundamental split in thinking about what the rise of One Nation signified, and they resulted in a rare self-consciousness and discomfort in the media about the political effect of their reporting.

After the 1996 election Howard, who had subliminally appealed to the new underclass and its resentments with his 'for all of us' motto and pledge not to govern for 'minorities', wanted a hands-off approach to Hanson. Let her have her say in the name of free speech, but don't respond directly. The other Liberal camp, with its base in Victoria, saw the seeds of appeasement in Howard's approach. They saw One Nation as a monster of racism and economic isolationism, a fascist organisa- tion that would only grow stronger if appeased. Hanson should be crushed immediately, they believed, by condemnation in the strongest terms by the nation's leaders, and by the unremitting exposure of her party's structural flaws. Victorian Premier Jeff Kennett was a leading proponent of the get-out-there-and-take-her-on school of thought, and planned a visit to Blair to argue his case on the ground.

The third way, constructive engagement—an attempt to understand what was causing this incredible and potentially self-destructive scream from the politically apathetic—was never really tried. So the barriers went higher. Hanson said something shocking on the 'Midday' show; the audience clapped and cheered. Media interviewers tested her out, she faltered, and her popularity went up. Pauline's People felt battered by those who governed them and those who reported the governance. Our sense of national coherence ruptured.

That evening back at the Nine Network studios Hanson recorded an interview with Ray Martin for 'A Current Affair'. I hitched a lift with Hanson and James to the ABC studio, and on the way asked Hanson why she'd taken such a risk by producing Easytax. James was contrite about his disastrous performance at the press conference, but was still confident about his brand of political judgment. 'Strategy, Margo. People will only hear the 2 percent, and they'll like it. Strategy.'

Hanson had to enter the ABC in darkness through a side door into a staff games room. An outside studio broadcast unit had been set up on a verandah. Hanson would be interviewed overlooking the Brisbane River and the river lights, all so John Howard wouldn't have to see her when he left the main studio after his interview.

As we were leaving three press gallery radio journalists who were following Howard emerged from the darkness. They'd come from the ABC's front entrance, where they'd asked Howard about the bizarre procedures in place to avoid a meeting with Hanson and received only a grunt in reply. They wanted to talk to Hanson, who was in her car and about to drive off. I knocked on her window, explained the proposed questioning, and said she should do it because she had nothing to lose. Hanson told them she hoped Howard wasn't trying to avoid her, and she would have liked to say hello.

'Don't stay too long on this campaign,' Louise Maher from Sydney Radio 2UE said to me as she left. I knew what she meant. It was nothing new to me after my Queensland campaign experience to organise things with Hanson directly—but gee, I did look like her media adviser in that little exchange, and she seemed open to my advice. Louise was afraid I'd get 'too close' to be objective, although it was hard to see how you couldn't get close when there were no minders between you and your subject. And after all, the political journalist's job is to get up as close as possible, to get inside the story, to get inside the head of the person you're watching. But the established codes of conduct between the major parties and the media had suddenly been replaced with a void, and I was on my own. I had to find my own balance.

TWO

Please go away from me

DAYS 2, 3 AND 4

Hanson's electorate office was smack bang in the centre of Ipswich, an old Labor city an hour's drive from Brisbane. Once rich on coal and railways and woollen mills, Ipswich was now on the ropes thanks to the decline and fall of Australian manufacturing. The building in which Hanson was housed was named after Bill Hayden, the former local copper turned federal Labor leader and Governor-General. The council room in which she had launched her tax policy was called the Barry Jones auditorium, named for the erstwhile federal Labor president. Centrelink had an office next to Hanson's, and unemployed youth trooped in and out all day looking for hope.

Today the job seekers were joined by a media pack wondering what Hanson would be doing on day two of her official campaign. She dashed out of her office and sped off to a shopping centre, where she ran in and rushed about thrusting her Easytax papers into people's hands, urging them to 'Have a look at it'.

The sight woke me up. On the road during the Queensland election, her secret was to let people come to her. She'd wander along and they'd approach her, whereupon she'd bend her head, cross her hands and listen. Hanson excelled as a channel for grievances. Now she looked like just another politician hawking her wares. The growing, panting media presence—as journalists began to catch up with her—was also taking its toll on her bond with voters. People hung back and looked on.

I tried to find out what she thought she was doing. 'Why did you put out a tax policy rather than doing something a bit vague like "I'll talk to the people about it after the election"? Why did you take the huge risk of putting out a tax policy when you knew the reaction would be all bad?' I asked.

'But hasn't my whole political career of two and a half years been a risk?' she countered firmly. 'Why should I change? I've been against the establishment—what they've done with their own policies, and their views and issues—right from the beginning.'

'So you're prepared to risk all?'

'You're putting yourself up to say right—this is what I stand for. This is what it's all about. Give people out there an idea of what you're about.'

'But why did you become not the alternative to the major parties, which some people liked, but loopy? Why did you put out a loopy tax policy?'

She bristled. 'Who's loopy? Excuse me, I don't like to be called loopy.'

I had thought we were having a private conversation, but the TV cameras swooped. The next day, *The Daily Telegraph* led page one with, 'Don't call me loopy'.

Hanson drove to a suburban street for some Easytax doorknocking. About half the media contingent tracked her down, but not the TVs, who needed time to pack up their gear. Photographers Dean and Grant lined up in the first front yard she approached. An elderly woman pressed her face against the glass of a front window. She did not answer the door. (Snap—page one photo in *The Weekend Australian*.) At another house, a little dog jumped up behind the glass door, again not answered. (Snap—page one of *The Daily Telegraph*.) Hanson kept trying doors without success, shook her head, and told her police escort, 'This isn't

DEAN SEWELL

This image is a news photographer's dream, capturing the divorce between Hanson and many of her voters after Easytax. Her spontaneous doorknocks in Ipswich after announcing Easytax opened her eyes to the impossibility of free-form campaigning with the media present.

working'. She informed *The Australian*'s Leisa Scott that she wanted a meeting with journalists in her office.

Sitting in her anteroom, journalists had a good look at the people who would form the core of the 'Please Explain Tour' for the first time.

All media except *The Sydney Morning Herald* and News Limited had assigned Brisbane reporters, and only Helen and I were expected to file daily. The press gallery, it seemed, through a combination of cost pressures and disdain for Hansonism, didn't want a look for themselves, despite the fact that many of its members commented on Hansonism constantly. *The Age* sent no one on the grounds that Hanson was beneath its dignity and its middle-class readers would prefer to ignore her. *The Australian*'s Leisa Scott—despite urging her bosses to assign one person full time because the campaign was so different—lost the battle. Outside Queensland, the paper's State bureau writers jumped on and off the trail, looked stunned, got lost and wrote another colour story.

ABC Television assigned their senior State political reporter Lisa Millar (to be replaced mid-campaign by press gallery journalist Fiona

Reynolds before the ABC decided a full-time Hanson watcher was an advantage) along with press gallery cameraman Marty and soundman Dave. ABC TV's approach to Hanson, as with everything in the election campaign (everybody knew the Liberals would be waiting to pounce with a bias charge), was scrupulous fairness. They didn't run Hanson often—about as often as the Democrats. ABC Radio chose Brisbane current affairs reporter Anne Delaney—'AM' and 'PM' wanted only news with a hard edge, focusing particularly on preferences. As scheduled, Sydney reporter Stephen McDonell replaced her mid-campaign and more colour stories got a run.

The Nine Network assigned Melanie Wendt, another State political reporter, because Hanson had black-banned the omnipotent Laurie Oakes; and Oakes wanted someone with 'access' to Hanson to smooth the way. Nine didn't want to cover Hanson regularly—'It's conscience, I suppose,' Melanie said—but tracked her everywhere just in case. Nine ran the least Hanson of any TV station.

Seven chose Peter Doherty, a nice guy who'd followed Hanson around Queensland ever since she hit the scene. Unlike the other commercial TVs, who picked up local camera/sound crews in each capital city, Seven assigned veteran Brisbane cameraman 'Ollie' full time. As a result, Seven rarely missed newsworthy footage. The demographic of Seven News is older and more attuned to Hanson, and it ran up some embarrassing figures mid-campaign, with Hanson getting a run thirteen times to the Democrats nil.

Ten assigned no one, relying on the occasional pop-in. Ten News chases a younger audience not generally attracted to Hanson, but the main reason for Ten's lack of presence on the campaign was cost—Ten is the most cash-strapped network.

Here we were, with strikingly different briefs for a federal election campaign, about to embark together on a trip in which it looked like there'd be none of the usual ground rules. It seemed there would be no mutual accommodation of each other's interests through set-piece itineraries and joint travel arrangements, and little or no acceptance by either side of the public hostility/private understanding dichotomy of the standard working relationship between politicians and journalists.

DEAN SEWELL

A despondent Hanson makes her first speech to journalists to sort out some ground rules. She publicly sacks Peter James as her media adviser, at least for the day.

After twenty minutes, Hanson stood before us to make a direct plea for special treatment. 'What we're doing now is because it did not work out very good today with my doorknocking. That's what I planned to do in my electorate. I'm going to spend quite a bit of time next week in the electorate of Blair, and I was going to do very much what I started out to do today—which hasn't worked. Now what I want to do is, we're getting different points in my electorate to organise meetings so that the people can come and hear me, and ask questions of me or my policies. Plus we'll have my Senate candidates or any other candidates there with me. So we're virtually leaving ourselves open for the public to actually ask questions of us and they can sort of come to me. So that's what we're trying to organise now, with dates and times to actually give to you, so you know what you're doing.'

'As I've said, this is all new to me, a federal election campaign. It's different to the State one, because then I wasn't actually out there trying to win my seat. It's very important that I'm electioneering in my own seat as well as trying to do it for everyone else. So I want to work in with you the best I possibly can. I know I'm a pain in the butt, and probably different to what you're used to from working with Howard or Beazley or anyone like that. I'm not trying to give you the slip, if that's what you're thinking. I move, that's it, and I go, and I'm on the move, and that's what I do. So I'll try and give you as much information as I possibly can, and let you know what we're doing. We'll sit down and work this out this afternoon and give it to you.'

She said Peter James had lost the job of her media adviser (he looked down), to be replaced by her number one Senate candidate Heather Hill, who would be on David Oldfield's old mobile phone.

We were stunned. Political leaders never admit that they don't know what they're doing. The paraphernalia of political process was tumbling down. No one spoke for a few seconds.

'Okay, in this new spirit, is there anything else happening today?' I asked. Yes, an interview by local high school kids organised before the election. In a normal campaign this would be considered a picture opportunity, a chance to look good. But for Hanson? She worried about the kids.

'Well, this is unusual for me. I'm just trying to gauge it from their point of view.'

'They'll be rapt,' said Melanie, and the first on-the-spot agreement between Hanson and her media was struck.

Hanson suggested we write down our mobile numbers—'and if we've got something happening I'll get Heather to give you all a phone call and let you know. This has got to work out better.'

'We agree,' Helen said, and everyone laughed.

Hill didn't answer her mobile phone from day one, and when her husband did—which was rare—he never knew anything. Peter James continued as media adviser unless Heather Hill turned up on the trail. One Nation never got its story straight, because it never knew what it was doing. Within days, none of her regular media followers ever asked for itineraries or believed them when they did appear. We were beginning to adjust to a very different election campaign.

Hanson spent Saturday, day three of her campaign, as the official guest of honour at Linville's 21st annual country races. Linville is a tiny town in the west of Blair, near Wondai, where John Howard had faced an angry town meeting after the Queensland election. It is in the State seat once held by the former Premier Sir Joh Bjelke-Petersen, and now held by One Nation.

It was a glowing Queensland day in the bush, and for six bucks you were entertained all day and into the night. The event was a big draw-card around the sparsely populated mid-west, and more than a thousand people arrived with chairs and rugs. All the candidates for Blair—including the forlorn National Party candidate, Brett White—were there. So was the One Nation State member, Dorothy Pratt. Waiting for Pauline.

Hanson was absolutely dressed for the races—transparent shoes with gold strips, a little gold handbag, and a startlingly white top and flowing skirt. Although it was sweltering, she sauntered through the appreciative crowd like a film star, cool amid the sweat and chainsaw dust. The races compere introduced her with, 'Great to have you here at Wondai last Saturday too—now what was the evening like last Saturday?' She looked blank. 'I don't know where I was—I think I'm all over the place.' She giggled, and the crowd forgave her.

All day long intricate chainsaw competitions raged, and a man stood nearby using his chainsaw to carve elegant birds out of chunks of wood, for sale at $65. In the afternoon, a rodeo—and the country Australian ritual of forcing terrified six-year-old boys to ride calves in the ring. Shooters Party types were sprinkled in amid the traditional country people—shaved heads, long beards, blue singlets, tattoos, black sunglasses. There were also scary, *Deliverance* types—jeans around their bums and shirts with the sleeves ripped off. The drinking was constant, and by mid-afternoon men were sleeping it off on the ground, oblivious to the chainsaws. Dean was too different for some tastes, with his McLenin T-shirt and long, tangled hair. A man approached him carrying a hunk of wood and asked if he was an animal liberationist. When assured otherwise, he said, 'Lucky for you, I was going to knock your block off'.

Journalists relaxed and enjoyed the day after a brief doorstop mid-afternoon where we quizzed Hanson on the torrent of criticism raining down on Easytax. 'I don't believe there is an adverse reaction to it,' she said, despite the fact that Peter James had announced a review. But even some of her many fans at the races raised doubts about Easytax with her. By nightfall she'd told an unconvinced supporter that she'd drop Easytax if people didn't want it. Helen happened to hear the back-flip—Hanson had said she'd 'stand by' Easytax at its launch—and *The Courier-Mail* ran it on page one. This turnaround on a key policy within two days proved that to get the story you had to be in her face all the time. Hanson, unused to being watched, did not seem to understand that as a politician she was accountable for what she said. She wasn't having a chat over the fence any more.

A wizened old cabinetmaker called Anton Myck approached and said he remembered me from One Nation's election night party in Queensland. 'I call her the redhead match, you know, and I voted for her to set the country on fire.' Why did he want to torch Australia? 'We've been in a stalemate for twenty years.'

A couple of loud and lubricated young farmers' sons called Scott Haynes and Matt Bahr sidled up to ask Hanson to the bar for a drink. Matt said to her, 'So you have to deal with these journalists in your face all the time? You're causing a stir, you're causing a shitfight. Great! Wake 'em up, wake 'em up.' And then to us: 'Don't put me in the paper, no way, focus on Pauline. The media gives everyone the shits.'

Hanson refused a request to enter the bra-flinging competition, saying she would have if only the media weren't here to make something of it. Scott gave Hanson her favourite drink, the sickly sweet rum and ginger ale. 'Ginger bitch, we all love 'em,' Scott said. Stunned silence.

'*What* are they called?' Helen asked.

Hanson blushed and muttered, 'That's the first I've known about that, anyway.'

Helen had her colour story for the Sunday papers. We decided that 'ginger bitch' had to be a set up, and were amazed that the blokes had been so convincing. We quizzed them later. The drinks really were called ginger bitches. They both *loved* Hanson, and stayed at the bar drinking to her for the rest of the day.

About then, I started to lose my bearings. Normal political instincts were going nowhere but up dry gullies. It was also unsettling how up close and personal she could be when she wasn't running away. As we walked away from Scott and Matt, she said, 'It's good to see that you're in a good mood, that you're happy today.'

'Yeah, I wasn't very happy yesterday; I'm happier today,' I replied, taken aback. Lines of communication open, I reinforced the need for basic rules of engagement. 'It's starting to come together—very good move yesterday. It's ironic, but if you organise your campaign you can actually get your privacy. You can say, "I'm going there, there, and there"—and then you're free.'

By day's end, difficult Hanson/media relations had transformed into something approaching the ease of casual acquaintances. She agreed to have her photo taken with Dean and Grant, and offered to buy a chain-saw bird on my behalf and bring it down to Canberra for me when she got elected as the member for Blair.

She tried to leave the races at dusk, but was corralled by a group of raucous young men, drunk and fascinated, who conducted their own doorstop. 'John Howard, have you met him? What's he like? A prick? He's got to be,' said one.

'No, when I won my seat he actually congratulated me,' she said.

'In other words he's brown nosing?'

'No, he's got a job to do and I have a job to do. The fact is, he is still Prime Minister of Australia, and I respect him for that. I may differ with the points of view, but always remember he is Prime Minister of Australia.'

'So you can't run him down, you can't say anything bad against him?'

'No, there's a difference. You have a go at someone if you disagree with their policies or their views. Don't denigrate the person just for the fact that you don't agree with him.'

'Hey, do you ever go into that big flash building that they're in? Where they all sit and argue and bitch about things?'

'Yeah, I've been there.'

'Hey, Pauline, I've just turned eighteen—should I enrol myself to vote? I don't want to, I reckon it's a pile of bullshit.' Another cut in: 'Do you pick the dresses that you wear?'

Refreshed by a day at a place where she was feted, Hanson drove herself home after stopping at the gate to touch up her lipstick. Grant and Dean rushed over, pushed their cameras into the window, and started shooting. At first, she put the visor across the window so her face was covered up. Then she moved it back and told the boys that, as she was leaving, a woman had said, 'Don't go on TV, it doesn't do you any good whatsoever—you're much better looking in person.' She laughed and continued with her lipstick, posing for the cameras she loved so much when on a high.

■

It was out to the country again on Sunday, to a candidate's training seminar in Gympie. One Nation was so young and raw that its candidates were learning to campaign *during* the campaign. She arrived wearing jeans, riding boots and pursed lips. 'This is off the record. Can I just have you all here, and the tapes off please?'

Overnight, she'd seen Saturday's page one *Weekend Australian* piece on her Friday doorknocking. The headline read: 'I hear you knockin' but you can't come in.' She'd also seen a poll in Brisbane's *The Sunday Mail* showing she could lose Blair. Hanson was about to withdraw Friday's olive branch to the media as it began to dawn on her what she was up against. Most people left their cameras running and tapes on, just in case.

We gathered around her, and she launched into a public flaying of *The Australian*'s reporter Leisa Scott—an excruciating spectacle for everyone. She held up Saturday's *Australian*, her eyes narrowed, and she let fly.

'Now *The Australian* newspaper, which I'm not impressed with, especially the story—JUST HOLD IT!' (A camera had flashed.) 'Now, to the story as you wrote it. "The first door Pauline Hanson knocked on yesterday in her bid to win the new electorate of Blair gave her something she wasn't prepared for—a knock back." True?'

Leisa paled. 'Yep.'

'"The woman in the old timber home in Ipswich popped her head up in the window, looked at her visitor, then the assembled media,

DEAN SEWELL

A frustrated Hanson in full flight, tongue lashing Leisa Scott in front of her colleagues for her doorknock story.

muttered something about being sick and refused to come to the door." Well, she did, but it wasn't really a knock back in the first place.'

She continued reading. '"Ms Hanson smiled, looked uncomfortable"—well, I didn't realise that—"slipped her Easytax policy under the door and retreated. It happened in various forms again and again." What's that—knock backs?'

'People not coming to the door, not being there,' Leisa replied.

'Right, but it sounded as if I was constantly getting knock backs. The truth of the matter was the people welcomed me, but because I had all the media around they weren't interested. And I wasn't intending to spend more than about two minutes there, because I wanted to get as much done as I could. That was the reason—just a quick hello, there it [Easytax] is. But it made it look as if I wasn't interested in talking to them and they weren't interested in talking to me. I had a lot of good responses yesterday, but you didn't see that part, and there's nothing in here saying that I got a good response. And then it goes on later in here to talk about the shopping centre. You know the story about the shopping centre, don't you? [We had no idea.] The fact is it wasn't organised, and the centre manager wasn't really happy about my being there in the first place. I just went there on the spur of the moment. A lot of people there actually did welcome me. Did you see it?'

'They were mostly polite, yet circumspect,' Leisa replied, almost in tears.

'I'll tell you something, Leisa—if I lose my seat, it will be on the basis that people don't want my policies, that they don't want me or what I stand for. But there's no way in the bloody wide world that I am going to allow the media to make me lose it. Such a negative story, when it didn't really happen that way at all. So if I lose this election, I'm damn sure its not going to be because of the media. Like I've always said, I don't ask for anything from you whatsoever—and I'm speaking to everyone in general here. All I ask is that you just report the facts. Let the people judge me. Don't put a spin on the story that makes me come across negative, and you'll get a fair go out of me. But I tell you what, if I see this completely negative—I don't know if it's your boss behind you that says "Right, we want something here that's going to put her down, and have a shot at it"—if that's the way it is then please go away from me now, I don't need you. If you give me a fair go, I'll give you a fair go. It's not easy for me, but I tell you what—if I see that it's going to cause me problems, then you won't know what the hell I'm doing, and I won't tell you what I'm doing. Either we have a good working relationship or we don't. But I'm not going to have you up there around me all the time, when I'm having a personal conversation, having a tape recorder stuck under my bloody nose so that people are not going to talk to me.'

Politicians usually leave admonitions to their minders, and the blast is usually private. Now a leader was personally, 'publicly' urging reporters to exercise their judgment in her favour.

A long silence. And no one had been in this situation before—a full-on threat to evade the media in an election campaign. An election is the one time when politicians court the media. Hanson also didn't seem to accept at all that the media had a rightful place as scrutineers in an election campaign. And she didn't seem to comprehend that it was she who was letting us get up so close through her spontaneity and her refusal to manage her relationship with the media.

The truth was, the media covering Hanson were almost overwhelmed by the reality she was offering us—the idea of a doorknock that wasn't carefully prearranged was a journalistic turn-on. Of course we'd be there if we could. She was just beginning to realise that our presence on her campaign altered her reality, and that she needed to find a way to deal with it.

Helen explained, 'Part of the competitive spirit is that if some of us are watching you, we all have to watch you. We sympathise with you, and we know you're under a lot of pressure having a lot of us around reporting everything you say.'

'It's because of who I am that I draw that much attention,' Hanson replied, now close to tears herself. 'A lot of people out there want to support me, but they're so bloody scared of getting their photo taken with me because it's One Nation.' She saw me taking notes.

'What are you doing, Margo—you're not writing a story round this are you?'

'After the campaign,' I replied.

'I won't be happy if this comes out, because I said this is *off* the record—'. A camera flashed and she swung round to face Grant. 'Are you still taking photos?'

'I didn't take a photo,' he said. (It was Dean.) Hanson demanded a straight answer. 'When I speak to you like this and say it's off the record, is it really off the record?'

A veteran AAP reporter on the trail for the day said, 'Of course it is. We're honourable people.' She calmed down a little. 'My job's not easy, your job's not easy, and I'd rather work in with you. I'm straight-forward, I'm honest.'

'Off the record is off the record—we would do that for any other politician if they asked that,' Helen said. (The meeting remained off the record until Hanson disclosed its contents in a radio interview with talk-back host Stan Zemanek in the last week of the campaign. She later gave permission for the ABC's 'Australian Story' program to screen parts of Marty's videotape.)

After 'the meeting' broke up, I said to Helen, 'Jesus, if we don't manage this campaign, this thing's going to fall apart.' Helen told me what Hanson had said to her as she left. 'A lot of people are depending on this, and if I don't make it, the whole thing will fall apart.' This led to the question I'd posed in a comment piece the previous day predicting One Nation's demise due to Easytax. 'If Hanson cannot repair the damage the frightening question arises: What happens when her people—those without faith in the established parties—lose faith in their Godhead?'

Letting off steam seemed to relax Hanson, who agreed to let us hear her address to her 24 candidates-in-training, in return for our agreement to leave her alone until the next stop, Noosa. Depressed and overwhelmed, her pep talk faltered. 'I can't do everything by myself, so this is where it's—it's an emotional time for me because, as you can imagine, it's been a battle for me for the last two and a half years.'

In Noosa, Hanson was ignored, booed or summarily dismissed on a street walk of the Melbourne holiday-makers' playground, and several people held up *The Sunday Mail* front page, predicting her defeat in Blair, as she passed by. Grant, Dean, Helen and I lunched at the Hyatt, where a nearby table of Melbourne visitors urged us to rid her from politics.

By now, Grant, Helen, Dean and I had become a team, an odd occurrence between direct competitors. Dean and Grant had got the job by sheer chance. The political photographers were with the leaders, and most of the other shooters were in Kuala Lumpur for the Commonwealth Games. Dean and Grant competed every day as the crime/action specialists of *The Sydney Morning Herald* and *The Daily Telegraph*, and were the closest thing to paparazzi in Australian newspapers. Their driving was superb and risky, better than most of the Hanson cops who tried to lose us throughout the campaign. Grant and Dean were on a political campaign that suited them to a tee and they loved it. I was beginning to adjust, slowly.

We sensed that we were in what should be a print-driven campaign —the first since TV had taken over. A fast, unpredictable, hyper-reality campaign was perfect for print, but the physical bulk of TV cameras and the technical difficulties of transmitting pictures put TV journalists at a disadvantage, especially on late-breaking stories. (Modern leaders' campaigns never have anything of significance scheduled after mid-afternoon so as to fit in with the timing of the TV news.)

The major parties' campaigns in 1998 were following the familiar tightly staged pattern, with voters locked out or carefully selected as a backdrop. The dominance of TV continued to choke reality and create its own, because of the medium's power to shape public opinion, the scale of its technical requirements (perfect light, perfect sound) and its need for stories to be visual and dead simple. TV producers want a particular look, a particular feel, to their news. The last thing TV producers want is a sweaty Kim Beazley—it wouldn't look nice. They want every item to have a similar flavour, shape, size or design, just like their news presenters. So cameramen have to make their political leader 'look good', even when it means advising him or her and directing certain scenes.

None of that was happening on this campaign. The voters were central and their contribution unpredictable. The technical needs of TV were completely ignored, and the style was too unstructured for television and its demand for fifteen-second grabs. The raw footage of Hanson's campaign was much in demand in Canberra TV newsrooms, just for personal enjoyment. The stories got to the public largely through newspapers.

To keep print on top and in control, and to cover our backs given the vagaries of her campaigning style, Fairfax and News Limited agreed to work together on the road, as war correspondents do in battle conditions. Our coverage, however, would be very different. The *Herald*'s election Web site editor, Tom Burton, sensed an exciting campaign ahead, too. He asked me to record a daily audio report on the Hanson trail and Dean to file his personal choice of best photos.

In short, Hanson was a local politician on the national stage and completely out of her depth. Anything could happen.

THREE

Welcome to Queensland

DAY 5

Pauline Hanson visited the livestock saleyards in the grand old farming city of Toowoomba on Monday morning, and a tantalising prospect loomed. Victorian Premier Jeff Kennett had pledged to chase Hanson down every burrow and while other politicians sought to suffocate Hanson by ignoring her, he was travelling the land during the election, spelling out the dangers of her policies. Kennett was also in Toowoomba on day five of Hanson's campaign—what price a meeting?

On the drive from Noosa Helen and I hit the phones to our colleagues on the Kennett tour. I called my sister, Gay Alcorn, from *The Age*. She said Kennett wasn't averse to a meeting, but didn't want to seek one out. He was due at the Grand Central shopping centre at 11.25 a.m. Helen phoned David Oldfield, who had taken to calling Helen, Channel Nine's Melanie Wendt and me nightly from Sydney for briefings from us on the day's events. He was keen to play ball. But journalists already at the saleyards said Hanson had declined their entreaties, using the ridiculous reasoning that a meeting would take the gloss off her primary industry policy launch in the afternoon. No one could swing her around.

The Age had told Gay to follow Hanson for a day after Kennett went home—its way of acknowledging her existence while looking down its nose. *The Age* wanted a 'campaign notebook' colour story but Gay felt at a disadvantage compared to her competitors on the Hanson trail full time, so she peeled off Kennett for a first look at Hanson. She was there when I arrived.

Hanson was still a definite no. She wasn't only worried about her primary industry launch; she didn't like the idea of chasing Kennett. She didn't see why she should. This was so politically stupid as to be beyond belief, as well as torpedoing a good story. Since it was in both sides' interests, I had no moral qualms about talking her round—at the time, anyway.

I took her aside. 'Look, this is look-you-in-the-eye advice. It's good for you to meet Kennett. It's the big bad Southerner thing—it doesn't matter that you chase him down.'

She agreed, and Dean, Gay and I raced to the *Herald* car. I drove so Dean could jump out the minute we hit the shopping centre. I drove up just behind Hanson's police car to get a prime position for the chase. Grant went one better, though, talking her into letting him travel with her. She drove herself, tearing off down the main road as Grant reinforced the point—if she wanted to get a run for her primary industry policy, a meeting with Kennett would drag it into the news. Without Kennett, it wouldn't run in the major media outlets.

She went through an orange light on a main street intersection. I put my foot down and went through my first red light of the tour. The Nine car behind me stopped—Melanie said later the cameraman driving was nearing retirement and wasn't in the mood. That left the other media cars stranded behind him.

At the shopping centre, Hanson still looked as though she might change her mind and walk out, so I said, 'Your primary industry policy will get out to the people who matter in your seat—this stuff is you getting back in the main game.' She frowned and nodded at the same time.

DEAN SEWELL

Hanson and Kennett show their nerves, as my sister and I beam at bringing them together. My T-shirt is a souvenir of Fairfax journalists' 1997 campaign to stop a Kerry Packer takeover.

I introduced Gay to Hanson, and Gay asked, 'What's happening here?'

'Pauline's just come to do a centre walk, and if she meets Kennett that's fine. What's Kennett's attitude?'

'He's fine. He's not against it,' she said.

Leanne White from *The Toowoomba Chronicle* joined us and Hanson stepped onto the escalator.

Just as she alighted, we saw Kennett, alone with a shopper, his back to Hanson. As she approached he turned and saw her. He seemed uncomfortable and messed up his lines. 'Ho, ho, ho, ho. How do you do?' he said, shaking her hand.

'Welcome to Queensland,' Hanson replied, beaming, but so nervous she trembled a little.

'I hope you come—I was going to say second [in Blair]. I think what I hope you do—'

Hanson dared to interrupt. 'What you really mean to say—you hope I come first!'

'I think—I hope and suspect you'll come third, fourth or fifth. Good luck.' Kennett turned away as Hanson protested, 'Noooo, this is QUEENSLAND.'

'Good luck,' Kennett repeated as he walked away.

'Thank you very much,' Hanson replied to his back.

The TVs, radio and some print journalists arrived at the very end of the brief encounter. The TVs had limited vision (none of the handshake), and little or no sound of the exchange. We crowded around Hanson for her reaction.

'I meant to ask him what he is actually doing here in Queensland, but he was in a hurry to get away from me again, like when I was down on the [Melbourne] "Footy Show".'

'Will he do more harm than good up here, do you think?' Gay asked.

'Look, he's really helping One Nation. I think it's wonderful.'

'Why do you think he's helping One Nation?' I asked.

'Because Queenslanders do not like to see Jeff Kennett, a Victorian State parliamentarian, up here—especially [not when he's] having a go at Queenslanders as he has done. He's tried to denigrate me, put me down, and he's forgotten that one quarter of Queenslanders voted for One Nation, so there we go.'

We raced round the corner to interview Kennett. 'John Howard and Kim Beazley have so far tried to avoid engaging her—aren't you doing damage to their cause?' ABC Radio's Anne Delaney asked innocently.

'Can I say, with due respect, that's a bit of a stupid question. If you actually saw what happened, she's obviously been following me and trying to track me down. If people try and track me down, they come up and grab me as she did, at least we can always be polite.'

Anne countered with: 'Do you feel a bit uncomfortable being stalked by Ms Hanson?'

'Not at all. I think it's a sign of desperation by Ms Hanson that she has had to go out of her way to come here to find out where I am to track me down.'

'Do you think she has some sort of fatal attraction to the Liberal Party after all?' Anne asked.

'Well, who knows, who knows—but I think her campaign is clearly running out of steam, and I think most Australians are realising that. One Nation is not an option for the future of this country and I strongly hope that that will be re-endorsed by the public as we go into the election.'

I put to him Hanson's claim that he'd done a runner. 'How ridiculous. I said good morning, I wished her well, I shook her hand, I had nothing else to say to her. She's not part of Australia's future.'

'So your political instinct is that One Nation's time has come, that it really is over for One Nation now?'

'I don't think anyone should be complacent. I welcome any individual and any party standing for public office—that's the strength of our democracy. And where we disagree with the views of an individual or a party, we've got to use that same democracy to drive that ugly black cloud off our political landscape, and what we are on about now is driving that black cloud off the landscape.'

'What was your reaction to her Easytax plan?'

'It's a joke. Again, it just shows how populist One Nation is. It's all about popularity. We know what they're against, but we don't know what they're for. And on any occasion on which they've been intellectually challenged to deliver something of value they have failed the test in the simplest form.'

The ABC missed out on any vision of the meeting and spent the afternoon begging other channels for a favour, which was finally delivered. To cover up, the TVs interlaced some footage of Kennett walking past Hanson while she had a coffee in a café. None of the TV producers in head office would accept the miss, and no excuses worked at all. It was incomprehensible to them—in election campaigns, nothing happens until the TVs are there. There is no reality without vision.

But we had our story, messy as it was, and it was all our own work. Hanson made all the TV news programs that night, and the meeting was the page one picture in *The Australian* and *The Age*. *The Age* picture was telling: Hanson and Kennett eyeing each other off from opposite sides of the photo, Gay and I in the middle, tape recorders out, beaming—at our handiwork, I suppose. Melbourne's *Herald Sun* story, written by a journalist on the road with Kennett, was headlined 'STALKED'. *The Sydney Morning Herald* gave the story a solid run inside the paper, as we would throughout the campaign. I made it clear in my story—the question was either not addressed or left open in most reports—that the media had set up the meeting. To me, to run the story without that information would fail to provide readers with the backdrop to the performance and reactions of both leaders. In other words, it would be dishonest.

We had our story all right, and I could tell myself all I liked that I was just doing my job—getting a story that would get a run in the paper. That's part of the internal reality of journalism. But now we were in a scenario where we had the power to make the story happen in a highly political context.

Such power was unthinkable with other political parties, who organise their campaigns so as to get the stories they want out of us. We ask the questions when we get the chance and look for the glitch in the presentation. (Even then the parties are not beyond intervening. During the 1998 campaign, protesters against the Jabiluka uranium mine bashed on the wall of a hall where Howard was attending a closed meeting— a Howard minder barred the way of *Herald* photographer Andrew Meares to stop him going outside to photograph the disturbance.)

So did we have a duty to refrain from using this unexpected power to create news when its exercise could lead to an increase in Hanson's popularity? The question only arose because it was One Nation—a party whom our editors, our friends, the experts, and we ourselves agreed was a negative force in Australian politics. That's the reason why the media has been so self-conscious about covering Hanson, a rarity in such an instinctive, hard-nosed profession. We're just the messengers, let the consequences be what they may, is the usual media refrain. And yet, from the beginning, the media relationship with Hanson was never that pure. Most media groups campaigned against her and her party, although they differed in their approach. The broadsheets led a campaign urging Howard to do something to stop her. The tabloids and commercial TV news showed a fascination with her difference and shock value, flamed by huge support from the public as demonstrated in talkback, the polls and letters to the editor. This mixture of grassroots popularity and media disapproval had thrown up more than one selling point for One Nation. The ubiquitous One Nation posters of Hanson wrapped in the Australian flag was initially the idea of a photographer, who considered it a send-up and talked her into it. And her signature phrase, 'Please Explain', was her spontaneous response to a '60 Minutes' interviewer asking if she was xenophobic.

After her explosive entrance into the main game at the Queensland election, the city media (several country and regional papers actively supported Pauline Hanson while others played dead bats) put Hanson and the party under intense scrutiny, resulting in the occasional sloppy and unfair story based on allegations without foundation. But she was still hanging in there, and her supporters increasingly blamed the media for her woes, seeing us as part of the 'elite' they were yelling at to 'Please Explain'.

She'd succeeded despite us, or perhaps partly because of us, and now we had to deal with the consequences.

The Hanson challenge to the media sent shivers down our collective spine, and saw some media groups making political rather than news judgments about whether running a particular story would 'help' One Nation. In short, there was crisis in news judgment over Hanson. And now, at the coalface of an election campaign, the fraught One Nation media dynamic had come down to Pauline Hanson and us.

Grant, Dean, Helen and I stayed at Vacy Hall, a big old mansion turned guesthouse in Toowoomba, and we sat by the open fire for hours going over the day. The TVs all had Queensland-based reporters on the road, working under their Canberra political correspondents' orders, and it was becoming clear that the running would be left to us. Should we keep doing what we'd do if any other party allowed us this much leeway, and create news when we could? Or should we treat her differently?

The next morning, Brisbane talkback radio featured outraged Queenslanders wanting to know why Kennett was there and why he was so rude. Senior Liberals castigated Kennett for his folly. Kennett, still in Toowoomba, countered with a powerful speech detailing why Hansonism would destroy Australia. A *Sydney Morning Herald* poll two days later showed Hanson's support declining across all States bar Queensland because of Easytax, with the national vote steady at 8 percent due to a 10 percent lift in her Queensland vote to 19 percent.

Hanson began telling her audiences how Kennett had once threatened to chase her down every burrow but that when she went to see him he ran away.

A remark by Hanson's former adviser John Pasquerelli about the Hanson/media relationship kept running through my head. 'She and the media are now locked together. It's like an embrace which both parties don't want to be in, but they're there.'

Helen and I were to lunch with Hanson the next day.

FOUR

Staying over

DAY 6

Pauline Hanson sat in an Ipswich restaurant with her head in her hands. Helen had raised the matter of campaign organisation. 'How do you think I feel? Don't ask me, no one will tell me anything. They're all trying to protect me, especially Peter, but it means I don't know what's going on.'

She was to work in her office all day, in what Peter James had dubbed 'a media-free day'. He'd announced the plan at her up-country primary industry launch the previous afternoon, where the free-range chooks that dashed about had far outnumbered the assembled guests. Grant, fishing for a day-off picture, had asked Pauline if she hung out her own washing. 'Yeah, I do. I do all my housework—my washing and ironing and everything.' A photo of that, then? 'Grant, Grant, Grant, I'm at the office tomorrow, working, and I don't take my *washing* to work. Have a day off; you need it, you're looking tired.'

It seemed strange that she'd agreed to the lunch until it dawned on us that maybe she was an isolated figure within her own party. Head still in her hands, she said she'd discovered at the last minute that her primary industry launch was to be held in a windowless room in Toowoomba. She had put her foot down. 'Have it on a farm, where it's for,' she'd told her party boys. Hansonites were a bunch of hare-brained amateurs without cash, talent or experience surrounded by a marauding media. I almost felt sorry for her.

She didn't know the half of what she was up against, and we didn't tell her. Hanson's main man, David Oldfield, the only person in the party with a political brain, was overtly contemptuous of his leader to journalists, oblivious to the damage he caused to the image of the woman he called 'the product'. After Easytax, Oldfield had told me that he'd tried his best to stop the policy seeing the light of day, but that Pauline could not be talked out of it, and that he'd rewritten her tax speech two hours before the launch. He'd then insisted that Peter James call me to confirm Oldfield's innocence on the Easytax issue. A party heavyweight telling journalists that its tax policy was stupid seemed simply bizarre.

Oldfield had told me the night before that he'd join the campaign soon in order to save it, and I asked Pauline whether she was looking forward to his return. She said she didn't like being seen with him because some people thought she was a puppet, and she wasn't.

We ordered steaks, and I asked who she thought would win the election. She said people were very disappointed in the Liberals but they weren't ready to go back to Labor. John Howard would win, but if a Paul Keating were leading Labor, Labor would win. She liked Paul Keating? 'Yes, I do. He's strong.' I did a double take, one of many during the campaign. Paul Keating—the demonised king of political correctness who, according to the Right, had propelled Australia into all this division and pain on race and multiculturalism—was admired by the woman who'd led the backlash.

I asked if she was a feminist. No, she said, because when married she had cooked a hot meal every night and had it on the table for her husband, regardless of what else she was doing. That was a woman's duty, she said.

'But you have lived a feminist life, Pauline,' I protested. 'Single mother, started your own business on your own, pro-abortion, no wish to marry again, you believe men are just for sex, you *are* a feminist.' (She'd mentioned her aversion to remarriage and her current preference for the occasional fling after our interview at her home after the Queensland election.) She laughed and said nothing.

'I've always tagged you "Ms" in stories—is that what you want to be?' She frowned at Ms but said she definitely wasn't a Mrs. Maybe Miss? Helen said Miss implied she was on the marriage market, when she'd said she definitely wasn't. She agreed to Ms, reluctantly.

We moved on to Wik. We'd been told the previous weekend that she'd be flying to Longreach on Friday, and we'd suspected that meant she'd play the race card there. Peter James had confirmed our suspicions the previous afternoon among the chooks, ramming home the need to be there. She'd be announcing One Nation's 'Aboriginal policy', which would be 'controversial', he'd said. The event would take place at the Stockman's Hall of Fame, the spot where Howard had made his famous pledge to angry pastoralists that he would never back down on his ten-point Wik plan.

Pauline was banking on race to rebuild her campaign, and the night before she'd even considered postponing the Longreach trip when she'd realised it would clash with the opening of the Commonwealth Games. After Oldfield had rung from Sydney with that bit of news, I'd suggested she'd have a media riot on her hands after all the scrambling we'd done to charter planes to be there, and she'd backed down.

Now, at lunch with the enemy—the dreaded Southern media and the only Canberra press gallery journalists on her campaign to boot—she asked why the High Court had come down the way it did in the Wik decision. I said most pastoral leases gave pastoralists no more than a right to graze, and that because the British colonists had taken the land from the Aboriginal peoples without legal authority, the Government must return it to the extent that it had not made land grants to others. Wik was a very conservative decision from the Aboriginal perspective, because pastoralists' rights under their leases would always prevail over the leftover native title. She asked a lot of questions about why people in the cities should be safe from native title. I said her policy to abolish native title on pastoral leases could never happen. You couldn't just abolish the property rights of one race and refuse to pay compensation for that loss, while continuing to grant compensation to other Australians whose land was appropriated. That would mean asking a racist question at a referendum to repeal the constitutional requirement that the Government pay just compensation for land rights it took away, but only for native title. Such a proposal would create a damaging scandal around the world. She said it was none of the world's business.

We couldn't seem to find a way to communicate on Wik, and she changed the subject by relating a run-in she'd had with her son Adam the night before. He'd returned a day late from a Gold Coast trip with his sister Lee, nearly fifteen. She'd been so worried she'd called the police, and had given Adam a good tongue-lashing about the need to 'respect' his mother. No easy road, that of a single mother during an election campaign.

After two hours and a couple of bottles of wine, Helen and I prepared to leave. Pauline said it was a shame she had to work, otherwise she'd invite us to her house for dinner. We were paying the bill when she offered to pick us up in the early evening.

Sitting at the restaurant bar, somewhat stunned by her invitation, Helen said, 'She's lonely, that's what this is about. She's surrounded by sycophants or manipulators. Maybe she's got no friends.'

Pauline's police escort picked us up at about 5 p.m., but she had to take us back to the restaurant twice—first to pick up my phone charger and then Helen's portable computer. She laughed at our disorganised state, seeing the joke before we did. She directed the police driver to a supermarket, where she bought a cooked chicken, wine, and bread. As we drove out of Ipswich towards her country property, I worried that there'd be no mobile phone service for me to do a radio interview, so she got the police to stop at a phone outside a service station. When I couldn't make the phone work, she laughed and showed me how to reverse the charges before returning to the car. On radio, I criticised her campaign in peace. It was surreal stuff—a political leader stops her police car to let a journalist do a critical interview about her, and even helpfully arranges the mechanics.

Pauline's home, built on her fish and chip shop money, was on acreage at the top of a hill near the hamlet of Coleyville. She'd designed the house herself. Big glass windows and doors, surrounded by verandahs, offered 360-degree views of her land and her bush, where she agisted cattle and horses. An enormous Australian flag flew from a corner of the verandah outside her bedroom. She'd designed one wing for herself and another for Adam and Lee, both at boarding school but regular visitors.

It was idyllic, and you could see why she'd drive for hours after a full day's campaigning in order to sleep at home, rather than somewhere on the road in the huge seat of Blair. There were vast, empty tracts of polished wooden floors throughout, and a general air of minimalism. The only eyesore was a big, overstuffed couch by the fireplace, covered in a rose-patterned chintzy material that looked like a Laura Ashley reject. 'You've got to get rid of that,' I said. She feigned outrage.

The lounge room, its walls filled with photos and portraits of Pauline, was dominated by a huge open fireplace. It was still a surprise to see that the camera liked her face and that she liked the camera. When *The Sydney Morning Herald* had run images of a smiling Hanson during the Queensland election campaign, some readers and many press gallery journalists were taken aback. The more familiar images in the media were those glowering, hard, raw-boned shots taken when she'd been shunned, sullen and out of her depth in Parliament House—Hanson as the unwelcome outsider.

Her fans sometimes painted her and gave her their work as a tribute, and a glamorous 'pretty' portrait had pride of place on one wall. It was too glibly attractive, more a boring idealisation, and Helen said she didn't think it accurately reflected her. Pauline said she liked it. Her original Pro Hart painting, a gift from the artist, was propped on the floor near the TV.

She was house proud, and took us on a tour. She complained that she had no garden because she had no time to make one.

In reality, her home was not a haven. It was a fortress, due to the regular threats against her since the formation of One Nation. Inside the front gate sat a caravan in which a federal police officer with intercom access to the house was on duty 24 hours a day. This was the entry point—no one drove up the long, winding track to the house unless Hanson gave the word. It was a warm Queensland evening and she took us outside to see the glorious night view, opening complicated double locks on double doors. Every door and window had them, and each time I wanted to go outside for a cigarette she had to work the locks for me.

Pauline was a perfect hostess and good company, with a dry, self-deprecating sense of humour. But we felt uncomfortable. She treated us like friends, when we couldn't be. She was a sitting duck. This level of openness was outside my experience, and I was completely taken aback at her lack of façade. It would be no easy task to draw the line between public and private on this campaign.

We sat by the fireplace—Hanson on the couch, us on two chairs opposite. She broke up the chicken, sliced some salami, cheese and bread, and piled up our plates. We ate the chicken with our hands, drank red wine, and discussed Aboriginal affairs.

I said that even if one accepted her claim that she was not a racist, there was still no denying that there were racists in her party, that her party promoted racist policies, and that as leader she was accountable for that. If she wasn't racist, she could prove it on Friday and really shake everyone up by saying she wanted an official apology made to the stolen generations. That would make page one, I said jokingly. She smiled and said nothing.

Helen said no one disagreed that there were problems in ATSIC. She cited the ATSIC board's decision to fund legal action by its deputy chair, Sugar Ray Robinson, against the Queensland government for wrongful arrest after the High Court quashed his conviction for rape. But that didn't mean you should abolish assistance to Aboriginal people. Just because there's welfare fraud doesn't mean you abolish the social security system, or the farmers' biggest welfare hit, the diesel fuel rebate.

'I'm writing my race speech myself,' she said, adding that she would work on it when she went to bed.

I said to her a few times: 'I'm going to work you out by the end of this campaign.' She replied, 'I know, I know.' I found her a fascinating personality—as soon as you thought you'd found the box to put her in, she'd jump out of it with a remark that floored you. I'd made up my mind at the start of the campaign to try to maintain an honest dialogue with her on race, to find out if she really was racist by design. I felt that if people of differing views couldn't talk about race constructively, there was no chance of moving beyond divisiveness to reconciliation. There didn't seem any point in persisting with the media myth that she was some sort of monster who needed to be slain.

She had clearly surmounted enormous disadvantages to become successful in business, and now in politics. Pauline Hanson was a maverick underdog—normally an attractive Australian archetype—and I found it hard not to admire her guts, even though she had triggered a disturbing and sometimes frightening political climate. There was also an element of class putdown in Hanson commentary which I found extremely unattractive—exemplified by people sneering at her pronunciation of 'Australia', her lack of grammatical correctness, and her 'fish and chip shop' background. It was true enough that working-class politicians were now rarely to be seen in federal politics, but the elitist hypocrisy in accusing Hanson of divisiveness while engaging in careless class discrimination seemed to me not only poor taste, but inimical to the Australian egalitarian tradition.

The weirdest thing about the dinner conversation was that she didn't try to justify her views or use the opportunity to give us a positive spin on her politics. She just listened and chatted. Maybe people like us, who thought like we thought, hadn't engaged with her before; we were curiosities to her and she was a curiosity to us. Or maybe she wanted to size up the enemy. It was hard to tell with Pauline Hanson.

I asked for her home phone number so Radio National's 'Late Night Live' could call for my Tuesday interview spot with Phillip Adams. I did the interview in her kitchen, overlooking the lounge where Helen and she continued the discussion on Aborigines.

'I understand that your special candidate had the day off, so you've had some time off as well,' Phillip began.

'Maybe.'

'Why does Hanson take the day off now, when according to many a measuring rod she's not doing too well?'

'I think it's because there is no organisation to her campaign. It's an amazing experience. There's a big media presence, and if you've got no organisation then people can get hurt. Like if you've got to run a red light to get your news story or your news pic, like the pic of Kennett and Hanson yesterday, then it's starting to get dangerous, isn't it?'

'You're telling me that she doesn't have minders, that she's not surrounded by Oldfields?' Phillip asked incredulously.

'There's no one there. So it's a mad, wild, realistic campaign, all the pictures are real, there's no set-ups.'

'There's no set-ups, except this photograph of Hanson and Kennett was a set up.'

'It doesn't make sense, does it?' I replied.

'Is she running scared now she's seeing, perhaps, the tide turning?'

'We've got the Newspoll this morning which shows her down about 2 to 7.5. I think the Kennett pic will pick her up a little bit—who knows where she'll go? The first week of the campaign was a complete and utter disaster. She's trying to meld all sorts of agendas between her core base, which is extreme right-wing, and all those people who make her important, all those voters who are protesting. So if she comes up with an idea, people go, 'Oh my God, that's just rubbish'—but if she doesn't come up with an idea, people say, 'Oh my God, she's irrelevant'. So we're running around after someone who—who knows if she can get anywhere or not?'

'I've just worked this out,' Phillip said. 'The reason you've had a day off is because the media needed the day off, and Pauline Hanson's having the day off while you blokes are resting because you can't handle the stress.'

'Yeah, I wouldn't have a clue what's happening, actually. It's the maddest, most interesting campaign that I've ever followed, but it's also the most exciting journalistically, because the journalists are in control of this campaign. Unlike the last election—remember that documentary "Media Rules"? [This was an SBS documentary following the press following the leaders in the 1996 campaign.] Every journalist complained about being powerless. And remember, we're the representatives, we're the eyes, supposedly representing the public, and it's stage-managed out of existence. We were humiliated in that campaign. The image for me of the doco was Howard's boy Anthony Benscher telling the photographers that they had to stand behind a line that he had drawn, to take their pictures. And now we're on a campaign where there are no rules. It's hard to understand—it's a very personal campaign. To get the stories and get the pics on this campaign, you've got to have a relationship with her.'

At about 11 p.m. we discovered we were stranded. Pauline said no taxis were available out here at this time of night. We rang the boys, but they'd been drinking by the hotel pool for hours. So we stayed. She put Helen in the spare room and me on the couch, and I facetiously demanded a fire. She picked up a torch and took me outside into the pitch blackness to collect kindling.

The fire was still burning when Pauline woke me up at 7 a.m. Without make-up she was very pale and looked very tired. She said she hadn't quite finished her race speech. I had nothing to wear, so she took me to her room and began pulling out nice shirts. 'No, give me a T-shirt that you'd do your gardening in.' I finally chose a maroon T-shirt, and she told me to use her shower because Helen was using the one in the children's wing. Her bathroom was wall-to-wall cosmetics.

We put Pauline on the phone to Grant, by now at Ipswich, to give him directions. I joked about having to drink the same brand of instant coffee, International Roast, that my mother had when I was a child in regional Queensland. She laughed and disappeared for a makeover.

The boys arrived with my sister Gay Alcorn, on the trail with Hanson for a day for *The Age*. Gay couldn't believe her luck, and rushed around the lounge room checking out Pauline's taste in music, the photos, and the furniture. Hanson the politician emerged, looking like a million dollars, and began washing the dishes and wiping down the kitchen benches.

I disapproved of Gay's activities—but Helen and I were in no position to argue. Staying with the politician you are following is beyond the pale, although I'd dare any journalist to turn down such an invitation from a mainstream leader. The thing is, it just wouldn't happen.

Gay was just itching to open the colour story of her day on Hanson with two campaign journalists staying over. She knew she couldn't. After all, I'd done her a favour by letting her travel in *The Sydney Morning Herald* car, and that's why she was here. She could hardly return the favour by creating a scandal about us staying over, however inviting the prospect. She suffered over the decision, though, as journalists do when personal loyalties conflict with getting the story. Still, the consequences of a family split outweighed writing such a delicious lead paragraph, which would have graphically illustrated the oddity of Hanson's campaign.

The police car arrived and we followed Pauline Hanson to Gatton. On the way, Oldfield rang Helen asking for details of the Sugar Ray Robinson imbroglio. Pauline had mentioned it to him, he said, and wondered if it could be mentioned in her race speech.

FIVE

It's like I'm a mother

DAY 7

By day seven, the media's appetite for Hanson stories and pictures was voracious. As the major parties lumbered through their set-piece ballets—this day would find John Howard in Melbourne showcasing Liberal unity and the 'social justice' of his tax plan, and Kim Beazley in a Perth industrial zone attacking the lack of it—Hanson was like a shot of oxygen for a jaded media reporting to a jaded public.

But between the heavyweights' choreography and Hanson's sideshow, there was no middle ground. This was a road movie without a director. At times, the chase became the story. Yet any moment might turn up some scene or utterance that would reverberate around the nation. You just never knew where or when.

A heavier media contingent than usual turned up at the Gatton One Nation office that Wednesday morning for a day's campaigning in Blair. Hanson's stock had soared thanks to the news value of her Kennett confrontation. Inside, the poverty of her political organisation was plain to see; the party leader was struggling in vain to operate the fax machine, while local volunteers put together her itinerary for the day.

Without a word, Hanson flew out of the office and careered off in her car at a high speed. The TVs and other journos new to the trail trundled off to the first official stop, a shopping centre. Distrustful print and radio journalists careered after her. She stopped outside a small weatherboard home in a suburban street and asked us to wait outside. This was a 'private visit'.

Minutes later a frenetic-looking woman of about sixty appeared on the front porch. Her husband had emphysema in both lungs, had just had a triple bypass operation, and had asked to see Hanson as his dying wish. Could we please come in to witness the meeting and could we please take pictures? She waved us in, saying her name was Dot Cornwell and her husband was Mervyn. We could hardly say no.

About eight of us filed into a tiny and faintly musty sitting room that could have been a set for a 1950s movie, decorated with black-and-white family photos on doilies. Hanson was in an armchair, hands folded on her lap, leaning forward, eyes filled with sympathy and concern. Mr Cornwell reclined on the couch, and there were tubes everywhere. Frothing slightly at the mouth, he spoke slowly but without pausing, and was barely comprehensible. Hanson's eyes never left his face, though her jaw set in annoyance at the sight of us. We sat on the floor, silent and acutely uncomfortable. Dot started calling out questions to her husband—trying to get him to say something about being denied a war service pension—but despite several game attempts he couldn't get a grasp of the topic. Hanson nodded occasionally as if she understood everything. As we were leaving she scolded me for coming in. She hadn't been aware of Dot's invitation, and shook her head in disbelief when I told her.

Hanson cruised on to a battered light industrial shopfront, the first of dozens we would visit on her campaign, where men who once employed workers now struggled on alone, staving off defeat for a while. Calls were pouring in from journalists at the shopping centre worried they'd been sold a dud. I found Hanson inside looking helpless, still having no luck sending that mystery fax. Sue Gordon, a woman with

DEAN SEWELL

Hanson embraces a dying fan, Mervyn Cornwell, as uncomfortable journalists look on. His wife Dot transformed Hanson's favour into a surreal media event, perhaps hoping to help her idol in the polls.

big platinum blonde hair who was One Nation's number three Senate candidate in Queensland, appeared to be her minder for the day. Gordon said the fax had to go to Hanson's Ipswich office, but the fax machine there was always jammed with appeals from people asking her to help them. Today was not the first time she'd paid a visit to a sickbed. The photographers lined up outside the shop to shoot her exit. She refused Grant's request to pose beside a blackboard marked 'Specials' and sped off.

A group of supporters clapped and chanted 'Pau-line for Blair' as she finally arrived at the shopping centre. In their midst was Dot Cornwell, who we discovered was the local branch secretary. A Nine Network cameraman quipped: 'We missed you Pauline.' Hanson smiled knowingly and shot back: 'It's nice to know I'm missed.' She had cut the media down to size, but now came the down side.

The TV people, still smarting over missing the Kennett vision, were rattled that they might have been caught out again. They crowded around her like moths to a flame. She was enclosed; her supporters had no way in. So Hanson wanted to escape? Let her try. Nothing is guaranteed to fixate the media more than a reluctant subject, let alone one who could blurt out something newsworthy at any time. A voter keen to ask Hanson some questions came up to me and said: 'Could you ask Pauline if I could see her another day, when she's not busy?'

The media suffocation of Hanson had begun. Running red lights, illegal turns, and broken speed limits became the norm that day as the pursuers and the pursued settled into their respective roles at a cracking pace, shattering the peace and calm of this fine old Queensland town.

Hanson sped to a nursing home for tea and scones. When she sat down with a group of residents, reporters either joined or surrounded the party. The Reuters reporter needed to ask about her suit because readers in Asia were obsessed with every detail of Hanson's appearance.

Hanson was unsure of the colour. 'How do I know—pink?' Fuchsia, suggested my sister Gay. And the fabric?

'I don't know,' Hanson said. Was it silk?

'Oh no, not silk,' she replied, as if shocked by the suggestion. She might dress smart, but she had an eye for a bargain.

A reporter asked a woman of 83 seated next to her what she liked about Pauline Hanson. 'She'll take the money off those abos, those abos who aren't real abos. Them bloody ones with more white blood in them are getting the money and that's not right.' All eyes were on Hanson. Her face didn't move.

Outside, Hanson wanted to ditch us while she had lunch, but no one in her party could tell us how to get to the next stop. We agreed to take time out and eat together at the Tent Hill pub without cameras and tapes.

Some reporters logged tapes or wrote stories over lunch, but most sat at the table where Hanson presided. Someone started the discussion by asking for more campaign organisation. Hanson waved her arms and smiled. 'You just want me to be a mother chook, rounding up her hens.' But didn't she care that the campaign was getting dangerous? Her tone hardened. 'Look, I'm not stopping you leaving. I'm not going to change—I've got too much to get done.'

She said she knew the media was 'a necessary evil' which had 'brought me up and can bring me down'. But she'd play her own game her own way. I started recording these remarks on a scrap of paper. She told me I looked pale and should get something to eat. While I was ordering, she winked at reporters and put my piece of paper in her handbag.

I asked whether she ever missed her fish and chip shop days. She sighed and relaxed, reminiscing. It wasn't really a fish and chip shop, she said, it was 'a seafood takeaway'. So she was a bit of a snob herself. 'I introduced fresh fish to Ipswich.' Before her shop opened, people were happy with frozen cod, and at first they kept asking for it. She'd suggest fresh fish, and promise a refund if they weren't satisfied. The shop became famous, growing all the time, but had gone downhill since she'd sold it. She took after her Dad. Jack's Café was famous for his chicken rolls—chicken, cabbage and rice in pastry she'd made with her own hands when she'd worked for him.

It was mesmerising. People couldn't get enough detail. How often had she gone to the fish market? (Four times a week, at dawn.) And how many hours had she worked? (Fourteen hours a day, six days a week.) Melanie recalled that a school friend used to buy his fish and chips from her and liked them, and Hanson beamed. She was much happier chatting about her shop days than politics.

Our fascination was such that she could have been from another planet, but it was also an uncomfortable reminder of the class divide. When was the last time a semi-inarticulate, 'ordinary' person had blundered onto the stage where power is played out, and stayed there? On that stage, Hanson's unsavvy working-class persona made her an exotic, a curiosity, which was one reason why her media coverage had always been so enormous. She was the unthinkable setting her sights on the impossible.

Gay asked whether she was a Ms or a Mrs. 'I'm a Miss,' she said. Stunned, I reminded her she'd agreed on Ms. 'Alright, Ms,' she said. Out of the blue, she leaned over and offered to take me to the fish markets tomorrow morning to show me how to choose fresh fish. I asked when she wanted us there, assuming she meant a media event, the sort of photo opportunity politicians revel in. No, she said, it would be a 'private' visit. I couldn't comprehend her meaning. How could she expect to organise such a thing with the rest of the media present?

They'd be there regardless of what she wanted. The blurring of public/private boundaries went with the territory in Hanson's world, but it never ceased to be disconcerting. The fact that Hanson seemed to like me, and even trust me in some way, made the standard politician–journalist game much more personally confronting. Since she didn't know the norms of the game, should I, in fairness, fill her in?

Hanson kept up the pace till nightfall, which brought her first public meeting of the campaign, at the Gatton senior citizen's hall. The place was nearly full; tapes were rolling just in case, but we were all dog-tired and hoping there'd be no news. Hanson, waiting unattended in an anteroom for a local official to turn up, was edgy. 'I like to be on time. I don't like to keep people waiting,' she said. You never saw Pauline Hanson lose her cool, never saw her bawl out her helpers, even when their cluelessness brought her grief. She was not a complainer.

She'd had to call off the fish market expedition, she told me, because Oldfield had wanted the TVs to come. 'You're exhausting us,' I said. 'I haven't started yet,' she replied.

Why were we here? Why were we trying to make sense of something that didn't make sense? 'We're here because of the unknown, because we don't know what will happen,' Helen said.

Hanson launched into her speech in style. She stood like a country singer, all her weight on her back foot, hips forward, hand on hip. Her delivery was rousing, emotional, and well timed. Gay, looking suitably tortured, was impressed—the same reaction I'd had when I'd first seen Hanson perform before a friendly crowd during the Queensland election campaign. 'She's good, isn't she? Quite inspirational, in a way,' Gay said. Personally, I thought Hanson sounded a bit down, realistic about her fading chances and asking for sympathy.

'I'm still not that polished politician,' she said, a reference to her self-description in her maiden speech. 'I've probably learned a bit along the way [in my] understanding of the political process. I remember one time they called a cyclone "Cyclone Pauline". The media here are the same—they haven't worked me out either.'

To race. 'The Aboriginal people always will be part of the Australian history,' she said, and they should stand by 'us' now, because 'we all work too darn hard for our dollars to see it wasted.' Gay and I looked at each other and rolled our eyes, but it seemed low-key stuff on race overall. I asked Network Seven's Peter Doherty, who'd seen Hanson speak many times in Queensland, how he saw it. 'It's a bit softer than usual,' he said. 'And it's a much longer, slower speech than usual. Her battery is running down.'

'Please give us the opportunity to keep on going,' Hanson continued, voice cracking. 'The polls may tell you we're going down. I don't believe it. So really, the future of this nation is in the hands of the Australian people. I hope you'll give us a go. I'll tell you what—we couldn't do any worse than they have.'

I joined one of her police officers outside for a cigarette. He said that in the car that morning Hanson had noticed a newspaper report saying that she'd tour Western Australia on Sunday. 'So that's what I'm doing—and I didn't know,' she had said.

I returned to hear, 'I know I've got a fight on my hands. I care, and I care so passionately about this country, it's like I'm a mother, Australia is my home, and the Australian people are my children, and I have to look after my home that's in the best interests of its children.'

Peter Doherty hadn't heard that one before. Like a lot of Hanson lines, you could read it either as a bit of weirdness or as something sinister: an emotional reaction to visiting a dying man, or Hitler's Fatherland become Hanson's Motherland. We all filed for the late editions and the morning news.

Oldfield rang very late for his nightly chat, hyper from too little sleep and too many hours on the phone hosing down political bushfires lit by idiot One Nation candidates around the nation. I relayed the mother of the nation remark, and said it didn't work for me. He sighed, theatrically I thought, and said the phrase was all hers. She'd said it a few times before at meetings, despite his suggestion that Australians might not like to be seen as children. When she was emotional, out it popped.

I said I'd been offended by her remark that Aborigines were an important part of our history. Laying on the sarcasm, I asked whether the race policy announcement at Longreach on Friday would entail exterminating the blacks and building a monument to their memory? 'Yes, in the shape of a boomerang that won't come back,' he replied jokingly. But then he got angry, saying I was completely out of touch, that only 5 percent of Australians thought like me on race, and that surely even I could see—if I wasn't deliberately blind—'that isn't what she means'.

One could only go by the text surely, I replied. No—what people like me did was print the words, but interpret them against her by twisting her meaning. I protested that I hadn't reported the remark and was just giving him my personal reaction. 'Well, you've got something to look forward to,' he yelled down the phone. 'You're going to stand on your head and spew green vomit when you hear her speech on Friday.'

The next day, Hanson as mother of the nation took off on talkback radio, and the political heavyweights suddenly had lots to say about Pauline Hanson. John Howard, in his usual sanctimonious fashion, said, 'I have always regarded myself as the servant of the nation.' Peter Costello remarked, 'She's not my mother. I can assure you of that.' Jeff Kennett dubbed the concept 'hideous'. Kim Beazley said: 'My mother had a philosophy, and her philosophy was there was always room for one more. And the view of Australian mums, as I have found, is that while you love everybody, there's always the vulnerable in your family that you take care of most. That is motherhood Oz style. It is not motherhood Pauline Hanson style.'

SIX

Don't put the blame onto me

DAY 8

Thursday was bright and hot in Laidley, a little rural town in Blair where Hanson knew lots of first names. She was greeted like an old friend in the main street as she wandered along shopping and buying raffle tickets. Like Gatton and many other Blair outposts we'd see during her campaign, Laidley was a place where time passed slowly among the traditional country architecture, wide streets, big old pubs and settled ebbs and flows of doing business in the country.

We were starting to settle into a campaign rhythm—after a rushed high-stress day, a chance to chill out. Besides, tomorrow was race-policy day in Longreach, and we were getting the feeling that the promise of something new there was a hoax—a ploy to get all media possible to overcome the logistical dramas and be there to watch her play the race card. It was time to save energy and get relations with Hanson on an even keel before the inevitable confrontation on race. Hanson ordered journalists to buy themselves some of the fresh peas on sale at a road-side stall and they obliged.

While a spontaneous interaction with a member of the general public was so rare on the major parties' campaigns as to be big news, Hanson's campaign produced several a day. This time, an opal miner who wasn't finding many—dressed in black jeans and a black shirt, and a little unsteady on his feet—wanted to have his say. A Czech immigrant, he was passionate about the dangers he saw in Hansonism. He said she'd made Lightning Ridge a ghost town, with only 40 full-time miners left after overseas customers had pulled out because of her. She took up the challenge. 'Why would that be? What are my policies that caused that?'

'I agree with a lot of what you say but I don't agree with a lot either. *You* are creating racism in Australia.'

'No, excuse me, you made a statement, now you back it up.'

'Yeah I am backing it up—you are creating racism in Australia, really badly.'

'You tell me what my policies are that have caused that in Lightning Ridge. And I'll tell you something—I went to Lightning Ridge and I've been down those mines and I've spoken to people there. And they are looking at me for the answers because they can see that they're losing their industries there, not because of me. Have a damn good look at the Government—'

'Well there were customers in China and Cambodia and all over South East Asia; they are all gone because of you—'

'No! Excuse me, it's not my fault and don't put the blame onto me, because I'm only one independent backbencher—look at the damn Government.'

'No, you are the one that's creating problems in Australia—I have worked with Chinese, I have worked with Vietnamese, and they were great—'

'And *I've* worked with them too, and I had an Asian woman who ran my business. So what's your next question?'

'My next question is—'

Hanson was angry now, hands on hips, head forward, spitting out her words. She was more articulate in street brawls than at doorstops. A small crowd had gathered, mostly nodding when she spoke. She was shaking a little and Peter James intervened. 'That's enough now, sir, let Pauline get on with it. You've had your go, okay?' I began interviewing the man as she walked away, but she came back for more.

'You have no understanding. I've been out to Lightning Ridge—and you know something? Those people out there are turning to me to help them because it is a failing industry; there is a failing business out there. And it's got nothing to do with me, so you get the facts straight and know exactly what you're talking about because I'm trying to save a lot of Australian businesses and industries here.' They began speaking over each other and she walked away again.

Coming after the mother of the nation remark, it struck me that maybe she really did take on some of the pain all these people shared with her on some sort of emotional level, and she really did see herself as a saviour figure. Certainly the suggestion that she had been complicit in hurting the people she wanted to save seemed to shock her.

She agreed to do a doorstop outside a senior citizens' centre if we'd leave her alone for the rest of the day, and we agreed with relief. Selina Day from AAP began. 'It is two years to the day since you made your maiden speech—' Hanson laughed. 'Oh really?' What was her best achievement since then?

'Umm, getting Australians to wake up, and not be so apathetic about politics and the direction of this country, to realise that they really do have a voice. What I've said all along is you can only have good government if you've got good opposition. I've been a voice that has raised issues that have been on the lips and minds of Australians, but now they are the ones who are the opposition because they're the ones who are making the Government take heed and listen to them.'

'John Pasquerelli said today that your campaign is a bit of a disaster thus far and he's offered to come back to you. What would be your response to that?' Selina asked.

Hanson laughed. 'I mean to say, he's a man who's where? Down in Melbourne, and he's talking about my campaign? No, John Pasquerelli won't be on my campaign trail and David Oldfield will be coming back to be my right-hand man, my media adviser.'

Was she concerned about the lack of organisation? 'I think we're all so unused to each other. I mean to say, this is my first campaign of this size, as you can appreciate. And even yourselves, you've never worked with anyone like me before, so we've had to get used to each other, haven't we?'

I was next. 'You had a confrontation with a man worried that your ideas were splitting Australia. He's seen first-hand what can happen in Europe when racism takes hold—' Hanson interrupted with 'There is no racism in Australia.'

I couldn't believe it—a carbon copy of the statement made by Paul Keating in Singapore, the man she so admired, both of them peddling convenient delusions from opposite ends of the spectrum.

'You're saying there is no racism in Australia—there is not one racist in Australia?' I asked incredulously.

'If there is, there is a lot of reverse racism that is happening.'

What on earth did that mean? She cut reflexively to Aborigines, avoiding her Czech accuser's point about offending Asians. 'People out there are actually being told that this land belongs to the Aboriginal people, and there is a lot of racism that is out in the streets. You ask a lot of Australians out there that are made to feel this is not their country.'

White people were being discriminated against? 'Yes, they are being discriminated against through government policies; it's clearly there, but you can't discuss it because it's politically incorrect. Let's just throw the whole blasted lot out the window, let's treat people equally and on a needs basis. That's everything I've ever stood for.' She flounced off, flustered.

In the evening, we flew to Rockhampton on the central Queensland coast, en route to Longreach, and Hanson was rushed to a local fundraising dinner. Journalists adjourned to the bar at the Leichhardt Hotel, where we were staying, but I went along to soak up grassroots One Nation ambience. Guests were dressed as I remembered from my childhood. There was the usual One Nation sprinkling of toupees, the suits were well worn, the women knew their place and the food was old style—baked lamb, roast potato and pumpkin. There was no wealth in the room at all.

They sang 'Advance Australia Fair' with enthusiasm. One of Hanson's police officers at my table said Hanson had read my 'danger on the trail' piece on the Gatton chase and 'had a good laugh'. She was enjoying our humiliation I supposed, and why not? A Hansonite said the venue for the night's public meeting had shifted at the last minute, so the numbers might be a bit low. Typical One Nation.

The candidate for Capricornia, Len Timms, was a squat man who said he was an accountant but sounded more like a used car salesman. He made a long speech, talking a great deal about himself without saying anything. Hanson gave a tired call to action before the room filled with the sound of Queen's high camp 'We are the Champions'.

Hanson arrived late at the faded red-velvet Grand Ballroom of the Leichhardt for her public meeting. When I'd lived in Rocky in the mid-1980s it was the town's best hotel, but now it was past its prime. Two hundred people and two hundred empty seats awaited Hanson. Timms gave the same speech even though it was to many of the same people. Hanson entered from the back, fresh make-up and fresh dress illuminated by the television lights. She gloried in the attention.

Rockhampton is a regional city with a long Labor tradition, and here Hanson focused not on race, but on the evils of economic rationalism for ordinary workers. She'd keep Telstra because it made lots of money for the public rather than shareholders, and a sale would see thousands of jobs lost. She'd stop the growing dominance of big business by freezing competition policy so it wouldn't run over independent pharmacies, newsagents and service stations. Her subsidised apprenticeship scheme would allow people without an academic bent to leave school at fifteen and learn a trade. She repeated her demand that Australia pull out of negotiations on the Multilateral Agreement on Investment, a secretive treaty process designed to guarantee compensation to multinationals in Australia and other OECD countries if government policy, even environmental laws, adversely affected them. (The Government abandoned the MAI after the election.)

And I'm not for this free trade, and I've spoken about that for the last couple of years, and just recently Bill Clinton's done a turnabout on it. We hear Dr Mahatir is actually doing a turnaround because he says now that free trade is destroying his country. Is it all right when they say it, but when Pauline Hanson says it I'm wrong or I'm simplistic? A lot of the things I've spoken about are now being addressed.

Pauline Hanson addresses her followers in the ballroom of the Rockhampton Leichhardt Hotel. I took this picture as one of a series of her performance—it had an unusually decadent feel.

And it's only because they're concerned at losing their seats, they're afraid of losing their control of Parliament, because for the first time there's real opposition in this country.

So I'm not simplistic, I'm not stupid, and someone called me loopy the other day—well I'm not loopy either, it's just that I have a different way of doing things. I'm addressing issues and how I would make a difference. They've done no good in this country; I don't think I could do any worse. If I haven't got the answers, I intend to find them.

She told a long story about how when she was on the Ipswich Council, her first political job before standing for Oxley, she'd listened to the council labourers to work out what needed doing on the city streets. She made government sound like running a shop guided by the grievances of honest toilers.

You have to bypass the bureaucrats because they'll only tell you what they want you to know. And you go and listen to the workers, the people at the grassroots, and they'll tell you. You'll get the answers from them, and that's where you can make the right decisions. I don't intend to do this job any differently, and I haven't. You go to the sources, you find out what you want to find out, and then you toss up the information you've got and you come up with the answers for yourself.

She'd just about lost her voice and looked about to drop with tiredness. She apologised for needing to cut question-time short and a man called out, 'Have a rum.'

'You know I drink rum, do you? The message got around.' It had, courtesy of her 'ginger bitch' at the Linville races.

As she prepared to leave, a young man approached. 'We are three Central Queensland University students doing a poster project on how the media manipulates you. Can we speak to you?' Hanson: 'I'd *love* to speak to you.' The crowd cheered.

SEVEN

Go and tell the people of Australia the truth

DAY 9

At Rockhampton airport in the early morning of race-card day, Len Timms told me casually that he and the National Party member for Capricornia, Paul Marek, had agreed to swap preferences—a big story if it was true. The Queensland Nationals were still in agonised discussion about whether putting One Nation last would split country conservatives so badly that seats would fall to Labor.

A wild-eyed Heather Hill, Hanson's 'media adviser' for the day, said she was still working on a family policy for release the following week. How was she coping? 'I just keep moving, just keep moving.' We left in our charter plane early to beat Hanson to her first stop, the central-west coal-mining town of Moranbah, a Labor stronghold before Hanson rode into town.

DEAN SEWELL

Preparing for her race speech, a lonely Hanson takes instructions by phone in Moranbah. Dean's Sydney colleagues judged the photo a brilliant set-up—in fact, Dean shot it through a glass door after Hanson barred media entry. He chose this picture to sum up her disastrous race-card day in Longreach.

It was hot as hell at the Moranbah Community Centre, heat waves shimmering across the flatness of the company-built town. Hardly anyone had turned up. A youth in Moranbah State High School uniform stood outside waiting for the hall to open. He wore a thick chain on his belt that hung below his right knee. His face was pale and blank, and his long greasy hair hung below his hips.

As Hanson arrived, a mining union man called Geoff Bail called out, 'If you're the mother, then how many fathers are there? Hitler would be one, wouldn't he?'

Hanson was early. She entered the empty hall, closed the glass door, and made phone calls. Through the door Dean and Grant shot what would be the pictures used in *The Sydney Morning Herald* and *The Australian* to depict her race-card day: head down, defeated, alone.

Outside, Geoff Bail had just had a verbal stoush with a Rockhampton One Nation official travelling with Hanson, an ex-miner Geoff saw as a class traitor for joining the party. 'Piggy's his nickname. Riverside and

Goonyella used to be two separate pits in Moranbah. I worked at Goonyella and he worked at Riverside. I have no time for him and nor does the rank and file.' Geoff had worked as a fitter in Moranbah for 22 years. 'I'll rely on you to protect me,' he said.

'I'm as scared as you are of these people,' I replied.

His black-button eyes were watery and glazed, as though he'd been on a bender that wasn't over yet, or the heat and isolation of Moranbah had gotten to him. He spoke gently.

'What about that statement, the mother, that was enough to get my blood boiling. The whole racial issue, I suppose that's the one I follow the most, more than anything else. The racial attitude that she's floated, whether she totally denies it or not, it's what she puts up.'

Was there much support for her here?

'Doesn't look like it, no. There is a fragmenting, because of the gun legislation and her position on that. Being an ex-sporting shooter myself, I've done a lot of shooting locally. But I've got to admit I totally agree with the laws. I lost all my guns through it, but if it saves one domestic violence turning into a murder, I've got to support it. I've got two daughters, and for their lives and everybody else's I think the gun laws had to be tightened, although it had a big effect on me and what I did.'

One Nation, guns and Wik. What a combination.

An elderly woman standing across the road held up a rough banner, 'Good mothers don't discriminate—say No to Pauline Hanson'. She shook as I approached. 'Oh no, the media—I didn't do it for the media.' Mary Leslie lived in Dapto near Wollongong, and had seen a flier for Hanson's meeting while in Moranbah visiting her miner son. She apologised for her banner. 'I couldn't find a big enough piece of paper.' Why did she go to the trouble?

'Because I don't like Pauline Hanson and I don't like her policies. I think she's a stupid woman, and she's manipulated, and she's only a Liberal in disguise as far as I'm concerned. Look at John Howard, he's not going to say too much about her because he relies on her.'

'So you're on holidays and decided to make your own sign. Fantastic,' Helen said. Mary began to shake again. 'Oh dear, I've got a headache.' We left her alone.

Only 60 supporters turned up to see Hanson. Battling the flu and facing long rows of empty seats as the prelude to her big race-card moment in Longreach, she faced sceptical questions on Easytax, which she conceded could 'break One Nation'. Then came requests for reassurance that she'd bring back guns. Hanson never raised guns off her own bat, and twisted and turned in her answer, contradicting One Nation's soft line on all gun ownership. 'I don't want a loaded gun in the home, by no means, but the man on the land needs it as a tool for his business.' (David Oldfield admitted later in the campaign that the gun lobby had donated $100 000 to the One Nation election campaign.)

While she was speaking, our head offices called with the news that Queensland National Party director Ken Crooke had just announced that North Queensland Nationals Bob Katter and De-Anne Kelly would preference One Nation. (Two Queensland colleagues, Paul Marek and Paul Neville, officially joined the pair later.) Crooke had also made the startling allegation that One Nation had offered to preference National Party leader Tim Fischer in his New South Wales seat of Farrer in return for National Party preferences in Hanson's seat of Blair. The allegation had not been denied.

Hanson had made it crystal clear to all and sundry since her Queensland election triumph, including during this campaign, that One Nation would put Tim Fischer last. It was a matter of personal pride to her, and an assertion that One Nation would replace the Nationals as the party of the bush. Was it appropriate to report what One Nation's leader said on such things as fact, as we had assumed? How did you cover a campaign when the leader wasn't the leader? The offer was also a sure sign of One Nation's fear that Hanson could lose Blair.

We left for the airport to force a doorstop, and surrounded her taxi on its arrival. ABC Radio's Anne Delaney put the Crooke allegation and Hanson drew breath.

'No. No. No way in the wide world. No way. Not from me...Tim Fischer would not get One Nation's preferences. No way in the wide world would I put Tim Fischer second preference in his seat, or [deputy

National Party leader] John Anderson. They have been two—especially John Anderson—have all but destroyed the country, and the industry, and people on the land.'

'So you did not authorise that offer to the National Party?' I asked.

'No. No.'

The Nine Network's Melanie Wendt asked, 'Pauline, are you worried that preferences discussions are going on behind your back without your knowledge?'

'There are people—look all my candidates, I've said to them, have input into this—'

Melanie interrupted, 'So what about your seat, the seat of Blair, are you worried that your officials are talking to the National Party without your knowledge?'

'Listen, nothing will happen without my okay.'

'So will you sack the people who have been offering to save the National Party leader if the National Party saves you?' I wanted to know.

'Listen, Margo, you're putting these questions to me—until I hear from people, and I speak to my own people about what's going on—'

'So you haven't been told what Ken Crooke said yet?' I asked, incredulously.

'I haven't had a chance to. I have been on the road for so long, and so busy—the phones don't work in every area that I go to.'

'But what directions have you given so far on what deals you're prepared to make? What's your overall concept of it, or are you just allowing your officials to do anything they like?'

'I do have an input into this, and when I get back it will be finalised, and then only, so thank you.'

She staggered off to her plane looking shell-shocked. *The Sydney Morning Herald*/News Limited plane took off first, but her plane was faster and passed us. So now, a plane chase.

AAP's Queensland State political reporter, Sam Strutt, hitched a ride, and related wild stories about the behaviour of One Nation members in the Queensland Parliament. When the new Labor Government wanted to soften the State's industrial relations laws, it was on the cards that the six One Nation members in former Labor seats would vote yes, while the five in National Party seats would vote no. But the One Nation leader,

Bill Feldman, offered Premier Peter Beattie all the votes if One Nation MPs got more staff. So much for the people's voice.

Sam was at the centre of a One Nation/media scandal born of an incident in a Queensland Parliament House corridor. She'd been walking along with Debbie Beaven, press secretary to Bill Feldman, when the One Nation member for Ipswich West, Jack Paff, called Beaven over to say, with respect to Strutt, that 'I'd like to knock her off'. Feldman had sacked Beaven for advising Sam of Paff's sexual threat, and *The Courier-Mail*, in an unprecedented move, had offered Beaven a job as a journalist then published her exposé of One Nation's Queensland MPs. That offer—proof, if any were needed, that some media played by different rules when it came to One Nation—had understandably outraged journalists on staff. Beaven, now a *Courier-Mail* 'journalist', was suing One Nation for unfair dismissal, and had told Sam she'd have to give evidence.

Our pilot was flying on full throttle and Dean sat beside him urging him on, but we were falling further behind Hanson's plane. Our pilot radioed hers and got his agreement that, if possible, he would circle before landing to give us a chance to catch up. We landed minutes after her plane, and Lisa Millar told me days later that Hanson had sat sweltering in her plane to await our arrival. A first.

At the Stockman's Hall of Fame with its towering bronze statue of a stockman, you could see why our presence was important. A mere 30 people were scattered on the curved steps in the shade, some of them tourists. There was no welcoming party or formality at all, and British ITN TV's Australian correspondent, Libby Wiener—one of many international media reporters on hand to see Hanson play the race card—greeted the One Nation leader.

This 'race speech' was purely a media event, and a botched, surreal one at that. John Howard had come here in 1997 to face more than 1000 angry pastoralists who were incensed at his ten-point Wik plan and insistent that he abolish all traces of native title from pastoral leases. At Tim Fischer's request, Howard had answered their questions and given them his word of honour that he would compromise no further—although One Nation's success at the Queensland election forced him to do so in the end. One Nation, by choosing the same venue for a speech on race, and thus elevating it to a symbolic level, needed to match Howard's crowd and approach its genuine passion. Instead, it was relying on empty symbolism, and the hope that the media would fill the vacuum and create something from nothing. We knew by now that there was going to be nothing new in Hanson's 'Aboriginal affairs policy speech'. You have to have a story or a damn good spectacle to successfully stage a political 'media event'. Unless One Nation had something new and startling to say, it was either very dumb or very desperate.

One Nation's lack of planning contrived to emphasise the sham. The lectern and microphone from which Hanson would speak faced out from the Hall of Fame directly into the full glare of the stiflingly hot sun. Her minuscule 'audience' was gathered behind the lectern in the shade. Hanson would thus have her back to the people, speaking instead to the cameras she so mistrusted. (Oldfield later said of Heather Hill's performance as media adviser that day, 'I don't mind Abos but I hate stupid people.') When Hanson mounted the lectern she looked startled at the arrangement, and turned her back to the cameras to ask her audience for forgiveness. 'I don't like having my back to you, but I can understand why you're sitting there, because you want to be in the shade. So please, I do apologise for the way this has been set up, with my back to you.'

She turned to the front to face the enemy and began. 'So welcome each and every one of you being here today. I've never been to Longreach before, so it's my first time, especially standing on the steps of the Hall of Fame.' She saw Marty—the ABC cameraman deputed to film for all the Australian TV networks due to a shortage of charter planes—running towards her. 'Is everyone ready, is the media?'

'Two minutes please, Pauline?' begged Lisa Millar. So Hanson started again.

Hanson read a text shaped by Oldfield two nights before. 'Does an Aborigine who is the same age as I am, and was born here as I was, have any more feel for the land or cherish its beauty and ruggedness more than you or I do? Would an Aborigine fight any harder to defend Australia than you or I would?'

There were a few Aboriginal people in 'the audience', but Hanson plainly did not include them in the pronoun 'we'.

The political bleeding hearts and others who seek to line their pockets through greed will only destroy our nation and our people. We are all sorry for past wrongs but no one group has a monopoly on heartache and despair. This shameless grab for land is not about reconciliation, but in fact an exercise in remuneration. We should sit down as a nation and talk through these issues not as Aboriginal and non-Aboriginal, but as Australians.

And what was this Australian's version of equality and talking through the issues as Australians? Take everything away from Aborigines again and replace the loss with nothing. Abolish native title without any compensation and abolish the Aboriginal Land Fund which was set up to buy land for Aborigines no longer connected to their land because of dispossession, and thus not eligible to claim native title. Remove the constitutional power to legislate for the benefit of Aborigines, giving power back to the States which had maltreated Aborigines for so long. Remove all Aboriginal benefits, and question whether some people on those benefits were actually Aboriginal.

'The Aboriginal population is growing faster than the population generally, despite terrible infant mortality and a generally shorter life span,' she said. It was grotesque—a statement of shocking racial disadvantage used as proof that assistance should be withdrawn. It was the same old One Nation line, the standard appeal to whites that they, not Aborigines, were hard done by. The inherent racism of the appeal was made even more transparent by Hanson's failure to announce any new plan—in what One Nation itself had billed its Aboriginal affairs policy speech—to address Aboriginal disadvantage once everything in place was dismantled. Yet she'd said during the campaign that One Nation had troubles in city areas 'because of the perception that One Nation is supposed to be a racist party', and had supported a planned Government election policy to gut ATSIC and decentralise responsibility for service delivery. Yes, said Hanson then, 'bring in the elders, let them have the respect from their community to deal with the issues there.' But these ideas, however flawed, never made the light of day. I remembered David Oldfield telling me just after the election was called that he'd have no trouble beating his competition for a New South Wales Senate seat, the

Aboriginal leader and Democrats candidate Aden Ridgeway, because 'Australians are racist'. Whatever Oldfield's strategy, the race card wasn't going anywhere, and after Hanson's Longreach debacle the Government dropped its big anti-ATSIC policy announcement. A counter to a One Nation race card wasn't needed any more.

The promised 'controversial' announcement in the race speech was in the same vein as the crazed blend of cynicism and naivete in Peter James' claim that voters would lap up Easytax because their eyes would shine at the words '2 percent'. Hanson claimed that the *Native Title Act* would allow a future government to make freehold subject to native title, based on an untenable reading of a regulation made under it. This assertion totally ignored the High Court's definitive ruling the day before in the Larrakia case that a grant of freehold extinguished native title forever.

Not only was the claim ludicrous, it profoundly misread the power of Wik as a political issue since the settlement. After a pitched and divisive battle lasting nearly two years, all stakeholders apart from the Aboriginal people and reconciliation groups were relieved. Wik was dead as an election issue in the bush. And here was Hanson, her back to the gullible and the sightseers, trying to convince the media she was saying something important.

She finished to stuttered applause and retreated to the steps for the shade. Her Aboriginal affairs spokesman and number two Senate candidate in Queensland, Len Harris, who turned his back on the cameras occasionally to address his leader sitting behind, detailed the 'Your backyards aren't safe from the blacks' line. Hanson looked devastated, and *The Age* used a picture of her head bowed between the bare dangling legs of two children above her.

After the speeches were over a reporter from Brisbane radio 4BC ran up, panting. She'd managed to get a seat on the plane flying One Nation House of Representatives and Senate candidates from Brisbane for the big event. The plane had been delayed by fog, and Hanson had not waited for the people who had come to applaud her to arrive.

Hanson wandered down the steps and reporters gathered around for the expected doorstop. Libby Wiener was interested in the generality of her racism for her international audience. The Australian media knew all about that and wanted to quiz her on the farce we'd just witnessed.

Libby began. 'People say your message is actually racist, by saying you want to take funding away from these groups.'

'Did I say that?'

'People are saying that it's racist.'

'You heard my speech—did I say it?'

'But you want to take away funding from certain groups?'

'You heard my speech, don't try and make something else that I didn't say.'

When the Australian media started asking questions, she said, 'I'm going', and walked away towards a small group of supporters waiting to meet her. We followed. Anne Delaney asked if the speech was an excuse to kick Aborigines in order to revive her campaign. She sighed and kept walking. 'Was it an excuse, the whole purpose of this?' Anne retorted. No answer. Helen asked, 'Ms Hanson, do you consider that there's anything new in that policy launch at all?' Hanson said hello to a fan, gave him a hug, and began shaking hands. Helen repeated her question, but Hanson kept meeting and greeting.

Then she turned, walked back to the pack, and said, 'Look at my speech, have it analysed, and really try to understand what is sitting in that [Native Title] Act now. Then you might start to understand what I'm trying to say.'

She turned away again, but Libby brought her back with the question, 'So you think John Howard has underestimated you then?'

'You're from what?'

'British television ITN. We're very interested to see the impact One Nation's having.'

'Yeah? Well look, I have enough problems keeping up with the Australian media, let alone the international media being here.' She turned away once more.

I addressed her back. 'Ms Hanson, why did you make the speech today?' Silence. She looked at me, frowned, turned away, and looked back again.

'It's clear what I've said, and it's clear that I—'

I interrupted. 'But why did you play the race card today, Ms Hanson?'

Her voice rose and she began to give me a lecture, emphasising her point with her rolled-up speech notes. 'I've made it quite clear that Australians have the right to know before they go back to the polls what is in that Native Title Act. And people have been deceived over it. And it clearly states that through a regulation it can be changed, that there can be native title claimed over any part of Australia.' I tried to interrupt her with the facts about the Larrakia judgment, but her voice rose another notch.

'We cannot afford this because $210 million dollars has been spent so far on native title claims and only four have come out of it, and two were actually sold off within 45 minutes of coming out of that court. And apart from all that, there are another 2000 claims in Australia under native title. We cannot afford it as a nation, it will divide us as a nation, and I'm going to fight every inch of the way. If people think that they're going to divide this nation—' The crowd which had gathered around us clapped and cheered, her voice rose another notch, and she faced the pack.

'Now if you cannot understand that, well I feel very sorry for you, because you are the voice of the people in what you print in your papers and what you put across on your TVs.'

She started screaming. 'So it's about time—go and tell the people of Australia the truth. Now with this ten-point plan, as Howard stood here on these steps he actually changed, and he lied to the Australian people. Go and print the facts and go and tell the Australian people the truth, and let them make up their minds. Because October the third is a very, very important time in Australian political history, but Australians have the right to know. And as far as I'm concerned—GET THIS CLEAR—we are AUSTRALIANS, and it makes no difference whether you are from Aboriginality, or whether you were born here or whether you were a migrant. We are all Australians together. And DON'T try and divide this nation.'

To more applause and cheers, Len Harris put his arm around her and led her away.

It was fabulous TV vision and the TV people fled to file before deadline. It made all the TV news, although the Nine Network at first decided not to use it because the sight of Hanson upset at the media could increase her support. A political judgment, in fact, but they'd changed their minds and went with news judgment instead. The vision of Hanson's dummy spit was too good not to use.

Helen, Leisa Scott and I trouped down the road to the Jumbuck Hotel, where another very poorly attended public meeting was to take place. Hanson, looking distressed, made a dash for the hotel dining room.

David Oldfield had rung Helen several times trying to get to Hanson, panicked about her reaction to the Fischer preferences allegation. He was denying only that he had made the offer, not that it had been made. When she came outside, I asked if she'd spoken to Oldfield yet. She said no, because her phone didn't work. I gave her my phone. She went over to a corner, and I tried to follow to record the conversation. But one of her federal police officers, playing media minder, said the conversation was private. You couldn't blame him, really—everyone's roles got confused in this campaign.

When she returned my phone, Helen asked what Oldfield had said. Just that preferences hadn't been decided yet. And the offer of a preferences swap with Tim Fischer? 'I didn't ask him about it at all.'

I was stunned. 'You didn't talk about that?'

'No, I didn't talk about that.'

'Are you the leader of the party, Ms Hanson?'

'Get it quite clear. Yes I am. There have been no deals done.'

I was calling my editor, Paul McGeough, from the hotel reception desk for advice on how to write 'the story', whatever the hell it was, when I overheard two female employees who were watching Hanson making a speech to all of ten people outside.

'She could have at least worn something nice,' one said.

'She looks all right,' replied the other.

'No, jeans and boots and a T-shirt—we see that every day. I wanted to see her all dolled up, like she is at other places. Isn't Longreach important enough for that?'

I was completely freaked out by the day—the revolting speech, the disturbing image of Hanson talking race just to the media, the shocking sense of being in a foreign country, the boy with the chain on his belt, the plane chase, the sheer incompetence of it all...And now, a Longreach voter's desire that Hanson stick with the cheap glamour and forget substance. Paul told me to take a step back and just report the day, as it happened.

I sat down next to a big, ruddy, red-haired man to listen to the rest of her speech. He looked at me with disgust, and moved. It reminded me of my reaction when I'd moved away from a bloke I'd classified as a Deliverance type at the Linville races.

After the speech, Len Harris demanded to know if I'd read the Wik legislation, but I was too tired to argue Wik, so Leisa Scott filled the breach. David Anning, a polite young Hanson acolyte and number four on One Nation's Queensland Senate ticket, gave me a tape on the evils of economic rationalism and made me promise to listen to it.

As debate on Wik raged around me, Christopher Zinn from *The Guardian* asked if he could interview me for a piece on Hanson and the media which would air on the Nine Network's Saturday morning current affairs show.

'What happened? It's been a very strange event,' he began.

'I've never seen anything like that, as a political event, in my life. Pauline Hanson, in the ultimate irony, spoke to the media with her back to the people. To me, that is the image that suggests One Nation is dead.'

'What about this mad air race that's going on. It looks like the whole thing is just set up for the media, and not for the people at all.'

'That's another irony of this most ironic of campaigns. Ms Hanson has made no arrangements for the media whatsoever, but with Ms Hanson you've always got to be with her because she might blow at any time. Anything might happen. So we were forced to chase her. Now we had a slow plane. Her plane went past. We tried to make arrangements with her pilot to slow down. Luckily, her plane did slow down. So when we got there, there she was—and we were there to see the death of One Nation.'

'So why come all this way just so she could give a speech she could have given in Brisbane...?'

'Because it's a symbolic speech, a speech about saying "John Howard made a speech to the pastoralists last year on Wik, I come back to the pastoralists and make them a pledge that I will get rid of Wik, that I will get rid of native title, get rid of land rights." Remember Pauline Hanson's fight here is with the National Party, as to who will be the party of the bush. What she is saying is that the Coalition will not deliver for the bush, I will. That's why she's here. And it has been a complete and utter disaster. And I think in most quarters in Australia, including all of us in the media, it will be a great relief.'

Later, I asked Hanson for a lift to the airport because Grant and Dean were still at a film-processing laboratory in town. Helen and I expected a knock back after the day's aggression, but she said, 'How many of there are you? Hop in.' She seemed happy, whether because she thought she'd scored well on the day, or because the ordeal was over, I didn't know and couldn't tell.

'Are you coming to the dinner with me tonight in Brisbane?' No, we were stuck in Rockhampton overnight. Would she tell us what she'd be doing tomorrow?

'Yeah, I've got a street walk on, at nine o'clock, in Rosewood.'

'So, what are you going to say about preferences tomorrow?' I asked.

'Bloody nothing!' She giggled.

The airport was packed with journalists returning to Brisbane on charters and other passengers on the commercial flight Hanson would fly home on, which was booked out by the time she'd told her media what she was doing. Grant and Dean tried to get on her plane to take a shot, but the flight attendants refused to let them on board. They stood on the tarmac and waved till she spotted them. She looked out and gave them a thumbs up.

With nothing new on race except for the laughable claims on free-hold title, the dummy spit and the low turnout became the race story. But that night back in Rockhampton, where the Please Explain journalists were staying, our Queensland politics experts Melanie and Anne said the dummy spit could bring her back from the electoral brink, that she could get a popularity lift because of the hatred of the media in Hansonville. I kept seeing her thumbs up and worried that maybe I'd been precipitate in publicly predicting the demise of One Nation. After Easytax beached her campaign at birth, and without the race card, could the sympathy vote turn her fortunes around? With Pauline Hanson, you never knew.

EIGHT

You've seen a bit on this trip, haven't you?

DAY 10

With a two-hour flight from Rockhampton, and a long, fast drive to a hamlet outside Ipswich called Rosewood for a Hanson street walk, it wasn't going to be an easy morning. Amid the buzz of rollicking street fetes and Saturday morning shopping mayhem, Hanson threw me a hard stare and turned away with, 'I did not turn my back on my people; I apologised for that.' She'd read *The Sydney Morning Herald* for once, and she wasn't happy.

When there are no minders around, you have to restore relations personally—and after a bitter day like Longreach, that was a hard ask. Dressed in gingham, and looking unusually country matron, Hanson sat outside a café eating a pie for brunch under the adoring gaze of a young Rosewood mother and her daughter, Alice. I put Marion Wilkinson's

Hanson and I debate the merits of the Moranbah picture. She hadn't bothered to read the Herald's *exposé, 'Who's afraid of Pauline Hanson?'*

feature, 'Who's Afraid of Pauline Hanson?'—the cover of the *Herald*'s Saturday 'News Review' section—on her table, and pointed to a stunning half-page picture Dean had taken of her walking along the beach at Noosa. 'What's wrong with that?' She pointed to the news picture of her alone and defeated in the Moranbah community centre and retorted, 'That one looks like I'm crying, but I'm actually on the phone.' The old 'perception is reality' problem. I said the picture could create sympathy among potential One Nation voters, and her friend, who trailed Hanson whenever she visited Rosewood, piped up with, 'Yes, I think it's lovely'. The door opened.

In the butcher shop buying her meat, she tried to talk Helen and me into buying some too. 'Well, I got you to buy peas the other day, didn't I?' She asked the butcher how business was going. 'A bit quiet, but as good as you'd expect in the climate we're in. We need more jobs I feel.'

'I think every Australian thinks that's what we need,' she replied.

She broached another complaint as we walked out. 'Now it came out on TV this morning that you were chasing us by plane and all the rest of it—what do you mean, a plane chase? I *did* wait for you guys at Longreach.'

'But you didn't tell us you'd be waiting.'

'I don't tell you everything, Margo.'

How to get her to understand? 'But if you don't tell us, then we have to chase—that's why you might like to tell us.'

A woman behind us yelled out, 'Get out of the way you media people, she's come here to talk to us.' Hanson lived a few miles from Rosewood and did her shopping there, so she knew everyone and everyone knew her. She had a pre-lunch beer at the bar in a gorgeous old pub, a very under-age Alice beaming beside her on a bar stool, bought every raffle ticket in sight and spun lucky-number wheels with abandon. The photographers and cameramen fell in love with the reality of it all—there was no need to set up shots because they were there for the shooting.

She had lunch at the only pub in an even tinier hamlet called Marburg before a Blair candidates' public meeting in Lowood, about an hour's drive away. Journalists ordered steak sandwiches and I asked her to join us on the pub verandah. 'Well, I was going to play pool, but all right.'

Hanson gave me another blast over the plane chase, I protested again, and my colleagues told me to shut up and eat. Melanie asked Hanson what she thought of her opponents in Blair. She said the National Party's Brett White was nice, and the poor bloke was worried because his wife was just about to have their first child. She didn't know anything about her main rival, Liberal Cameron Thompson, and said she'd see what she thought of them all at the candidates' meeting before deciding how she'd personally distribute her preferences in Blair.

Anne Delaney said Thompson used to work for the ABC. Was he any good, Hanson inquired. 'I couldn't possibly comment,' Anne said stiffly. Typical ABC. 'Well, he won't get my preferences then, if he worked for the ABC,' Hanson said jokingly.

She told us, we thought in jest but couldn't be sure, that she might go to a disco tonight. She looked pointedly at my jeans and T-shirt. 'They wouldn't let you in.' I'd begun to enjoy her flashes of snobbery.

'You could turn around and say, "You've got to let her in, One Nation's for all Australians".' Ha ha.

Hanson returned to her table inside and began reading Marion Wilkinson's piece. The TVs were keen for a preferences doorstop—the

major political topic regarding One Nation, which had still made no official announcement. She'd said in Longreach that she'd say 'bloody
nothing' on the topic of preferences, but I approached her to advise the
questions we wanted to ask, 'so you can think about them', and assured
her we'd give her lots of space. She walked out to the verandah and
allowed herself to be directed.

'A little to the right,' Peter said, and she shuffled across.

'But not far right,' I added cheekily. Anne grimaced and Hanson
smiled and shuffled back a little. Sound checks, light checks—the TV
journalists explained why—and she began the smoothest doorstop of the
campaign.

Under questioning, she said she would put Tim Fischer and John
Anderson last, and give One Nation preferences to three Queensland
National Party renegades—Bob Katter, De-Anne Kelly and Paul Marek.
No one really believed her.

Lowood's community hall was packed when we entered, but the light
was too dim for TV. A clash of cultures was about to begin. Having
been on the road with Hanson for more than a week now, the TVs were
used to making do. The ABC was deputed to light the hall and install
a microphone on the stage. As is the usual practice, the cameramen set
up on stands in the middle aisle up the front.

The candidates were nervous as hell about all the media attention.
They all—Greens, Democrats, Christian fundamentalist, National,
Liberal, Labor and Hanson—had five minutes each to have a say, then
the floor was open to questions. The second speaker had just begun
when an old man in the audience called out, 'Why are those cameras
there? I can't see. Get them away.'

The room froze. Marty looked across and I nodded—it seemed silly
to risk ugliness—and he led the retreat to the side of the room.
Throughout the campaign, many country people were antagonistic
towards the space occupied by the media. Some were incensed that the
media—in theory their representative—seemed to think it had the right

to occupy a central place, believing it was they, at election time at least, who had top priority.

The meeting chairman noticed that candidates were worried about the microphone—Dave from the ABC adjusted its height as each candidate spoke—and ordered that it not be used. Several members of the public ostentatiously shielded their eyes and grimaced and groaned when cameramen shone their spotlights on them for a crowd shot.

When the Greens and Democrats candidates spoke of their economic policies, there were surprised mutterings of, 'They sound like One Nation'. When the candidates were asked about foreigners not paying tax, the Greens candidate, Libby Connors, got ambitious. She suggested that the international bodies so demonised by One Nation as a threat to our sovereignty might well provide the answer by negotiating a world tax on the flow of international capital. Silence.

Brett White—who would have been a shoo-in in Blair before One Nation split the National Party vote—looked as if he needed a blood transfusion, and stared hard at the back of the room as he trembled his way through his spiel. He said he'd never agreed with the sale of one third of Telstra, delivered by the Government he was seeking to join as it had promised at the last election. He'd vote against selling off any more, too, despite the National Party's agreement with the Liberals to sell off the rest in exchange for increased spending on telecommunications in the bush. He looked like a loser.

Someone asked ALP candidate Virginia Clarke to explain Labor's planned capital-gains tax changes. She said, 'I don't know, and I'm tired,' and sat down. Labor was thought to have a slim chance in Blair because of the three-way split in the conservative vote, but how could they hope to win when their candidate appeared so weak? The rural poor—who Labor kept saying should be Labor voters—were getting no hope from Labor here.

Then some more real-life drama. Hearing a loud thud at the back of the hall, Melanie and I hurried down to investigate, fearing someone had hit Grant. An autistic young man had fallen over. He got up, walked onto the stage, faced the audience, and slowly drank a glass of water he took from the stage table. He sat next to Hanson. The meeting didn't skip a beat.

ABC TV had to leave midway through the questions because its deadline was pressing. They had no choice, but it meant the lights and microphone were dismantled mid-question time, leaving people blinking in the darkness. Hanson's jaw set at this further proof that the media was hurting her in Blair.

Despite the morning's work to keep her calm and happy, when she left the meeting she hit the accelerator, and the chase was on in driving rain.

The public had had no problem with print media at the meeting but they hadn't liked the intrusion of the TVs. Maybe the future in covering this sort of campaign, in the unlikely event it happened again, was the small hand-held camera. If the light was dim, well it was dim, and viewers would see it dim. If the sound was bad, then it was bad. But TV always demands technical excellence—a show tinted just for them—and TV always wins in the end.

The problem went much deeper for Hanson. She had to win her seat—no small ask when your major rivals have put you last on their preference tickets—and lead a national campaign to drag up a brand new party's vote across Australia, thus pulling in big cash returns from the election-funding scheme. Winning Blair meant lots of these fetes and meetings, and Blair voters didn't want the media around. They got scared, and felt that Hanson might be becoming such a 'star' that she wouldn't listen to them any more. It would have been just manageable to juggle a grassroots local campaign with a national campaign profile if she'd had a strong political and media advice team around her. But she was on her own.

Our next destination was Karalee State School in Ipswich for its annual fete. It was a beauty—packed to the rafters with children, and alive with music and dancing, fairies and clowns. Hanson made her standard apology about the media's presence to her hostess for the afternoon and got some advice in return. 'Pauline, you've got to think of the positives. Just ignore them.'

The school principal, Ron, welcomed Hanson over the sound system. Peter James made his first appearance of the day and reminisced with Ron about that golden day in 1996 when Hanson was elected the independent member for Oxley with the biggest swing in the nation. 'Two and a half years ago, Ron was down there running the polling booth and I was sitting there scrutineering, and there were people with tears in their eyes, weren't there? Labor Party people.'

Children ran up asking for autographs, and a boy offered her a Malteser. 'You're getting followed around by everyone,' he said. She laughed. 'I know. I can't lose them either.' Grant, always the interventionist (Dean preferred the purist approach of shooting what happens), told her there was a face-painting stall around the next corner. 'Forget it!' she said.

Grant and Dean were bored big-city boys, but I loved that fete. There was a classroom filled with fluffy toys—children had brought them from home, and there was a jar in front of each where people voted for their favourite with coins. Through the window, I saw a man outside pounding a car with a blunt instrument. At a dollar a minute, lots of people lined up for the pleasure.

In the next room, people proudly displayed the intricate craft of building miniature rooms filled with miniature furniture. One adventurous soul, Dawn, had built a video store and a private theatre, complete with piano. She said she'd vote for One Nation. 'Let's face it, the Labor Party's doing nothing for us, the Liberals have done nothing for us, so I think she's in with a real chance.' Nearby, Fred showed off a handmade miniature steam train—five types of native wood, 600 hours of work, 630 parts, and 125 parts inside the cab alone. He'd been the woodwork champion of the Ipswich Show in 1996. 'No, I don't think I'll vote.'

A feature of the fete was that whenever you bought something you'd get 'funny money' which you could then use to buy other things. Grant scored with that when Hanson agreed to hold up funny money for a picture—evoking memories of the call by her fundraiser David Ettridge to print more money to solve our economic problems.

She watched and clapped as children performed Irish and Scottish dances, but there was no sign of any non Anglo-Celtic culture on display. Ipswich, like most Queensland towns, is largely homogenous, apart from indigenous Australians.

I played a game where you pick a paddle-pop stick from a sandbox and whatever money is printed on the end of it you get. I won 50 cents and asked for funny money. The woman behind the table said, 'I saw you on TV this morning [the plane chase again]. Good report. It sounded hilarious.'

'Did you see her dummy spit at Longreach?' I inquired.

'Yeah, she didn't have good control, did she? You could hear the wobble.'

I said that maybe that was why the media was so fascinated with her, because she wasn't manufactured.

'Yeah, she sure wears her feelings on her sleeve.'

'That makes it a really interesting campaign trail, plus we get to go to country areas I've never been to before.'

'I bet you've never heard of Karalee,' she said wistfully. 'Not many people have.'

I was eating sausages and onion when Hanson's hostess came over to buy a curry. 'Welcome to the real world. You enjoying yourself?' she asked as Hanson joined her. 'You've seen a bit on this trip, haven't you?' Hanson quipped.

'Yes, at least you've forced the city media to come and have a look at the country. Win or lose, that's a good thing.'

Even Grant and Dean had downed tools. Hanson was free.

Just before dark, she sipped tea and waited for the fireworks. Her journalists did a deal to leave together after I extracted a promise from Hanson that she wouldn't be doing anything else tonight, including going to a disco, without calling me. A man was bashing the car as we left.

On the highway to Brisbane, Dean related the aftermath of the Noosa beach picture he'd taken the previous Sunday. As she'd left the beach, one of her ever-solicitous federal police officers fetched some serviettes from an ice-cream parlour to dry her feet. Dean shot off a frame and she'd freaked out, saying, 'If you're going to be sneaky like that you'll get nothing off me, I'll burn you off.'

'She gives you access, but then if you do take something she'll go off at you,' Dean said, nonplussed. 'If you're right in front of her you can't be that sneaky. It's a natural shot. That's not sneaky, not when you're there right in front of her, and when you have got the sort of access that we have to her. You'd never get that with Beazley or Howard.'

I told Dean about her chatting to someone at the fete, my tape under her nose as usual, when she'd picked up my wrist, moved my arm away, and dropped it. Within five minutes I was doing the same thing again and she was fine. 'She was nice by the end. When I got interested in those bloody miniatures I could do no wrong.'

Throughout the campaign, colleagues would assume Dean's best pictures were set up. They were so fresh that no one in the game could believe they were reality pictures. That's how staged-managed the media is these days on the election trail. Beazley picks up a fish as part of a message on the evils of a GST on fresh food—snap. The pollies had thought of all the symbolism and subliminal messages and references before they invited the photographers in. Andrew Meares, the photographer I'd toured with during Hanson's Queensland election campaign, had resorted in this campaign to shooting Howard from above his head and to taking close-up shots of his hands holding a cup of tea in order to find a fresh angle of vision. (He was castigated mightily by Howard's minders for the bald-with-protruding-eyebrows shot.) But on this campaign there was an embarrassment of wonderful, natural pictures each day.

By this stage, *The Sydney Morning Herald* was starting to demand a picture and a story every day. The pictures were so sparkling and the stories so different that some readers began following the Hanson campaign like episodes in a tall tale. For all my outrage over Hanson breaking all the standard rules of engagement, her campaign was a constant adrenalin high because of its sheer unpredictability. As political journalists, we were doing real work for a change, which required personal judgment on the stories and the pictures. It was a fantastic antidote to the precisely directed charade of the major campaigns. It was lucky for Dean and I that our readers were interested—because we were hooked.

PART TWO

TEST OF WILLS

NINE

Just a little redhead from Ipswich

DAYS 11, 12 AND 13

David Oldfield prowled the aisles throughout Sunday night's flight to Perth for Hanson's first interstate outing of the campaign. He moved people around so he could sit and natter to journalists one by one, annoyed passengers with his loud bombastic banter, and dominated the trip. The man who'd told us he'd come to save Hanson's campaign because 'my personal success is entirely linked to hers' was about to transform it.

Oldfield was nothing if not in-your-face. He was a tall, solid, blandly good-looking and well-preserved bachelor of 40, and very fussy about his appearance. His style was Sydney yuppie casual and he patted himself down, combed his hair and applied lip balm before TV interviews, which he then recorded to play and replay so he could improve his 'performance'. His on-air persona was still and calm, his voice even and expression 'concerned', regardless of what vicious or derogatory words issued forth. Some people thought his angry xenophobia was the result of his father's experience of torture in a Japanese prisoner of war camp during World War II.

His eyes were small, dark brown and expressionless, and his gaze direct, as if he was trying to see right through you. The most striking thing about his personal presentation was how light he was on his feet. He crept up on you, and almost soft-shoe shuffled through the day. I sometimes saw him as a mischievous devil, delighting in causing trouble wherever he went before stepping back to rub his hands and act the interested observer.

Oldfield portrayed himself as Hanson's knight in shining armour, the brains behind 'the product', and that's how he portrayed his first meeting with Hanson—which he swore was not premeditated—at a Canberra bar on the night of her maiden speech. According to Oldfield, a nasty young Liberal was haranguing her in the corner. 'I went over and pulled him away and apologised to her on behalf of the Liberal Party. I told her no one had the right to treat her that way. We started to talk and became friends.'

Hanson had never met anyone like Oldfield before—superficially urbane, solicitous and savvy—and she was impressed. Before long, he was secretly working for her, masterminding the formation of One Nation and a unique party structure which would entrench his power.

Pauline Hanson's One Nation was a company with three directors—Hanson, Oldfield and Oldfield's old friend David Ettridge, a professional fundraiser who took a cut of party donations. No director could be sacked without the vote of the other two, squeezing Hanson between the two Davids and stripping her of independent power in the party which bore her name.

The two Davids ruthlessly crushed grassroots opposition to their edicts, and insisted that each member of what was effectively a mere party support group hand over a signed, undated, letter of resignation on joining up. Pauline Hanson's One Nation was a corporate brand, selling protest politics for the benefit of three shareholders.

Oldfield gleefully despised the Liberal Party, where he'd learnt his politics before jumping ship to Hanson when he hadn't made the grade in seeking political office. 'They're an awful mongrel lot, but I'm paying them back in spades,' he'd told me.

Oldfield could not hide his contempt for One Nation members or their leader either. He considered himself vastly superior to that lot, and as a comfortably middle-class boy from the Sydney beachside suburb of Manly seemed to need the respect of 'the elites' that One Nation members so despised. He'd say to Liberal acquaintances, 'You'd have to say I've done a brilliant job with her,' and it was true he'd converted her personal popularity into a political party with real clout. The Canberra press gallery consensus was that Oldfield was a manipulative genius.

Hanson, from what she'd said to Helen and I at lunch on Tuesday, was well aware of the damage Oldfield's image as puppeteer could do to her popularity, and we waited with interest to observe the dynamics of their political partnership.

Oldfield's most obvious characteristic was his need to construct and display a notorious public sexual persona, despite his constant critique of media interest in Hanson's, and indeed his own, personal life. He made no distinction between public and private space, to the extent of invading other people's personal space as well as obliterating his own. He professed himself addicted to young blondes, admitted to using telephone dating services around the country, and told anyone who'd listen that his perfect woman was a cross between Jayne Mansfield and his mother. 'Women find me extremely attractive,' he'd tell female journalists. He was, in his own words, 'a playboy'.

Before the election, knowing he was being photographed, he'd put his hand up the skirt of a Sydney date and seemed pleased that the photo appeared in *The Daily Telegraph*. Before the election, he'd volunteered to me the information that the published photo was the first his 'Brisbane girlfriend' had known of the liaison. God knows if the Brisbane girlfriend knew about his 'Aboriginal girlfriend in Brisbane', whom he'd mentioned as some sort of proof that he wasn't racist. Not that she was into land rights or anything—'She's white in everything except her skin colour.' Oldfield had even gone so far as to give a

DEAN SEWELL

Oldfield and his date dance in Adelaide. Oldfield later boasted of his conquest to journalists. While Hanson complained to Grant and Dean about them taking pictures when she was trying to relax, Oldfield revelled in the attention.

photograph of himself with a young woman to a newspaper for publication.

The first time I'd dealt with him on such matters was after the Queensland election, when *The Sydney Morning Herald* wanted a profile. That morning, the *Telegraph* had run a page-one story speculating that Hanson and Oldfield were having an affair. I told my Sydney editor I wouldn't ask about his private life, only to find that Oldfield's opening lines were, 'I'm completely heterosexual and I am not sleeping with Pauline Hanson.' To claims he was a womaniser, he said, 'I certainly used to bring a little cheer to the lonely, but now I don't have time.'

'The Liberals push that I'm gay, but that is typical of the right wing of the Liberal Party. Now you and I know there's nothing wrong with that, but to them there is.' It all seemed compulsive, as if he was trying to prove something to himself as well as everyone else.

He'd already asked Helen, a blonde, to dinner more than once. Once on the campaign, he even arranged to book a plane seat next to hers, which she discovered in time to change her seat and avoid the ordeal.

He'd also rung a Brisbane journalist close to One Nation to ask if a female colleague covering Hanson was 'worth trying'.

During the flight to Perth, Oldfield suggested Grant sit next to Hanson because he needed to talk to Helen. Hanson asked Grant if he was seeing anyone, and when told he lived with his girlfriend gave him a lecture on the importance of getting married, professing an absolute commitment to the institution despite her two failed marriages.

Meanwhile, Oldfield asked Helen to write a positive story on him in the campaign's last week. Taken aback at his brazenness, she asked for the impossible, a Hanson interview on her relationship with Oldfield. Sure, he said. Helen knew she wouldn't—Hanson never spoke publicly about her private life. At the request of my head office, I'd questioned her as she boarded the plane on whether Clinton should resign in the wake of the Kenneth Starr report into his affair with Monica Lewinsky. 'Actually, I'm disgusted by the whole lot, by the way it's been such a media frenzy. This is between him and his wife, and it's a private matter,' she'd said.

Hanson's first venture outside Queensland was to a State greatly attracted to her message, and polls taken after the Queensland election had shown Labor leader Kim Beazley in danger of losing his Perth seat to One Nation. Network Seven's Brisbane cameraman, Ollie, had warned me to be careful because the West hated Easterners even more than Queenslanders hated Southerners, and the police could be dangerously overzealous. While the State was largely conservative, the Left was very active and had spearheaded tumultuous, sometimes ugly protests when Hanson visited Perth.

More than a week into the campaign the Western Australian Liberal Party was, alone of all State Liberal branches, still holding out against putting One Nation last on its how-to-vote cards. It was the most hard-line right-wing branch in the country, and its expelled former powerbroker, Senator Noel Crichton-Browne, had dined more than once with Hanson in Canberra, giving her a detailed, hard-headed blueprint on how to transform her post-maiden speech popularity into a new political force. He was one of many hard-right figures who had courted Hanson in the early days when John Pasquerelli, lent to her by the expelled Western Australia Labor member Graeme Campbell, was her adviser, until she'd chosen Oldfield as her champion.

Conservative politics in Western Australia was awfully murky. Two prominent Crichton-Browne opponents in the Liberal Party, Margie Bass and Mary Louise Wordsworth, had defected to One Nation, whose candidates looked and sounded like Liberals. They were a world away from the homespun amateurs we'd seen in Queensland. I asked Oldfield if Crichton-Browne was involved in the One Nation branch in Western Australia and he denied it, saying Crichton-Browne had rung him recently to ask One Nation to preference a mate of his in the Senate. One Nation had refused. Hanson didn't like him because he was too pushy, Oldfield said. Given Oldfield's form, the mind boggled, but Oldfield played a more seductive game with Hanson than with the media or party members.

Monday morning, day twelve of the campaign, was unseasonably cold in Perth, but Hanson arrived at the airport for a sweep through the south of the State in a bright yellow top and black skirt that sat above the knee. It was the same outfit she'd worn to enter the tally room in triumph on Queensland election night, so maybe she was feeling upbeat with Oldfield by her side. I suspected Oldfield might have chosen her attire, but she insisted later it was all her own work.

Helen had a feeling the tabloids would love what journalists immediately dubbed 'the miniskirt'. Grant knew it, and focused on getting the 'Princess Di' shot—skirt lifted by the breeze as she alighted from the charter plane at her first stop. He believed Hanson had worn the skirt to score a 'page one splash' over the tough competition of Clinton's travails and the Commonwealth Games.

I started to get a sinking feeling about that skirt, fearing the extremity of her difference from the main players was escalating her election publicity. The day before, Brisbane's *Sunday Mail*—which routinely splashed with Hanson on page one because it lifted sales—had opined in an editorial that Beazley and Howard were running evasive, shadow-boxing campaigns, and that 'Pauline Hanson seems to have caught the public's attention more'. For the tabloids, the miniskirt was pay-dirt.

Dean recalled covering the last Russian elections, where the official billboards had pictures of all the candidates bar the ultra-right

Nationalist, Vladimir Zhirinovsky, in colour. Zhirinovsky had mocked his official black and white image and had worn a bright yellow suit. Hanson's skirt was the equivalent, but assuming she was engaged in a cynical grab for publicity, did the media need to play ball? It seemed it did.

It was a tiny plane—the pilot and a federal police officer sat in the cockpit, Hanson and Oldfield in the front row, Grant and Dean in the second row taking pictures, and another police officer and me at the back. I asked Hanson what she thought of the Marion Wilkinson feature on the inside workings of One Nation that I'd given her in Rosewood.

'It was too long. Even though it was about me I lost interest in wanting to read it.' I burst out laughing. She was amazing, so disconnected from her own party's internal machinations—often conducted without her knowledge—that she couldn't even muster enough interest to read about it. Her position was so detached it was beginning to seem not innocent but deliberate, part of a Faustian pact with Oldfield to allow him to run the machine while she drew in the unsuspecting masses and kept her hands clean.

One Nation in Western Australia verged on the professional, and a media bus was waiting when we touched down in Albany, a former whaling port in the State's south-west. A bumper Monday morning crowd of 400 awaited Hanson in the town's basketball stadium.

She was already late, but Oldfield kept her audience waiting another half-hour. Outside, at the back of the stadium, he put on a white business shirt and began fumbling with a tie, using a police car's rear-vision mirror. An impatient Hanson twice went out to the car. 'Hurry up, David, hurry up.' Finally, a uniformed cop tied the tie on himself and then handed it to Oldfield. 'God, this is a joke,' Hanson complained. Oldfield's behaviour was starting to seem a little weird.

Paddy Embury, a local grazier and the candidate for the seat of Forrest, made his first-ever public speech to cover the delay.

This is a wonderfully exciting day for all rural people in this part of Western Australia. For too long, Australian politics seems to have concentrated federally around the cities of Sydney and Melbourne. We have a wonderful, very brave lady, who gets horrific press, and we really welcome you, Pauline. Being a bit of an old male chauvinist, Pauline really has served it up to the men of the Australian community.

He looked around desperately, but there was still no sign of Oldfield, who was to introduce Hanson. 'I read an interview just recently, an Asian lady from one of the countries to the north, and she was asked, "Have you ever heard of Pauline Hanson?" I don't know if she's a fortune-teller, but she replied, "Yes of course. She's the Australian Prime Minister, isn't she?" The crowd roared and Oldfield took the floor.

I met Pauline Hanson approximately two years ago in 1996, on the night of her maiden speech. And she was an Australian that I saw on that day stand up and say all the things that were not so much visionary or brand-new, but unsaid. Pauline Hanson, just a little red-head from Ipswich, stood up and said all of these things in the face of incredible attacks, vilification, threats, and politically motivated insults. And she's stood all through that, and today she's going to stand before you, and I hope you give her a warm welcome.

Oldfield looked and sounded like a smug city slicker—the antithesis of what these people were yearning for—and his patronising description of Hanson ensured his place in the day's tabloid 'miniskirt' story. We were learning that Oldfield made sure he was in the story, if not the story itself, every day.

Hanson, buoyed by her biggest crowd to date on the campaign, delivered her most upbeat speech yet, focusing on the evils of free trade, competition policy, big business and foreign ownership, and the lack of secure jobs for ordinary workers.

Maybe a few more of these politicians need to get out into the streets of Australia, instead of behind their closed doors and big desks, and realise what's going on. I'm pleased to see now that after I've been around and putting a little bit of pressure on them about what the Australian people want, they're starting to wake up to themselves. But I don't trust the buggers. Have you been reading lately [that the major

One Nation's top Senate candidate in Western Australia, John Fisher, confers with Oldfield on stage at the Albany basketball stadium. Fisher scored a substantial first preference vote but the Democrats candidate—a gay activist—won the spot because the Liberals and Nationals put One Nation last.

parties are saying] 'Well we've got to get out there and talk to the grassroots people?' Why would they want to bother starting now? I'll tell you—because I'm here, because Pauline Hanson's here. Without putting pressure on the politicians that are there now, nothing will change.

She descended down to the basketball court and was mobbed. It was like an evangelical meeting, the true believers gathered respectfully around her, waiting for her to lay hands on them.

'You're the best thing that's happened in Australian politics.'

'Good on ya Pauline.'

'I'm a Christian and I am praying that you get in.'

An elderly woman brought a letter from Hanson she'd forgotten to sign in July 1997. 'You've got such lovely handwriting,' she said. 'Best of luck Pauline.'

'I think you're much more attractive than the other buggers.'

'Thank you for coming.'

A teenage boy said: 'I'd just like to say you're a much prettier person here, in person, than you are on television.'

'Thanks for speaking out for us.'

'Bless you.'

'My brother met you in Hobart, I had to do the same here.'

'A ton of guts, congratulations and good luck.'

'I had my doubts, but I'm much more positive after hearing you.'

'You're one gutsy lady.'

'We'll join the party and we're with you all the way.'

An old man introduced his wife with a shy grin. 'This is one of your ardent supporters. She calls you the brave lady.'

Amid the adoration, a few policy questions and some announcements. Yes to a referendum on capital punishment. No to closing down taxpayer-funded abortions. No to foreign aid, except of Australian-made food and products.

Then, lengthy discussions with Gloria Quartermaine, eighteen, an out-of-work Aborigine who lived with her baby in a caravan park. She asked her questions with diffidence and turned the tables. 'So how come everybody's got the idea that you're a racist?'

'I have no idea, that's why I say to people, is there anything I've ever said that is actually racist?'

'So how come half the Aboriginals think you are racist?'

'Because of what's been put out by the media. Now there's some media here. You see all the tape recorders—they're all the media, so you ask them.'

'But you must have said something to make it sound like you were racist.'

'I put it to you and any politician to actually state where I have ever said anything that is racist. Do you find calling for equality for all Australians being racist?'

'No.'

'Neither do I.'

'So what was this about Aboriginals supposed to be cannibals years ago?' (In 1997 One Nation published an anonymously penned book, *The Truth*, featuring the claim.)

'That was written up in a book about it—'

'But it's the same as you saying about the media—they write things that are not right and say things about you. What's in a book isn't necessarily right, is it?'

Hanson drew breath and turned away.

As the plane was about to take off to the city of Bunbury, I asked whether she thought her campaign was back on track. 'No—what do you mean back on track?'

Surely she'd agree that nothing had gone right till today?

'Wait a minute, right for who—you or me? Whose point of view are we talking about? Just because we had a bus there for you today or what?'

We couldn't continue this fascinating discussion on the role of the medium in the message because she got off the plane to do a radio interview on her mobile phone. Helen joined me on the tarmac and we did an impromptu doorstop.

'Now what do you think of being called "just a little redhead from Ipswich"? That amuses you or upsets you?' I asked.

'No, it doesn't upset me; you just have a chuckle over it. And I *am* from Ipswich and I'm proud of Ipswich. It's been my home, I've run my business, I've reared my kids [there].'

'Do you think you've got more to offer than "just a little redhead" and a fish and chip shop owner, the owner of a seafood takeaway?' Helen asked.

'Fish and chip, my God. Umm, that's *me*, you know. Look that's me— they can try and put me down, have a go at me, whatever way they possibly can—'

Helen cut in, with disbelief, 'But that was David saying that!'

Hanson got back on the plane, where I tried another line of questioning. Why had she worn that skirt?

'I've worn this before. I thought it was going to be warmer down here. And this is not what I call a miniskirt.' How would she describe it? 'Well it's just above the knee, it's regulation height when I went to school.'

In Bunbury, Oldfield asked Helen and me for 'genuine advice'. Should he agree to a date with Emma Tom, a professionally outrageous young writer who'd asked him out for her debut column in *The Australian*? Of course not, we said, it was an obvious set up. We reasoned that we weren't betraying a colleague by telling the truth because he'd be incapable of resisting the publicity. We were right.

In Perth later that afternoon, Western Australia began to turn nasty, when a Hanson mall walk became a run through screaming protesters from the left-wing youth group, Resistance. Hanson gave up and returned to her hotel.

It had already been a long day and One Nationites, police and journalists lolled about at the hotel bar writing, recharging phone batteries, eating and drinking. Helen took calls from *The Daily Telegraph* editors demanding more miniskirt quotes, and Oldfield suggested Hanson say she had better legs than Beazley or Howard. She didn't want to say anything, but when pressed hard came up with the line that if she had good legs at 44 then that was good going. (*The Daily Telegraph* ran Hanson on page one with the headline: 'Forget policy, I've got great legs.' The Melbourne *Herald Sun*'s boys-own sub-editors rewrote the story to have Hanson declaring she had the best 'pins' in Australia. She did not wear a skirt above the knee for the rest of the campaign.)

That evening, Hanson took off for her meeting in the town of York, more than an hour's drive south, without Oldfield, who was forced to take a taxi. York produced a big crowd of 600 as well as 50 Resistance protesters. Hanson began:

> It hasn't been a real easy road to have travelled over the last couple of years. Just listen to the rabble outside and you'll understand why. What they're espousing out there is that they believe that there should be no racism, that everyone should be treated the same. That's exactly what I have been saying right from the beginning, and I have not changed my views or ideas at all—

A young man jumped up to counter that she was falsely assuming Aborigines were on a level playing field with whites. Several men rushed forward, a woman threw her sheepskin coat over him, and the crowd jeered as he was dragged out. After the commotion had abated, Hanson said with perfect timing, 'There's a spare seat now, if anyone would like to sit down.' The crowd roared.

But she'd been rattled—as she often was on race—and her speech was almost incoherent, a grab bag of her favourite lines strung together at random. There were no spare seats, and Oldfield sat with us on some steps to the left of the stage. He chatted while she spoke and showed us a badge supporting East Timor that he'd bought from the protesters. When Hanson started talking about her beloved Easytax he groaned audibly, put his head in his hands and said loudly, 'Oh God, I've got to go home.' Many in the audience were now looking at him and he groaned again, said, 'I can't take this,' and stormed up the steps and behind the stage curtain.

Grant and Dean ran backstage and saw him set up the playing of the Seekers' rendition of the bicentenary song 'We are Australian', an ode to multiculturalism which One Nation had turned on its head. (One Nation had been warned a year before that if it used the song again at public meetings a writ would issue for breach of copyright.) Oldfield's aim was to restore the buoyant mood of the meeting, but no one, not even Hanson, knew the words to the song.

Oldfield's desire for attention seemed to know no bounds. Another young man in the audience stood up to yell, 'We need a real opposition to that economic rationalism of the major parties, but all One Nation offers is racist scapegoating.' After escorting him out, Oldfield strode onto the stage to deliver a rave on the just cause of the East Timorese people—proving, he claimed, that Resistance didn't know what One Nation was on about. The audience didn't seem to know either, the meeting ended in confusion, and Hanson drove off without him again. It was her way of asserting, perhaps even to herself, that she was the star.

He got a lift back with us and it was my turn for the hard sell on writing a positive Oldfield story.

'There were middle-aged women coming up and giving me kisses,' Oldfield said.

'Oh, you're a sex symbol at last,' I replied, but the sarcasm didn't penetrate.

'Well they were only middle aged—but what do you mean, "at last"?'

Dean and I agreed he was unpleasant company and that we wouldn't give him a lift again.

Oldfield had been telling us for days that Hanson would go clubbing with us at her favourite Perth nightspot, but she went straight to bed. Hanson's journalists were at the bar when Oldfield joined us seeking company for a clubbing expedition. Everyone said no. He began complaining that people kept saying he was gay when he wasn't. After five minutes of this, I said no one cared if he was gay or not and could we please move on, but he couldn't—until he began eyeing a couple of women at the bar.

■

The Western Australian police lived up to their Wild West reputation. The next day passed in a whirl of highly dangerous, breakneck-speed chases and altercations that made me feel like I was in a cops and robbers movie in reverse. It was crazy—Hanson wanted the media with her in Western Australia because she needed all the local publicity she could get in two short days. And she needed us to follow her because by midday she had to decide on the run where to go because Resistance trouble had forced her to abandon her itinerary. The Western Australian cops, however, ran decoy cars, blocked our access to exits when she left a shopping centre, and threatened to 'get' Grant if he didn't stop following her. Maybe they thought if the media weren't where she was, there'd be less Resistance trouble. Whatever their reasons they played hard, and Dean thanked the lord he'd convinced head office that booking four-cylinder hire cars on the Hanson trail was not on. The police adrenalin/testosterone rush was a response to dogged protests by Resistance, but it propelled Hanson's road show beyond anyone's control.

At Karrinyup shopping centre Resistance protesters disguised in suits jumped out unexpectedly on her arrival to surround her and panic the cops. The suits screamed, 'You're a racist Pauline', and 'You're a disgrace to Australia'. Hanson almost ran through the centre, cameramen running backwards in front of her, police at each side, journalists and One Nation candidates scrunched in the middle. Resistance protesters ran along each side of the flying scrum screaming taunts and scattering customers to the periphery, where the occasional fan waved as she rushed by.

Hanson remains calm and smiles amid worried police faces as she runs through rampaging Resistance protesters at a Perth shopping centre.

An enormous uniformed cop of about six foot five, who I'd seen in York, started pushing me.

'Excuse me, I'm from the media,' I yelled at him above the chants.

'I don't give a shit who you are,' he said. I think my clothes—T-shirt and jeans—must have made him see red.

'Who are you?' he demanded to know as he grabbed me. 'Who do you represent?'

I told him several times as he pushed and shoved, and the federal police officer I'd travelled with on the plane vouched for me, but the giant was ready to play. The elbowing kept up, and finally I said, 'I'm a citizen, what are you, some kind of fascist?' It was pretty weird, like a scene from 'Wildside'—everyone shouting at each other, no one listening. A metaphor for the Hanson phenomenon.

At the Galleria shopping centre the nightmare was replayed until Hanson ran into a coffee shop on the mezzanine floor and a line of police blocked the entrance to protesters.

Hanson told her federal police and candidates, 'I'd just rather get out because it's not fair on the people here,' before retiring to a table for morning tea. I was at another table showing my emerging bruises courtesy of the giant to a reporter from *Der Spiegel* magazine. She looked across and said she hoped I didn't blame her. 'Maybe I should get a media sign made for you, then you'll be all right.'

A man asked her to autograph his upper left arm for the purpose of same becoming a tattoo, something of a tradition among male Western Australian fans. 'I notice you keep smiling, you keep a smile on your face,' a local reporter said. 'Is that hard to do or do you think that is the best way?'

'No it's *not* hard to do, because I believe in what I'm doing,' she said indignantly. 'Do you think I'm going to let a few rabble like this deter me when I went to a meeting last night with 700 people there that were telling me to keep going?'

Mid-evening, Helen and I were about to board the return flight to Queensland when Oldfield ran into the Qantas Club to say Hanson had just cleared his preference strategy—double-sided tickets so One Nation voters could make up their own minds who to preference. In the Senate, half of One Nation's preferences would go to the conservatives, the other half to Labor. So much for all Hanson's contrary announcements, so much for all the wheeling and dealing One Nation and the major parties had been doing in back rooms since the election was called. We filed over the phone for page one.

On the way to Sydney, where Oldfield would drop off for a few days before returning to the campaign full time, he again stalked the aisle, saying he'd told Hanson she'd gone 'soft on Abos'.

TEN

Your reporter's trying to destroy me

DAYS 14, 15 AND 16

After two weeks chasing Hanson, events and sights and words had blurred into a fog of images and half-formed thoughts. But there was no time to make any sense of them, if there was sense to be made. I took a day off to write an analysis piece on One Nation's preference strategy.

The Party was trying to establish a new political alignment by leaching support from all three major parties. Hanson wanted Labor battlers suffering the squeeze on blue-collar labour. From the Nationals, she wanted family farmers watching the disintegration of their independence and way of life through the relentless momentum towards big corporate holdings, and rural workers rendered jobless with the introduction of new farm technology. From the Liberals, she wanted struggling small business people, especially in the regions, and older, socially conservative self-funded retirees.

It was potentially a serious political movement in a world where the old divisions of labour and capital were breaking down and the gap between rich and poor was ever widening. People in all political camps were losing their living standards while some—'the elite' in One Nation parlance—benefited, sometimes obscenely, from the new global system they kept saying was good for everyone. But One Nation could not afford to be seen by Labor supporters as a front for the bosses, nor by conservatives as a Labor front. Hence Oldfield's decision—rammed through a hostile branch membership—for double-sided tickets. On the ground, though, One Nation people were more committed to preferencing their mates than complying with a strategy, and breakouts of resistance and one-sided tickets occurred throughout the campaign.

To beat the majors, One Nation needed discipline and a national strategy. Yet its membership was largely comprised of people who wanted their own say. Western Australian One Nation Senate candidate Colin Ticknell had discussed Hanson's vision with me on the flight from Bunbury to Perth. 'Pauline says she wants a party of independents,' he said. 'Me, I'm not a gun man. I'd cross the floor to stop looser gun laws.'

Yet with Hanson as the sole drawcard for voters wanting to protest, as distinct from the 5 percent of hardcore far righters who just loved her policies on guns and blacks, she needed to control policy, the grassroots membership, and her candidates. She was incapable of doing so, begging the question of how formidable a charismatic leader like her—so instinctively in tune with so many grassroots Australians—would have been in Australia with the added ingredient of strong political skills. Perhaps as formidable as Jean-Marie Le Pen and his National Front in France. Maybe Australia was lucky that our figurehead of the renaissance of far-right politics was a political novice.

The major political parties had quickly discovered the nightmare of dealing with One Nation according to conventional political norms. Backroom discussions on the ground in tricky seats—triggering public bushfires as Labor and Liberal members were caught bargaining with their declared enemy—had now proved pointless. That was easy for Oldfield.

TAX PANIC. Hanson defends Easytax at its launch. She told me later people had spruiked three tax plans to her, and she'd picked Easytax because it lowered bread prices. DEAN SEWELL

HAVE IT ON A FARM. Hanson is interviewed for 'Lateline' among the chooks at her primary industry policy launch, as Peter James ponders playing the race-card. DEAN SEWELL

JUST US. *Husband and wife duo Just Us entertain shoppers at an Anglican Church fete in a hall on Rosewood's main street. Dean was entranced, seeing the scene as epitomising Hanson's world, where the Queen is revered and Australian culture remains romantically embedded in the 1950s.* DEAN SEWELL

RELUCTANT FAN. *One Nation supporters in Ballarat dress a sheep in Hanson clothing at the sale yards. When the poor thing won't rise to greet her, a steel prod comes in handy.* DEAN SEWELL

EVEN DOGS DON'T LIKE IT. *This picture, the best of Hanson's visually compelling and politically disastrous Easytax doorknocking session in Ipswich, helped make Dean the Nikon press photographer of the year in 1998.* DEAN SEWELL

TOO GOOD TO BE TRUE. Dean took this picture as a parody of the leggy shot of Princess Diana when her dress flew up on her first visit to Australia with her Prince. DEAN SEWELL

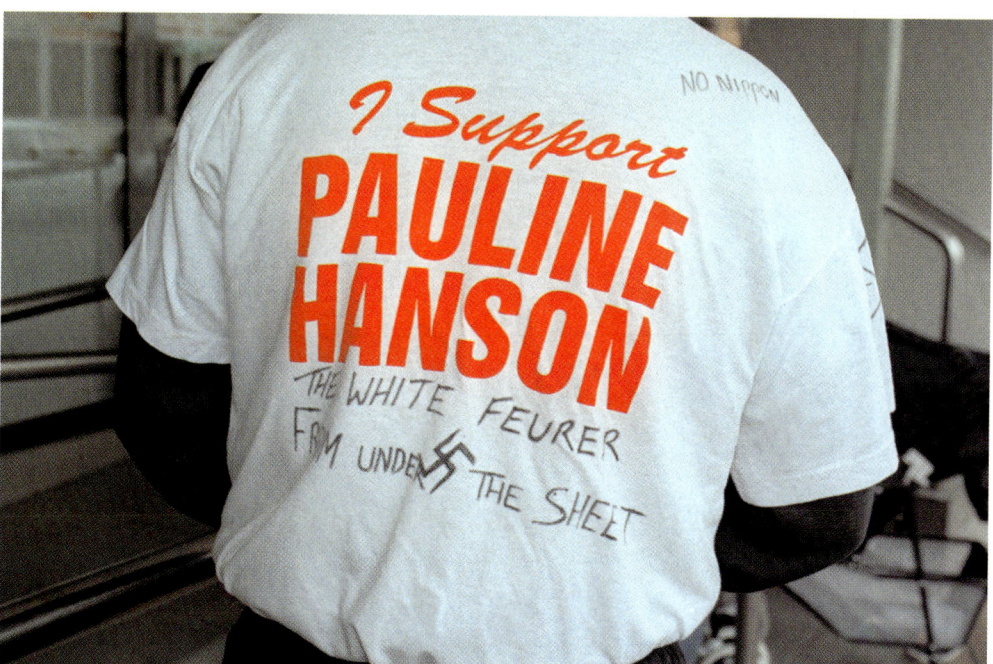

CLASS ACT. *Pauline's People lined the main street of a New South Wales central coast shopping strip to meet her. This bikie supporter grabs a young mother's attention, but got stroppy when Dean shot him front and back.* DEAN SEWELL

WHO AM I? *Hanson plays her version of a 1950s film star, revelling in her police chauffeurs and male fans' adoration.* DEAN SEWELL

RELUCTANT EMBRACE. *Hanson enjoys the attentions of her personal paparazzi Dean Sewell, left, and Grant Turner. I took this picture just before dusk at the Linville races and gave Hanson a print on election day.* MARGO KINGSTON

LIFE IS BEAUTIFUL. *First they placed their surfboards behind her as she tried to film a TV commercial. Then Ocean Defence surfers stole the show with spectacular leaps from the Bluff in Devonport into the cold, cold sea.* DEAN SEWELL

LOST CAUSE. *After One Nation evicted the media from its election night party, Dean shot this One Nation supporter from the outside looking in.* DEAN SEWELL

I'M BACK. *After casting her vote on Election Day, Hanson thought she'd won it, and resumes contact with the media. A similar shot made page one of a London broad sheet newspaper the next day.* DEAN SEWELL

WOMAN ALONE. *One Nation supporters left their election night party early, leaving the media outside looking in. This is Dean's last shot of Pauline Hanson's election campaign.* DEAN SEWELL

'Unless the parties are talking to me, it doesn't matter. Don't talk to candidates or officials, the buck stops here with me,' he said.

I protested that Hanson herself had spent the past week making announcements on preferences that bore no relation to the final decision.

Oldfield's explanation? Hanson was 'confused' and sometimes responded to questions asked, 'without connecting the question to her answer'.

By now I wasn't surprised by his dismissal of meaning in Hanson's words. The major parties put all their efforts into appearing coherent and never appearing contradictory, making an election campaign a mind game between politician and journalist, seeing if the bubble would stand the pinpricks of scrutiny. But Hanson's campaign was all mood swings and endless contradiction. And unlike the major parties, with One Nation there was often no 'inside', where the minders get together and work out their strategy before they face the media. With One Nation, you were in the same bar where the minders were working it out, amid Oldfield's running commentary on all his colleagues' limitations. Hanson's campaign was post-modern—text was meaningless, she was all over the shop; everything was personal, everything was subjective, and the journalist was both prisoner to her mood and controller of it. But just as the campaign seemed to be settling into a mutual understanding of sorts, it all fell apart.

Hanson had gone up country to Nanango in the north of Blair. She'd chatted up the locals and played pool all day while journalists wandered around antique shops and caught up on their postcards to the outside world. Peter James told them then that the next day was a 'media-free day' which Hanson would spend in her office.

The next morning I'd confirmed the 'media-free' status of the day, after Heather Hill had leaked to *The Courier-Mail*'s Christine Jackman an outline of One Nation's family policy—to be announced the next day. It reeked of significantly advantaging men, and I thought it was therefore legitimate to raise Hanson's history—her two divorces and a substantial property settlement from her second marriage. It was a tough decision because I stuck to the traditional Canberra press gallery convention that protects the private lives of politicians from scrutiny unless there was public hypocrisy involved. I felt she should be warned of what was coming as a matter of courtesy, and rang James in her office. I asked to speak to her about the family policy but he said she was doing no media at all. One could but try. Meanwhile, Helen had confirmed with Oldfield that Hanson had no engagements.

But by day's end it was humiliatingly obvious that we'd been duped. Over dinner, Hanson's journalists matched together bits and pieces of information we'd gleaned during Hanson's media-free, office-only day. She had shot an open-air television commercial in Brisbane. Oldfield had arranged a Nine Network interview on the family policy. Hanson had recorded an interview for the ABC's 'Compass' program at the ABC studio, and had done an interview with the BBC under the mistaken impression it was the ABC. She was at a Queensland Senate candidates' meeting as we ate.

Dean and Grant were severely rattled. A reporter can usually scramble together a missed story, but if a photographer wasn't there, he or she was finished. They felt the Oldfield–James scam was an attempt to freeze out print, which had so far dominated her campaign and its coverage.

For me, One Nation had just erased two established conventions of election campaigns—that the travelling media is present at all media appearances, and that parties do not lie to the media about the leader's engagements. The majors would never consider such a stunt—it would breach the pact between us. Without any trust, we'd have to track her from her home every morning, and no one wanted that. Everyone, presumably including Hanson, wanted some distance, some time off. Nothing One Nation did ever made sense.

Oldfield would be back on the campaign full time from Saturday. I was worried that he'd play all sorts of dirty tricks unless he was convinced there was a big down side to lying to the media and manipulating which of us reported the election campaign.

We decided to have a go at rattling him more than he'd rattled us. I rang and gave him the results of the next day's *Herald* poll as he'd requested.

I then said, 'I was actually giving you a ring to tell you we're going to declare war on your campaign tomorrow, because we have been given several promises by Peter James that there was no media today. If you want your people on the ground to lie to us, please don't expect us to be—'

He interrupted with earnest protests that it was everybody else's fault, while twisting and turning to justify his own deceit.

'Well what is One Nation?' I asked. 'What is going on, what is the purpose of these lies and what do you expect us to do about it?'

That gambit triggered a series of Oldfield calls to Grant and Dean blaming James and everyone else bar him. He professed himself distraught at being called a liar.

When he asked to speak to me again I put the boot in. 'Pauline Hanson will have no privacy because we've given her some trust and we've been lied to and made fools of. We have been genuine and treated you people like you're worthy of trust. It hasn't worked and we're on your case and we're not going to let you go, we're going to give you no quarter.'

During his fifth increasingly hysterical call he yelled at Grant, 'We're not going to respond to threats and abuse, we're just not going to. You're just going to have to face this fact. There's a lack of communication in this organisation—don't construe it as being lied to or fucked over.' Cold comfort—if no one was in control of One Nation's campaign, there'd be no choice but to stalk her.

▄

The next morning Hanson and Hill strolled across the road from Hanson's Ipswich office to the Barry Jones auditorium, scene of the Easytax debacle, to announce the family policy. Hanson wore a black suit with an appliquéd tiger on one shoulder. In yet another political first, she ensured she'd be asked no questions by sitting behind journalists with Peter James and her number four Queensland Senate candidate, David Anning. It was an apt vignette—Hanson, the leader, in the audience at a policy launch, probably hearing the detail for the first time herself.

The policy was much more extreme than *The Courier-Mail* story had indicated, and like Easytax amounted to the appropriation of policy from the fringe—this time the wish list of disgruntled divorced men's groups.

Like Easytax it was sociopathic, seeking not to improve the system but to tear it down, abolishing both family law and the Family Court.

Out of the rubble of the core protection of the citizen in our democracy—the rule of law not of men—would arise 'people's tribunals', comprised of 'mainstream Australians', who would make up their own guidelines and pronounce judgment on property, custody and maintenance disputes. All totally unconstitutional of course, mere irresponsible 'promise them anything' pie in the sky, like One Nation's Wik policy.

Legal representation would be banned and all legal aid for family law abolished. There were a few firm guidelines, though. One Nation would abolish the principle that, all things being equal, a child should be with its mother in the early years. This was based on 'outdated cultural values', Hill said. The sole parent pension would be abolished for all single parents when their child reached five, down from sixteen, forcing the woman to work so that the man's child maintenance obligations ended. In other words, Hill proposed the withdrawal of State support for a chronically disadvantaged group—parents struggling to raise a family alone. The centrality of the welfare of the child in decision making would also go down the tubes, through a massive scale down of the non-custodial parent's obligation to help maintain offspring. 'A child's standard of living cannot be maintained at the pre-divorce level,' Hill said, because fathers wanted to start new families.

The state, through new 'family centres' attached to the tribunals, would actively 'case manage' marriages 'from entry to exit'. All in all, a massive movement of the balance of rights to the father, and a Stalinistic proposal to allow the people in your street to tell you how to live, and end, your relationship. Images of Madam Defarge dropping a stitch as the People's Court cut off another marital head crossed my mind.

■

Like Easytax we were in sticky pudding, wondering where to start. We knew Hanson had only seen and approved the policy the day before. Unlike Easytax, the press conference became aggressive. Who would establish these 'guidelines', Helen asked.

'You're not going to have just One Nation members,' Hill said. Such a relief.

'How do you enforce the agreements when you've abolished the rule of law?' I asked, because without law there could be no judicial enforcement.

'Media free' man Peter James had already left Hanson's side and now sat in the aisle beside me. He got heavy, just as he'd done during Easytax when someone asked something Hanson couldn't answer. 'Excuse me, Margo, I think you've had a fair go. There are other journalists asking questions.'

A murmur of disbelief passed through the room at this crude attempt at media censorship, and Leisa Scott said: 'No, we're happy for Margo to ask questions.'

'Excuse me, you can't tell us what to say,' I said disdainfully. 'We're asking questions and we expect answers.'

Hill broke in. 'Okay, okay, I'm giving you the answer. I guess what we have then is a difference of opinion. I believe that the majority of parents are responsible enough that they will abide by that agreement.'

'You know as well as I do that there are a minority of cases that cannot be settled,' I retorted.

She waffled and waffled, then suggested the State Supreme Courts could do it. 'Ordinary people don't believe the Family Court gives fair justice, they don't believe it is a court that can provide justice. It just follows law.'

Anne Delaney broke in, 'And the Supreme Court will be different?'

'Oh yes, you're going to have judges in those courts that have a lifetime of experience.'

'Has Ms Hanson approved this document?' Helen asked.

'Yes she has.'

I followed with, 'So did she find her experience in the Family Court unfair?'

'To me that's personal, and that's not something that we need to draw up into the public eye.'

Helen protested, 'But family law is a personal issue.' Hanson shuffled up the back.

I queried the lack of legal representation, to be told that, 'You're stepping down the wrong road and what I think you're doing, which is really sad, is you're saying to me that whenever we're dealing with families we have to deal with the law.'

So who could argue the case for each party in the People's Court?

'They can take advocates with them—it might be Mum, it might be a church representative.'

Mum? Hanson marched to the stage, the colour drained from her face, and acted media minder. 'Last question,' she said, and fled amid a flurry of them.

The television reporters and most other media peeled off for the day, but after we'd filed our stories Helen and I caught up with Hanson at a Gatton street walk. I wanted to reinforce the threat we'd made to Oldfield—if we weren't going to be told the truth about her itinerary, we'd be in her face all the time. I was still steaming about Hanson's crazed and misogynous family policy, and she seemed angry about something too. We did not speak.

David Anning was chatting to a couple of school kids on the street, alleging in great detail that Hanson was not racist and that the TVs cut bits out of her sentences to pretend she was. Like the family policy, it was brain-scrambling stuff, and Helen marched up to the group to disabuse the kids of One Nation's latest conspiracy theory. Anning, the brother of ABC Radio's European correspondent Magella Anning, looked an innocent and was at least polite. He frowned, and said the TVs must make it up because Pauline Hanson was not racist. Well her party was, Helen said, reeling off some of Oldfield's racist remarks. Anning expressed disbelief and wandered away still frowning.

Amazingly, Hanson agreed to a doorstop in a side street. It was short and sweet. I began with, 'Why did you decide to abolish the sole parent pension when the youngest child reaches five?'

'Did I?'

'It's in your policy, Ms Hanson.'

'Right.'

'Are you aware of that?'

'As far as the family policy, Heather Hill spoke on that today, and she's the spokeswoman on it.'

Helen took over. 'Was your experience so bad in family law that you want to abolish the court system and the law system completely?'

'My personal life has got nothing to do with it. Yes, I have been through it, by all means—'

'—and obviously it didn't work for you.'

'That is not the case. As a Member of Parliament, and the number of people I have had come through my office with concerns over the Family Law Courts...'

'What about your personal experiences—how did the court go there?'

'My personal experience is *my* personal experience, and I will not discuss or debate about it with anyone. Let's address a fairer system that is going to address the concerns of the Australian people.'

'A People's Court with no rules and no laws, that sounds like vigilante stuff,' I said.

'It is far better to actually have a bit of mediation,' she replied.

'Would you have liked your mother to be the advocate in a custody battle over your children?' Helen asked.

Hanson looked scared and walked around the corner to a Commonwealth Bank. In the queue, head down, she looked ten years older. She looked like even she was beginning to doubt herself.

Only Grant, Dean, Helen and I followed her on a pub crawl of Gatton and surrounds. On the way, I returned a call from my editor, Paul McGeough, who asked how the day was going. I related her doorstop and he seemed nonplussed.

'When was that?'

Five minutes ago.

He said Hanson had rung a couple of hours before to inform him that, because I was miffed that she hadn't let me sit in on a BBC interview, 'Your reporter is trying to destroy me' by raising her private life.

What sort of rubbish were Peter James and David Oldfield filling her head with? It was laughable. And what was she doing answering my questions after making such a call? 'Oh well, she's over it now,' I said.

Paul had asked Hanson what I'd said that had upset her, but she'd become incoherent. 'I don't know, I didn't write it down,' she'd said. Paul said he'd ended the call with, 'Look, I don't care what Margo says, if you've got a problem with what she writes then give me a call.'

He asked what had happened and I said I'd been aggressive at the press conference but no more so than I would have been at any other if such garbage had been announced as policy. I said she must have been confusing my professional aggression with the private battle I was conducting to force One Nation to keep us informed.

'Sorry you had to be drawn into this soap opera,' I said.

'I had a feeling I would be,' he replied.

The Sydney Morning Herald senior writer David Marr told me on the campaign trail the following week that he'd seen McGeough straight after the Hanson call.

'He rushed out of his office as if he'd been flushed out by something, and his eyes were alight and he was a bit flustered and amazed. It was undoubtedly the first contact he'd ever had with her. So this was reality swooping into his glass cubicle via her. He said he'd just had Hanson on the phone, incoherent, saying something about her divorce and a question, so he'd surmised that you'd asked it. Marion Wilkinson explained that the question would have been 'How come you've done so well out of marriage settlements and now you're going to abolish them all?' In the end it boiled down to a usual dealing with an angry politician, but it certainly put some pep into his day. McGeough said, "She reckons that Margo Kingston is trying to destroy her—it's taken her a fortnight to work that out!"'

I wasn't out to destroy her, but I was out to put her under scrutiny. Still, at least Paul's charge was easier to deal with than that of Phillip Adams. He'd suggested on air that deep down I actually liked her. That charge was simply horrifying to my friends and colleagues, and the great bulk of *Herald* readers.

Before hitting the pubs, Hanson drove herself to a run-down tyre factory and chatted for half an hour to the owner inside while Peter James, reduced to an ignored, forlorn chaperone after baggings from Oldfield on the 'media-free' mess, stood outside on his own, head bowed. Oldfield rang Helen to claim that 'Peter James doesn't lie, he just fucks up.' Oldfield was great on blame, but why tell us? What was he trying to prove?

At the Grantham Hotel, the boys kept the pressure up by taking pictures of fans taking pictures of her. Oldfield began calling Helen

Hanson recovers her composure outside the Grantham Hotel in Gatton before tackling her afternoon pub-crawl. Peter James takes calls from David Oldfield, who blamed him for the previous day's media wars.

incessantly, saying she was the only sane one among us, and winding himself up into near hysteria over whether she thought he was a liar. He'd wound up with, 'Don't worry, I'm back on Saturday.'

'Wonderful,' Helen replied sarcastically.

'Do you think I'm a liar, do you think I'm a liar?'

'As the only sane one among us, I'm telling you there's some evidence mounting here,' she said. She hung up and said with feeling: 'I can't play this double-edged game forever. Best of friends and worst of enemies all at once. David can't go a day without having one or two yelling matches with one of us and a bitch session about other journalists as well. It's just too personal. They make us get involved. It's not our choice, it's their stupidity.'

A bloke who'd seen the Nine Network story on Hanson and the media illustrated the point. 'Hi, have you cleaned up her itinerary yet?' he asked with a smile.

'No, it's still just as bad,' I replied.

'Are you in the good books?'

'No, not in the good books today.'

When she entered the Tent Hill Hotel, where she'd told us of her fish and chip shop days a week before, she entered the core of Pauline's People's world. It was a warm, raucous country scene with kids running around the drinkers and raffles galore, a world away from the rough stuff of the day.

She was greeted as a mate and quickly surrounded by men at the bar. Her sex appeal to some men over 45 was palpable, and I recalled a conversation with a bloke who'd rung me after a gender analysis of her popularity on radio, in which I'd participated. He'd seen her at a meeting and reckoned her sex appeal to blue-collar, middle-aged men like him was about her aura of 'vulnerability, with attitude'. If Hanson ever got engaged or went out with someone full time, she'd lose lots of votes, he'd said, because, 'We all fantasise that she'll pick us'. In a Rosewood pub, behind the door, a pin-up of a woman, naked except for suspenders, with Hanson's head stuck on top took pride of place. Above the image were the words 'Fun Nation'. The regulars saw the poster as a tribute.

At the Tent Hill Hotel a short old man with a big hat gave her a posy. Another guy murmured, 'I'd like to get her flowers, too.'

His mate replied, 'No, get her pissed, get her pissed.'

Another bloke chimed in, 'Come on, Pauline, let me shake your hand.' His mate said, 'You're going to vote for her I hope, aren't ya?'

'I don't know, will I or won't I? One good thing about her, at least she shoots from the hip.'

A boy came up shyly and whispered his hellos. 'Hello. Now come on, a nice strong handshake,' she said. 'No, wait a minute, wait a minute. Now, look me in the eye. That's right. How are you?'

Helen and I adjourned to a side table, and a man who said he was a proud One Nation voter bought us drinks.

'How is she going, do you reckon she can win?'

We thought she was still in with a chance if she could garner a big sympathy vote after her campaign travails. David Anning joined us, and explained that he used to have a property near Winton in Western Queensland, then became general manager of a small aviation company.

'It was bought up by an overseas company, they ran it down, sacked the staff. Same old story,' he said wistfully.

An old character with a crusty voice called Col was dominating conversation with Hanson and I put a tape on it.

'Pauline, I want to know what have you got on you that nobody else could ever bring out? We had Liberal and National, we voted for 40 bloody years, and they didn't know where Queensland or us fellows were. Now seeing your name come up—Pauline Hanson—and all these people are here chasing you, and going on. How come they all come out of the woodwork? Before that they didn't know where we were, and you got 'em out of the woodwork. So what have you got? Have you got rat bait or what?'

She giggled. 'I think you should answer that question yourself. I don't know—what have I got?'

'You must have something, because you brought them out of the bloody hole, and now they're running around.'

Hanson looked at me knowingly and said, 'Jeff Kennett—remember he said he was going to chase me up and down the burrows? I had to go and find him.'

'What I didn't like was that business of you "stalking him",' Col said. 'You don't want his bloody stalk, anyway!' The crowd exploded with laughter, and Hanson warned him that my tape was on. He turned to me. 'I still want to know what she's got.'

'We're all trying to find that out, mate,' I replied.

The group launched into a laconic analysis of the performance of their former State National Party member, Tom FitzGerald. After eighteen years as their local member, voters had dumped him for One Nation's Peter Prenzell at the Queensland election.

'He's a hell of a good bloke, but every time he went to Parliament he put reams of sticky tape over his mouth. He didn't do anything for eighteen years, so he didn't talk a lot,' Col said.

'He did make a speech at the high school every year at speech night, and he did go to the kids' sports,' his mate countered sarcastically.

'He got a set of lights in Gatton in eighteen years, but it took fifteen years to get the cement, then it took three years to get the mould,' another bloke added.

Helen was speaking to a woman who said she didn't want to meet Hanson and would rather chat to us. She was a conservative voter but had voted independent in the State election to protest against FitzGerald's performance. She wouldn't vote One Nation because it wasn't good for the country, but like so many others in the regions she was prepared to distance Hanson from her party. 'It's the people around her who are the problem, not necessarily her.'

Peter James, posted by the door alone and looking dreadful, won a bottle of scotch in a raffle. He looked like he needed it.

We pulled out before her night time meeting to get some sleep before Hanson's nine-day interstate tour to Tasmania, Victoria, New South Wales and South Australia in the delightful company of David Oldfield.

ELEVEN

A lot happier time for the Aboriginals and the pastoralists

DAYS 17 AND 18

Pauline Hanson walked out of Launceston airport late Saturday afternoon into the usual media scrum and the tender mercies of a cutting-edge activist group called Ocean Defence. Michael Morehead, a tall, tanned young lawyer turned surfer, shook her hand as she began a doorstop and gave her a 'Please Explain' letter on her environment and Aboriginal policies.

He introduced himself. 'We posted you a letter last week—I fear that you might not have got it so we just wanted to hand it to you here. A few questions that we've given to all of the federal political party leaders, and we look forward to your response perhaps sometime over the weekend. We'll be attending public meetings while you're in Tasmania.'

'Thank you, Michael,' she replied with a smile. Hanson was a sucker for good-looking men.

The doorstop was dominated by One Nation's decision to preference the Greens ahead of conservative independent Brian Harradine in the Senate, justified by local One Nationites as revenge for Harradine's broker role in settling Wik. Strange—the Greens were way to the left of anyone else on native title.

Hanson wouldn't give a reason at first, then said under questioning, 'We have strong concerns on environmental issues.' Crikey, there goes her redneck Tasmanian vote if anyone in Tasmania took her seriously enough to report it. And here comes Ocean Defence to take her up on it.

A young woman called Claire Konkes introduced herself as an Ocean Defence activist and we gave her a lift to Hanson's hotel, where four Ocean Defence people would also stay. Funding itself through donations and selling postcards, Ocean Defence specialised in well-planned, peaceful direct actions. They planned to turn the tables on Hanson by demanding politely but firmly that she 'Please Explain'.

Helen and I were planning an action of our own. We'd decided on the flight to tackle Hanson on the views of one of her Queensland One Nation MPs, Jeff Knuth, reported in *The Sydney Morning Herald*'s *Good Weekend* magazine that day by senior journalist Frank Robson. Knuth had said he wanted to be Aboriginal Affairs Minister one day, and would return rural Aborigines to pastoralists to work for nothing in return for permission to camp and some food.

'They've tried to become white by adopting a flag, electric guitars and that...but it'll never work,' Knuth had said. The best thing was for the blacks to go back to the pastoralists, to ask: 'We don't want to take your land off you, but would it be all right if we did some work for you, and all you do is give us a bit of meat, or that?'

Knuth's views exposed the reality of the core racist element in One Nation beneath the cloak of Hanson's 'equality' rhetoric—the conviction that Aborigines were not equal at all, but an inferior race fit only for subjugation to whites or banishment to somewhere unseen. One Nation refused to even try to see the white–black relationship from the black perspective. Would Hanson back Knuth's policy prescription or disown it? And how could she explain?

I hadn't spoken to Oldfield since Thursday night's telephone exchanges on his concept of 'media-free days'. At the hotel reception desk in the small northern village of Ulverstone, Helen showed him the Knuth story to test his response and let him know questions could be asked of Hanson. Oldfield skimmed the article, said 'Oh yes' to Knuth's comments, and turned the page. 'Oh, that's a nice picture of me.'

It was a raw, cold Tasmanian night and Claire Konkes directed Dean to the Wynyard picture theatre for Hanson's first public meeting. Media identity passes were a problem again, and I got held up after the One Nation bloke on the door said he didn't believe there was such a paper as *The Sydney Morning Herald*, and if there was I certainly didn't work for it. If he couldn't keep us out, he wanted to charge us the ten bucks entry fee to hear Hanson speak. Claire went straight through after showing a homemade cardboard pass announcing she was from 'Undercurrents and News Unlimited Media'.

Helen, Claire and I sat together in an audience of only 60 behind a woman who turned round and began chatting. Janice Pfund, a plain-speaking Tasmanian of 60, was just back from eight years in Queensland. She said she admired Hanson for voicing people's kitchen-table concerns, and wondered if she had answers. Besides, 'I'm a bit of a stirrer myself.'

On stage, Hanson's six Senate and Lower House candidates—all men—settled in. Male domination was one thing One Nation had in common with the major parties.

'Why don't you ask her why there's no women?' I suggested.

Janice said she'd been secretary of the Meat Workers Union in Townsville many years ago, when one of the workers had taken to wandering around with his fly undone to bait her, saying, 'It pays to advertise.'

'You don't have to keep a dead bird in a cage,' she'd replied.

A young girl sang 'The Rose' beautifully, unaccompanied, as Hanson entered the hall. When she began to speak, Janice called out, 'I tell you what, Pauline, I'd like to see some more women up there.'

Hanson blanched and giggled nervously. 'My opinion is that regardless of what sex you are has got nothing to do with it—it is the best person for the job and it has been the branches that have selected the candidates to represent them. I'm not a woman who will push a woman into running for positions because they're a woman.' She got applause for that, but still looked uncomfortable. 'Although in some ways, I'd probably say women look at things totally different and I'd like to see more women there by all means. The men have had hold in this country for too long and see what they've done with it. But anyway, the best person for the job, that's the bottom line.' There was no applause, but Janice said 'Goodonya.'

When Hanson spoke of Australia's economy going down the drain, Michael Morehead interjected, 'Is that the Aborigines' fault, is it?'

'It's Michael, isn't it? I won't disregard you by no means. I met you this afternoon; you came and gave me a piece of paper. I've had a brief read of that. Now Michael, if you would do me the courtesy to allow me to deliver my speech then after it I will try and answer a couple of your questions.'

She gave a halting, defensive speech placing great emphasis on denying racism. But then she said something new. 'A racist means a person who considers their race to be superior to others. I have never, never stated anything like that whatsoever, and I never will, because I don't feel that way. I'm proud to be Australian, like any other race and any other people are proud of their own race and their culture.'

And what was the Australian 'race'? Her slippery rhetoric seemed to have slid into overtly claiming Anglo-Celtics as 'true' Australians, the rest as outsiders. With no opportunity to question Hanson, I wrote a question down and Alisha Moodie, a young Hobart schoolteacher from Ocean Defence, agreed to ask it.

Michael asked the first question. 'What is One Nation's view of Aboriginal people getting arrested at Jabiluka, on their own land, and what is your view of the multinational uses of uranium that comes out of Jabiluka?' Clever—combining an appeal to her antagonism to foreign companies with a curly race question.

Hanson took a breath. 'You presented me with these papers this afternoon, but I've only had from the airport to the hotel to have a look at it and I haven't had enough time to absorb it or make an opinion about it. It's not fair to the people up in Jabiluka or the Aboriginal people or the people of Australia to stand here and give you a position, because what I say here will be gospel and will be printed in the papers.'

The confusion in the room was such that she got the biggest applause of the night for announcing she had no policy. The audience could hardly boo Michael, since he was mixing his messages and she was being so solicitous. She continued. 'I take the point of what you're saying.'

'Thank you, Pauline, I look forward to receiving your response in writing to our questions as soon as possible—we've had responses from all of the other federal parties.' The audience clapped him.

Janice asked if she'd keep up freight subsidies between Tasmania and the mainland to stop Tasmanian youth leaving in droves. Freight subsidies were a burning issue in Tasmania and the One Nation Tasmania policy, which she'd release the next day, would have all the commitments in it Janice could want. But, as usual, Hanson didn't have a clue about her own party's policies. 'You would not appreciate my coming here from Queensland, my third visit here, to tell you what I think should be done here. This is where you need people, your representatives who are part of the community, to actually stand up and fight for you on these issues.' Janice decided she would not vote for One Nation.

Alisha asked the third—and last—question. 'What I want to know is, what is your race?'

Hanson threw her head back and glowered. 'I am Australian, and I am very proud of it. What's yours?'

'I'm from New Zealand.'

'You're a New Zealander?' The crowd groaned and tittered, and Hanson began an interrogation.

'Are you a naturalised Australian?'

'Yes.'

'You've become an Australian citizen?'

'Yes.'

'But you still call yourself a New Zealander?'

'I'm from New Zealand originally, born there and came here.'

'You call yourself a New Zealander, but you took the Australian citizenship?'

'I said I was from—'

'I thought when someone takes Australian citizenship that means to say they are proud to become that nationality, and I'm surprised you would stand up and call yourself a New Zealander... If you come here, be Australian, join us, be one of us, and be proud to stand up and say, "I am Australian".'

Hanson drew loud applause for that, but several people in the audience gathered round Alisha to apologise. She was in tears. Hanson had not only shown her ignorance in failing to distinguish nationality from race, but had also falsely accused Alisha of disloyalty to Australia. And the reaction of some audience members to Hanson's diatribe showed it wouldn't take much to convert her words on race into ugly abuse.

'I'm not going to lie about my past and my heritage, just because I live in Australia and am an Australian,' Alisha told reporters. I tried to comfort her, feeling guilty about asking an amateur to do my job.

Back at the hotel, the Ocean Defenders sat together in the café and a still-teary Alisha complained that she 'felt dirty' after her Hanson experience. The others hailed her a hero, but Michael accused the media of 'looking after Hanson'. It's a no-win game covering Hanson. You're too soft, too hard, or should be ignoring her anyway.

Oldfield joined journalists having a drink, but most left when he sat down and he spent the night debating politics with Michael. Michael had been then High Court Justice Sir William Deane's associate during legal argument in the historic Mabo case, which found for the first time that Aboriginal land rights survived white settlement. He said he'd learnt a lot from the Aboriginal people he'd met. Oldfield responded that he couldn't see that there was anything to learn—except, perhaps, after a nuclear war, when they could help find food in the desert.

■

Early next morning we drove to The Bluff at Devonport, once an Aboriginal men's site and now a wild, rocky park where Hanson would record a television commercial. Tasmania's north-west was the last place on the island where whites had rounded up Aborigines and slaughtered them. An Aboriginal flag and Aboriginal cultural museum marked the entrance—the perfect spot for a One Nation advertisement.

During the drive Claire mentioned a visit to Tasmania a few days before by Professor Henry Reynolds, Australia's leading historian of the Aboriginal–white relationship. In a State famous for being even more brutal to its Aborigines than its convicts, white Tasmanians had last century transported the remaining full-blooded Aborigines to a remote island to die out. Truganini was the last to do so. Reynolds had spoken of a famous Tasmanian massacre where, in retaliation for Aboriginal people pushing some sheep over a cliff, the settlers pushed the Aboriginal community off the same cliff. Reynolds had been helping a German film crew who were examining the massacre, but they couldn't get any locals to talk on camera.

'Hey, we're Germans,' they'd said. 'You can't shock us. We've owned up to our atrocities, why don't you own up to yours?'

'Easy,' I said. 'One Nation says, "It's not our generation." Stop. End of argument. John Howard says the same thing.'

It was windy and cold, but the light on the sea was wondrous, and Hanson wandered down a rocky path to see the view while she waited for her TV crew. We hadn't spoken since Thursday's family policy friction, and had instead tracked each other on the airwaves, doing back-to-back interviews on English and Australian radio. The old 'Are you racist—no; Is she racist—yes' thing. Now she shivered, and remarked, 'Remember the other day at Longreach?'

'Yeah, it's a hot and cold campaign,' I replied.

She laughed. 'Variety's the spice of life, Margo, isn't it?'

'Yep, I've learnt that from you, Pauline.'

'By the end of this we're going to have taught each other a few things, haven't we?'

'We are. Let's hope that afterwards we can still sit down and have a drink.'

She asked if I'd been to Tasmania before. 'I've been to Hobart three times for Labor Party conferences, but I've never stepped out of Wrest Point Casino so this is just fabulous.'

'I love it down here,' Hanson said.

'Then why don't you say something about saving the environment in Tassie?'

'Why do you think we gave the Greens the preferences? For the environment.'

I couldn't believe it. 'So you think it's important to protect Tasmania's environment for the sake of its economic future?'

'Not only in Tasmania, but around Australia—we definitely need to take a look at environmental issues.'

So what was her position on Tasmania's forests? She sensed trouble and laughed.

'We're not doing a doorstop here, Margo.'

The Nine Network's Melanie Wendt, an enthusiast of campaign scrapbook photos, suggested a media photo in front of the old white lighthouse on the bluff. I asked Hanson to join us, and she sat on a picnic table holding a TV camera the ABC's soundman Dave gave her. Snap. David Oldfield, who had developed a limp that morning, did a comical 100-metre dash to join in. Dean and Grant and the cameramen joined the pack, and a federal police officer and Claire took over the cameras. 'Please explain,' we said in unison. Snap. 'And I just don't like it,' Hanson retorted, sending up the line from Pauline Pantsdown's satirical song 'I Don't Like It', then all the rage in gay clubs and moving up the singles charts. Hanson had sued ABC's youth radio network Triple J for defamation after it played Pantsdown's first effort, 'I'm a Back Door Man', and an ABC appeal against a Queensland Supreme Court injunction against further airplay was pending.

When Hanson's TV crew arrived, everyone scrambled through the scrub down onto the rocks near the edge of the sea, where Hanson stood in front of her six male candidates making her pitch.

'Tasmanians, this election break the Liberal–Labor stranglehold. Save Australia before they sell it. Vote for change. Vote One Nation.'

The crew was amateur hour and they'd brought the wrong sound equipment to record in the wind. Dave offered to take over, and thus Hanson's despised ABC did the sound for One Nation's commercial. To Dave it seemed only fair—we were, after all, recording their recording.

During filming, the Ocean Defence boys appeared out of the scrub. 'Fancy seeing you here, it's where we surf,' Michael said, and they ran down to the bluff edge and jumped off. Dean took a sensational shot of surfer Simon van Zetten diving in, his body in the air and only his left foot on the rocks. His surfboard was held aloft with the words: 'One Nation, No explanation. The ugly Australian does not speak for me.' The light caught the ocean spray and the whiteness of his board, and Dean's shot became *The Sydney Morning Herald*'s campaign picture of the day. 'I don't think you need Hanson in it,' Dean said. "Please Explain" is just attached to her; there's no way she'll ever escape it.'

One Nation had set up a table in front of the Mersey River in Devonport for the Tasmania policy launch, but the youth action group Resistance silently protested behind the table with a big red banner, 'Actions not words against racism'. One Nationites picked up the table and carried it into the Char Grill and Seafood Bistro across the road, its friendliness advertised with a One Nation poster in the window.

In Tasmania, One Nation had the same formula for political success as the majors, topping their offers to forgive $150 million of State debt with an extra $50 million. One Nation promised to limit foreign purchase and control of fishing quotas to protect local jobs, local business and the local economy. It promised to 'ensure local timber mills have available an adequate supply of saw logs so as to re-establish a secure future for local industry and jobs'. In what was becoming a pattern at her policy launches, Hanson fobbed off questions on the cost of her promises and how she would pay for them with the promise that all would be revealed at her campaign launch, whenever that might be.

I asked how she reconciled her statement that she'd preferenced the Greens over Brian Harradine in the Senate because she was pro-environment, with her promise to increase logging.

'Maybe it should be a way of replanting, making sure there is a future, and we do have the trees,' she said.

Blancmange time again. So she would freeze the logging of old forests?

One of her candidates jumped in to save the day, saying the Greens had been favoured not because of the environment, but because Harradine had said he was standing for the Senate again solely to stop One Nation.

'But you told us earlier today that you'd preferenced the Greens because they were pro-environment,' I protested.

'There are environmental issues by all means, and I still stand by that. I do care about the environment,' Hanson replied, flustered.

Helen moved in on Knuth. 'One of your State members in Queensland yesterday was quoted as saying what he'd like to do in Aboriginal affairs is to return to the good old days when Aborigines camped by the sides of pastoralists' properties and worked without money. What's your view of that policy?'

'My policy is that I believe everyone should be treated equally and the same and treated on an individual needs basis. I'm not changing the policy of where I stand with the Aboriginal issues.'

'But this person's a One Nation person,' Helen protested.

'What this person has said, and I'll reflect on years gone by when the Aboriginals could and did roam on the lands, and they were pastoralists' lands by all means. And usually they worked in very well with the owner of the lands and they camped on the lands and they went about their own traditional ways and culture and they were very happy together with the pastoralists on the lands, and there wasn't these problems that are there today.'

Very happy? She painted a scene of idyllic frolicking by black and white in the days of slave labour, when Aborigines had no rights to be on their own land and pastoralists built their wealth on their backs. What had begun as pretty relaxed questioning after the morning's repair of relations began to heat up.

'But he's saying the Aborigines didn't get paid,' Melanie said.

'A lot of these people actually did—the Aboriginals were paid. They were either paid in food or clothing, and a lot of the Aboriginals that I've sort of spoken to and their families actually lived on the lands with the pastoralists—they worked in very well with the pastoralists. It was a lot happier time for the Aboriginals and the pastoralists.'

Everyone began asking questions at once. Stephen McDonell, on his first day replacing Anne Delaney for ABC radio, yelled above the pack, 'Should we go back to that now?'

Hanson tried to answer, but Oldfield, standing in front with the cameramen, shouted over her, 'Are there any more questions on Tasmania, any more questions on Tasmania ladies and gentlemen? We're in

Tasmania.' She kept trying to answer but no one could hear her over Oldfield.

Helen turned to Oldfield. 'Excuse me, this is a major issue, do you mind?'

Hanson again tried to answer Stephen's question, but one of her candidates spoke over her, using the classic One Nation 'make a mess and just keep moving' strategy. 'Ladies and gentlemen of the media, we do have a very tight time schedule, as we've still got to move on.' But Hanson was frozen in her seat, and we pressed on.

'Ms Hanson, you say your policy is equality for all Australians and yet you've suggested that it might be appropriate for Aborigines to go back without being paid—' I began.

'Excuse me, I never said that at all.'

So was Knuth wrong?

'That is not part of policy, our policy is to treat everyone equally and treat them on an individual needs basis.'

'Will you discipline him for those comments, in that case?' Helen asked.

A One Nation candidate lifted Hanson up, put his arm around her back, and almost carried her to the next room for lunch.

Confused by the messiness of the exchange, we ate hot chips near the bar, trying to work out what she'd meant. It looked as though Oldfield hadn't briefed Hanson on Knuth, then drowned her out when she was trying to disagree with him. Oldfield wanted to keep her hard on race, that was clear, and he did not appear to care if he publicly humiliated his leader to achieve his goal. Dean was sure we'd see a public blow-up sometime.

'She wants to be leader and he also wants to be leader, but he needs her face. He can't do it without her. He wants to be leader through her and that's what the conflict is between them. They both want control.'

Oldfield and Michael stood sparring at the bar, with Michael again demanding answers to his written questions. 'There's no chance of doing it in the course of this trip to Tasmania, there's no chance of doing it in the next two weeks. We do not have time between now and then,' Oldfield said.

'Really? You're talking to journalists, so you've got plenty of time. Why don't you go and sit down and write the answers to the questions?'

Oldfield's voice rose. 'My priorities are my priorities, they're not yours. I'm not here under your instructions—have you got that clear in your head?'

But Oldfield never walks away. He thrives on confrontation, especially with, or being watched by, the media. Michael was one of the few people who could beat him at his own game, and he calmly suggested Oldfield answer just one question.

'Don't ask me, I'm not involved, I just do behind the scenes,' Oldfield said, his standard response when cornered, transforming from self-proclaimed One Nation guru to humble adviser in the twinkling of an eye.

'Okay, who should I carefully ask?'

'Well, what's the question?'

'Let's try mining of uranium in a World Heritage area. What's One Nation's policy on that?'

'We don't actually have a formal policy on that.'

Hanson had finished lunch and now sat alone at a table away from the bar looking shell-shocked. I approached her to say that the story today was her support for Aboriginal slave labour.

She was shaking. 'I haven't seen the information, I don't know what he said—can you get me the story?'

I was stunned that she'd ask me and not Oldfield. I agreed, but Helen was appalled.

'We have the story, she was given the necessary notice, it's not up to us to spoonfeed her,' Helen said. 'If what you do means she makes another statement or changes her mind, that's an intervention in the story.' Helen thought Hanson had said what she believed and didn't see the need to give her a second chance. I thought that if Hanson really wanted to move the race debate to such an extreme position, then surely it should be deliberate, not accidental. Oldfield's yelling meant there was no clear quote of her rejecting Knuth's policy, but I could see Helen's point. I was uncomfortably close to assuming a media adviser's role, and I backed down.

We drove through immaculate, English-style scenery for an hour to Hanson's next public meeting in Campbelltown. Claire Konkes was tired less than halfway through a regular Hanson campaign day. 'There's so much reading between the lines—I've had a few moments today of a completely blank mind. Your brain is turning over so much, like, "Gosh, she just totally contradicted herself—again".'

Claire said the Resistance people were concerned that their silent protest wouldn't make the TV news. But it was a visually disruptive tactic, and it did, the moving table and the surfers' Bluff protest providing the TV vision of Hanson on the run in Tasmania. Resistance had achieved something else, too, a move from a beautiful backdrop that made Hanson look good on TV to being scrunched up in a dingy little restaurant. It would also have been much harder to sustain a hostile press conference in a picturesque outdoor setting.

A small crowd of 60 waited patiently at the Campbelltown town hall. Oldfield had finally agreed to answer all Michael's questions, and he retreated to a side room to write them out in longhand. Two federal police officers guarded the entrance to the toilet, and one of them called me over. Hanson stood just inside the door with her back up against the wall so she couldn't be seen, and beckoned me to join her.

Her voice was trembling. 'Where's that information?' she whispered. 'It was a stupid comment by him, of course I don't support that.'

But we told David about Knuth last night, I protested.

'He didn't tell me, he didn't tell me. Can you get me the information?'

I agreed and she left. When I'd gone to the loo and came out she was standing by the hall entrance.

'We're waiting for you, Margo,' she said.

She delivered a rave of a speech, pausing for neither breath nor applause, her timing shot to pieces. She tried to clean up the previous night's problem with the Australian 'race' by saying, 'I do not consider myself to be English or Irish, I consider myself to be Australian.' At the back of the hall I told Melanie and ABC TV's Lisa Millar that Hanson wanted to dump on Knuth, but the TVs needed to pull out almost immediately to file their story, so if she didn't do a doorstop quickly she'd lose her chance. After her speech we rushed up, I thrust *The Good Weekend* article into her hands, read out the key bits, and away she went.

'I'm not impressed with his comments whatsoever, and it doesn't reflect on my views or what I actually believe in for it. This is the comment that they should go back to the old system of working without pay. That's not right. As I've always said, I believe in equality for all Australians, and if you're out there working you should receive a fair day's pay for a fair day's work and Aboriginal people should be exactly the same. We can't go back to these times.'

What did she think about having a racist in her party? I asked.

'Well, I don't believe it's racist. He's actually looking at a way of doing things. I think it was a stupid comment that he actually made on that but it's not my views on it and I do not support those views whatsoever. I still say equality for all Australians. It is a stupid statement to have come out and said that by all means.'

Melanie missed the whole thing because her local camera crew was unused to such spontaneous activity, and she had to beg Hanson for another doorstop. Would Hanson speak to Knuth?

'It does need to be discussed because I don't support this whatsoever and he's made a stupid statement, and I will be having a talk with him and anybody else who comes out under One Nation. Whoever, I will be having my say to them, because it does not reflect what I stand for and what One Nation is all about. I won't have these stupid statements.'

At the Old Tudor Mill Hotel in Launceston, I wrote my story, which scored the headline 'Aboriginal slavery: Hanson can't make up her mind', then worried about my latest intervention in her campaign. Melanie had said that she and the other Queensland-based reporters hadn't seen anything newsworthy in Knuth's comments and hadn't planned to ask her questions on them because such outlandish statements from One Nation's Queensland MPs were now passé in the Deep North. This was the first time Hanson had tried to pull any of her State MPs into line, and for the Queensland-based reporters Hanson's rebuke was the story.

I'd gone on and on to Hanson during the campaign, justifying our right to cover her as an essential part of the democratic process. I'd argued that in one way the media also represented the people, and scrutinised politicians on their behalf. If that were really true, then if we got a story that we knew wasn't meant, wouldn't we just be reinforcing the blockages in the conversation on race in which Australia was now so painfully engaged? And in an atmosphere of total distrust by both sides in the campaign, any acknowledgment that the other side was human was a positive, wasn't it?

Helen was exasperated by these thoughts. 'She only said it because she knew she'd stuffed up the press conference. She didn't say it because she believes it,' she said.

As I collected my bags from Dean's car, Oldfield limped over wearing his 'concerned' look. 'Jeff Knuth never said it, it's repeated out of a book written by twelve Aboriginal elders.'

I couldn't see the relevance of what he was saying. 'Knuth did say it, didn't he?' I said, nonplussed.

'Yes, and so did the Aboriginal people,' Oldfield replied.

I rolled my eyes and walked away.

Hanson's journalists gathered in the bar to discuss the day before attending the night's public meeting. The Old Tudor Mill hadn't been touched since a makeover in the 1970s went for red shagpile carpet halfway up the walls, long brown vinyl couches and a bar in every room. Melanie reported that Hanson had been given a room with a mirrored ceiling.'

'Poor woman, she wouldn't want to look at herself after today,' I said.

We were talking about Oldfield's weird spin on Knuth when he arrived to resume his spruiking. He mentioned a book, written by twelve elders, called *Raparapa*, about the tragedy that befell Aboriginal stockmen and their families in the Kimberleys in the 1960s when pastoralists locked them out of their own land rather than pay them equal wages to whites. 'Apparently that's where it comes from, and Knuth's apparently got some ATSIC people that he's dealing with in his own area who agree with the comments.'

I snapped. 'What—agree that rural Aborigines should camp on pastoralists' land by permission and get a bit of meat in return for their labour?'

He nodded.

'That's ludicrous, David. No Aboriginal elder would say "Take me back to the land in exchange for a bit of meat". That is ludicrous.'

'I'm only telling you what I was informed of at seven o'clock this evening.'

'And we know to believe you, don't we? You tell the truth all the time, don't you?'

'Yeah I do. I'm not a completely, totally confused individual such as yourself, Margo.'

Melanie tried another tack. 'David, it doesn't actually change the fact that Pauline disagrees with it. That's the more important story for me, the fact that she disagrees with one of her One Nation MPs.'

Michael intervened. 'I think Pauline is feeling uncomfortable with some of the race stuff.'

There was a three-second silence. Oldfield broke it by pretending Michael hadn't spoken. 'I'm not suggesting it is right. I think it's interesting that it actually came from Aboriginal people themselves.' He was shifting his ground.

'Is Knuth denying that they're his views?' I asked.

'I didn't get that far.'

'I think that's fairly important, David,' I replied.

'It's obviously more important to you than it is to me.'

'So you're saying you don't care that they're his views?'

'I have my views. I'm more concerned with my views. If I was to be so concerned with other people's views, I would do nothing than be continually concerned.'

Melanie joined the fray. 'So you don't care what sort of views the Party is spreading?'

'I don't know what he said—'

'Well if you don't know what he said there's no point in even talking—' Melanie protested.

'—and I don't believe what I read which is put down by journalists.'

I couldn't believe it—he'd gone from agreeing with Knuth's remarks to denying Knuth had made them. 'Every single thing in that [article] was taped and you know it, David. How dare you slander someone—you're going to get a writ.'

'Oh, I'm shaking in my shoes.'

'Don't spread lies about reporters with no bloody evidence.'

'I think you need some psychiatric evaluation and I think I really should speak to your editor about your continual abuse to me over the telephone and your personal threats to One Nation.'

'Go right ahead, David.'

He walked out. I was shaken and decided, yet again, to ignore him at all times. Melanie said he was trying to wind me up to force me off the campaign. Helen said I just had to stare him out. 'There's something going on here. He's not briefing her; she's not speaking to him. Something's not right.'

That night's meeting was in a room that doubled as the hotel disco, with multicoloured lights and plastic plants hanging from a low ceiling. Hanson had lost the plot on her race rhetoric and said little on the topic except for the unprecedented remark that she wanted to know where the money was going, not just in the Aboriginal area but 'in other Government departments'. It was an acknowledgment at last that waste was not confined to the black bureaucracy, but Helen wasn't prepared to give her an inch on race. 'She's taken a battering on race today, so she backs off. Totally predictable.'

AAP's Tasmanian correspondent Don Woolford couldn't believe the change in her since her last Tasmanian tour. 'She was brilliant as a performer, she just milked her audience something fantastic and her timing was so good. But now she's stumbling. The woman I listened to in Campbelltown is not the woman I listened to in Hobart two months ago. You've got to scrutinise her, Margo, but not just kill her.'

After her speech Simon van Zetten, surrounded by cameras, spoke from the back of the room. 'Thank you for coming down here to Tasmania, and being approachable while you've been down here. None of the other politicians that have come here have actually been approachable to the people. So thank you for that.' Applause.

Unfortunately, our governments have failed to address the issue of reconciliation with the traditional custodians of Australia. Our refusal to accept our human rights atrocities against these peoples has been and still is shameful, even when most non-Aboriginal Australians accept this as true and they want change. Australia has been built on a multicultural society to our economic and cultural benefit, but only when we truly accept our past and embrace the beautiful and generous culture of the Aboriginal people can we really call ourselves a multicultural society and move forward as a nation.

Pauline, in two weeks' time it's quite possible that you could hold balance of power in the Parliament of Australia. I plead with you again, take this point into consideration please; for the benefit of Australia address this issue. I wish you luck should you decide to play your part in achieving reconciliation and a true nation status for Australia. Thanks for coming down to Tasmania.

Again the audience was confused by the politeness, and managed a sliver of applause.

The room fell silent, and an exhausted Hanson paused for thought as she leant on the lectern. Finally she said, slowly and quietly,

Thank you very much for your comments. I've noted them, and I've made my answer that I believe in equality for all Australians. And whether you're of Aboriginal descent [someone booed] or whether you were born here or whether you are a migrant from another country, we all are Australians and proud of this country and stand united and strong together. No matter what we do, we can never turn back the hands of time. We realise what has happened in the past and we learn by the mistakes. But the only time that reconciliation will happen in this country is if you can get rid of the resentment and the inequalities that we have...I was born here, this is my land as much as it is any Aboriginal's, and as I say, where the hell am I supposed to go? And that's how I feel about it. I respect the Aboriginal people, I respect their culture, and I've never wanted to destroy that. They are part of the Australian history by all means, but please, respect me as well, that this is my land as much as it is the Aboriginals.

Almost as many audience members surrounded Simon as they did Hanson when the meeting finished.

'You're about as Aboriginal as my socks, buddy,' a woman said. 'I'd like a 2 percent home loan too, but I'm the wrong colour to get it. So what have you got to say about that?'

A Launceston small businessman cut in to ask Simon whether he was 'mixed breed'. Simon said he was not Aboriginal and the businessman retorted, 'Well you're talking about someone else's business then.'

The Courier-Mail reporter Christine Jackman interjected, 'People said it was nobody's business about the Jews as well, didn't they?'

But this guy stood firm. 'I like Jews too, I like everyone. You're making an issue. We should be one nation.'

Simon tried again. 'These people have human rights violations against them right now. They have more deaths in custody by three times—'

'Why are they in custody? Because they're lawbreakers, that's why.'

'More Aboriginal children die from malnutrition and diseases than in most third-world countries.'

'That's not my fault, that's not the fault of anyone here. What you sow you reap. If you don't look after yourself, you can't expect other people to.'

A drinks session in Dean's room after a long day became an Oldfield photo shoot when he turned up despite his threat hours before to force me off the campaign. Whatever the photographers wanted, Oldfield delivered, even mimicking a puppeteer as Hanson spoke of her spiritual beliefs on TV.

'Imagine if you were ripped away from your parents. This is not 200 years ago, this was less than 30 years ago, and in the 1960s this was still happening. There's people my age who can't find their parents.'

'You can't change 30 years ago.'

'You can't change it, but we can address reconciliation.'

'Sowing and reaping in this world, if you don't sow right you won't reap right. Sowing and reaping. And sure enough they do. They die in jail because they're in there, they break the law.'

We adjourned to the bar, but there was no escaping Oldfield. He came in, bent his head over my shoulder, and put out his hand. 'Truce?' he asked. I shook his hand, reluctantly. I just wanted him to go away, but when we went to Dean's room for a drink he walked in uninvited and was the last to leave. While Hanson appeared on the ABC's 'Compass' program talking about her spiritual beliefs, Oldfield agreed to pose for Grant and Dean draped over the television set, smirking, acting the puppeteer. When John Howard appeared on the screen he lit a cigarette lighter in front of Howard's face for the cameras.

Oldfield asked how we could get along better, and I said we'd be fine if he did not insult my intelligence with crap spin and desisted from making racist comments to me. He nodded solemnly.

The next day, Hanson said Knuth's words were taken from a book and that she wouldn't speak to him after all.

TWELVE

It's a very private and personal matter

DAY 19

Pauline Hanson awoke to the news from Oldfield that her son Steven, 23, had told *New Idea* she was a bad mother who did not care that he had a serious illness. Oldfield had informed the media the night before.

Oldfield blamed Barbara Hazelton, Hanson's former friend and secretary, who he'd forced out of One Nation in one of his many purges of people close to Hanson and unsympathetic to him. (Hazelton's exit was at least more dignified than that of Hanson's official biographer, Helen Dodd. Oldfield had called her, told her to pack her things, and instructed a federal government security officer to escort her from Hanson's Ipswich office.) Hazelton had spilt her guts to *The Australian* newspaper when she was sacked after the Queensland election—alleging Oldfield and Ettridge had taken over the Party and treated its members with 'disdain and contempt'. According to Oldfield, Hazelton's revenge wasn't over yet, and she'd helped Steven sell his story. On the same day as *New Idea*'s story, *Woman's Day* published a lurid Hazelton interview detailing her belief that Hanson and Oldfield had had an affair.

At Launceston airport early Monday morning, *New Idea* quickly sold out.

I read the article with the sinking feeling I'd have to report on it, despite its irrelevance to her political credentials and the sickening breach of privacy in which her son had participated. The cover read: 'Pauline Hanson's dying son, "I can't even speak to her".' Inside, the headline read: 'Pauline's son begs "Please Explain!"'

The story said Steven had spoken out in protest at Hanson's 'It's like I'm a mother' remark, although there was no direct quote by him to that effect, or any sign of the magazine's cover quote, 'I can't even speak to her'.

Far from 'dying', Steven said he had an undisclosed illness that might be life threatening many years hence. 'Yes, I'm in trouble with my health, but considering how good I'm feeling at the moment who knows what will happen in the future? Mum's aware of my illness and she's upset, but I don't expect her to support me through this,' he'd said.

Hanson had married her first husband, Walter Zagorski, when she was seventeen and pregnant. He'd left her after she'd told him she was pregnant with Steven, her second son. Those were the days she'd spoken of over coffee at the start of the campaign, when she'd struggled to feed her children, and we'd wondered then how she could be so tough on single mothers given her experience.

'She was never the type of Mum who picked you up from school and baked cookies when you got home. She was always too busy, working to support us,' Steven had told *New Idea*.

His father never saw him, and Steven did not get on with Hanson's second husband, plumber Mark Hanson. Steven had described himself as the 'black sheep', and the story weaved an impression of a child hurt and confused in the transition from one relationship to another. 'I don't blame my mother. She thought she was doing the right thing.

I don't speak to her now because she's too busy, but I've often asked her to "please explain" my childhood—so far I haven't got an answer.'

That lament could be made by just about everyone I knew. Regardless of the cruel beat-up by *New Idea* to cash in on intense public interest in Hanson the woman, to sell childhood memories about your mother at a time that would maximise damage to her seemed on the face of it an archetypal act of familial betrayal. Like all family stories, there was clearly an intricate web of emotions at play.

But because of the timing, smack bang in an election campaign, and because Hanson was 'a phenomenon', the Hanson family soap opera was the story and the tabloid newspapers and television were salivating at the prospect. I felt more like an extra in 'Days of Our Lives' than a political reporter as we awaited the star's arrival at Launceston airport. Hanson, chin up but face drained of colour and flattened of angles, waved aside the waiting media and marched into the VIP lounge, where she read the magazine article for the first time.

When she marched out to board her flight I commiserated with her on *New Idea*. 'I won't say anything. It's private,' she said. I felt sorry for her, again.

As Hanson sat in the window seat staring out of the porthole, beside her, Oldfield opened *New Idea* on his seat tray and Grant, sitting across the aisle, shot off a frame. The next day, David Oldfield's visage dominated again in all the News Limited papers, and the picture ensured a good newspaper run of Hanson's family woes.

The hypocritical thing about this sort of story is that the 'mainstream media', as distinct from the tabloid magazines, wouldn't normally run it let alone pay for it, but would often follow it up. The only way for the subject to shut down such a story would be to say nothing, forcing the mainstream media to forget it (or run it only in their gossip columns). But it was impossible for Hanson to say nothing in an election campaign because the travelling media would persist until she did.

Robyn Spencer was waiting at Melbourne airport to escort Hanson on an impossibly packed two-day sweep of Victoria. She'd scored the number one spot on the Victorian Senate ticket in exchange for giving One Nation the immigration policy of her far-right party, Australians

Against Further Immigration. 'You look tired,' she remarked to me, 'but I bet Pauline looks terrific.'

'No she doesn't,' I replied.

We drove 150 kilometres south-west to Colac—named after the region's Aboriginal tribe, the Coladgin—a town set in one of Australia's richest farming areas. At a meeting of 200 at the Colac RSL, a pale Hanson lacked animation and could not control the quaver in her voice. She looked and sounded as if she was about to crack.

As luck would have it on bad-mother day, this public meeting saw the first and only question from the audience on the topic of mothers. 'You were quoted as saying that you are the mother of all Australians. Please explain.'

She paused, breathed in deeply, and supported herself on the lectern as she stumbled through an answer that left all eyes glazed.

'I didn't say I was the mother of all Australians, I said I regard this country like I regard my home and that I have a responsibility. It was taken in that context. It's like a woman who has your home and you want to look after it, and that's the context that it was in, pride and responsibility first and foremost to this country. If they want to make something out of it, it's just too damn bad. I know how I feel about it and I am responsible for this, like a mother, to actually look after the country first and foremost before worrying about your neighbours.'

Oldfield talked her into squeezing a doorstop on her son into a too-tight schedule. It was held at the premises of 'GA Grant and Sons. Maintenance and general engineers. Special welders.' The sign was so faded you could hardly read it, the machinery was cobwebbed, the floor was dirt and the owner and sole employee was the local candidate.

'I made this clear from the very beginning—my private life is my private life,' Hanson said. 'Once you start talking about it, it goes on and on. I'll take some knocks, I'll wear some things along the way, but I've made a decision and I'll stick with it.'

Under questioning, she said: 'It's a very private and personal matter and it is a family matter. I love all my children and I'm just so sorry that someone would pay him for the story.'

Was she upset that her son had said she was not a good mother?

'I just said it's a private, personal matter, and I will not discuss my private life or my children's life with anyone. I don't like to see anyone's personal life dragged through the media, whether it be Cheryl Kernot's, whether it be Bill Clinton, or anyone's…but it has happened.'

The problem with that line, of course, was that it was her son who had dragged her personal life into the media. My sister—Gay Alcorn from *The Age*, which had deigned to follow Hanson on her Victorian leg—agreed that Steven's comments in *New Idea*, as distinct from the headlines, said nothing overly adverse about Hanson as a mother, although being public they would be extremely painful. We wondered how *New Idea* would justify the timing of the story and the payment for it. After a long runaround, Gay finally got through to the news editor, Tony Velba, who referred her to the editorial director, Bunty Avieson. Velba called back: 'The editor and the editorial director are away so all I can say is we can't give any comment. It's entirely confidential.'

It made me depressed. Here was the media self-righteously insisting on its right to hold politicians accountable, yet while Hanson had been questioned on the *New Idea* story all day, the magazine couldn't be bothered answering any questions at all. Where was our accountability? No wonder the media was on the nose.

New Idea is hardly mainstream media, but when we feed on news from such sources, many journalists seem to throw away the rule book, or all that's left of one. A Victorian commercial radio station blithely reported, direct from *New Idea*'s blurb, that 'the One Nation leader's son Steven is seriously ill and doesn't expect his mother to support him through it. Her mother of the nation comment incensed her child, prompting him to go public with his hurt.'

On the return drive to Melbourne after a punishing day on the road, Hanson's party pulled into the Italian Social Club at Werribee for something to eat for the first time that day. In classic One Nation style, they chose a place where food was no longer being served, and the manager rustled up some old sandwiches. In hostile Melbourne, Hanson's night-time meeting would be for One Nation members only, and Robyn Spencer mentioned over coffee that she'd taken steps of military precision to keep its location confidential. But Radio 3AW's Steve Price had just announced the venue on air, and Spencer couldn't for the life of her work out how he knew. A spaced-out Hanson put her head in her hands and said thinly, 'Oh, I told him when he spoke to me on the radio. Nobody tells me anything.'

'There's your deep throat, Robyn,' I said. I told Hanson she should slow down; that the pace was too much for her.

'I don't organise this. This is no different than the last two and a half years,' she replied.

I had dinner in Melbourne with my partner, with whom I'd had many spirited debates about the media's role in the rise of One Nation. 'What does it tell us about the media when the media say Pauline Hanson's legs threatened to distract the public from the campaign? The media were distracted! It's the same as with her private life.' I couldn't think of an answer.

Hanson's son made page one in *The Daily Telegraph*, and the commercial TVs, apart from the Nine Network, loved it too. I suggested to my Canberra bureau chief, Mick Millett, that we not run anything and he agreed, but he rang back to say Sydney wanted it after all. I wrote a story that began: 'And now? *New Idea* magazine intervenes in the Pauline Hanson election campaign and farce becomes soap opera,' and ended with a dig at *New Idea*'s refusal to comment. It appeared on an inside page with a photograph of Hanson walking alone at the Melbourne shrine of remembrance, dressed in black, her shadow ahead of her. The caption: 'Mum's the word...Pauline Hanson beats the streets in Victoria.' The headline: 'The son also despises, as Hanson gets a New Idea.'

The next day the wave of questions on her son continued. Melbourne commercial radio hosts, in marked contrast to their Sydney counterparts, had always been aggressively anti-Hanson, and it didn't stop just because the running story was her private life, an area in which Melbourne is invariably more circumspect than Sydney. On Radio 3AW's breakfast show, Ross Stevenson and Dean Banks taunted her about polls showing her attracting only 3 percent support in Victoria, before asking whether 'those stories around about you having a boyfriend overseas are incorrect?'

'All speculations, isn't it?' Hanson responded.

They persisted. 'When you came in here you saw that I had a couple of magazine articles—'Pauline's love for David' [*Woman's Day*] and the story about your son. You indicated that if asked, you'd refuse to answer them. But I was really going to ask this—do you find it unusual that these sorts of articles are written about you and not about other politicians? Do you put that down to the fact that you're a woman?'

'There's a lot of gutter tactics that happens in politics and you are right. That is my private life and I won't discuss it with anyone, and that's just how I feel about it.'

She didn't read about other people's private lives, they asked?

'I'm not aware of what other politicians or any other people of the community do in their own private lives behind their closed doors. It's none of my business, I respect that and I call for the same respect to me, myself, with my private life...all this is gutter trash that is brought out about my personal and my private life and I don't like it.'

Did that mean the story about her son was untrue?

'Well, look, that is between my son and myself, and it's of no one's business whatsoever. And whatever I say and whatever I do, if I was to defend myself that means the story would continue on, and I don't intend it to. I love my son, and I care very, very deeply about my children, and I care about them that I don't want their private lives dragged out through the mud as well.'

The second talkback caller said her name was Dot. 'Don't worry about Ross, he's got a $100 bet that you won't get more than 3 percent in Victoria, but I think we've got news for him.'

Hanson: 'Can I take him up on that?'

Dean Banks: 'I'm not a betting man, but I might have $100 with you too, Pauline.'

Hanson: 'Good, am I going to get your vote by the time I get out of this?'

Ross Stevenson: 'We're only interested in your money, Pauline.'

And in her private life, Ross. (One Nation gained more than 4 percent of the vote in Victoria.)

By day's end, Hanson had bowed to the pressure, telling Perth radio that her son had pushed her away when she'd tried to help. 'I was trying to push him to go to the doctor. Sometimes you can lead a horse to water but you can't make him drink.'

The next day *The Daily Telegraph*, its appetite whetted by the mother and son story, decided to follow up the two-day-old *Woman's Day* Hanson 'scoop'. No one asked Hanson about the story, which wasn't really new, and *The Daily Telegraph* tried and failed to find her son. Oldfield saved its day, enthusiastically taking up Helen's request for an interview. It was very wink-and-nod. He repeated his denials that they were having an affair, and claimed for the first time that he and Hanson had 'discussed' having sex, but that he had said no because they were working together. That juicy tidbit, which also stressed his control over Hanson, was enough to put on page three a huge soft-focus photo of Oldfield fiddling with Hanson's collar on the bluff in Tasmania. The supposedly broadsheet *The Courier-Mail*, always looking for a cheap shot against Hanson, ran Helen's story on page one. No one else touched the *Woman's Day* yarn.

Helen strongly defended her paper's stance. 'This is a political partnership with considerable influence on the political landscape, and if the relationship is more than professional it is newsworthy,' she said. But was it relevant? 'Oldfield wants to talk about his sex life. He made it the story.'

I remembered standing on principle and refusing to ask Oldfield about his private life after the Queensland election, only to find that he'd blurted it all out unprompted. And I remembered Oldfield's conversation with Helen on the plane to Perth more than a week ago, when he'd asked for a positive story on himself and she'd suggested in jest an interview with Hanson on her feelings towards Oldfield. He got what he wanted in the end, in his eyes anyway, by breaching Hanson's privacy, just as Hazelton had done in *Woman's Day*. Since Hanson seemed to surround herself with such self-serving, self-publicists as Oldfield and Hazelton, in the end she had only herself to blame.

THIRTEEN

Never had this much political interest in Kyneton yet

DAYS 20 AND 21

Day two of Pauline Hanson's bumpy ride through Kennett country began with the appearance of a man in a chicken suit outside the 3AW studios in Melbourne. Chicken man was there on a dare from Melbourne radio station Fox FM, to win a ticket to Saturday's AFL Grand Final. He stuck to her gamely all day, squawking without a break throughout a trail of engagements that led us over 700 kilometres and stretched the length of the State.

In keeping up with her and winning his dare, chicken man did better than many of the day's huge media contingent, swollen by Melbourne reporters who turned up in droves. The official itinerary was an idiot's wish list of One Nation's Victorian regional branches, although almost nothing on the itinerary took place and new stops were added constantly.

It wasn't long before Melbourne reporters were calling Hanson's progress 'the headless chook campaign'.

On the day's frequent detours to rundown light industrial businesses, a familiar pageant was played out: the owner took Hanson's hand and professed undying devotion, and his family crowded into the office for pictures with Pauline. But if Hanson's people ever thought rural Victoria would offer her the same spontaneous reassurance she was used to in Queensland, the delusion took a battering almost from the start.

After a visit to the Ballarat sheep saleyards, where a cowering sheep wearing a Pauline Hanson poster refused to be prodded into standing up and greeting its heroine, Hanson retreated to the city's magnificent old RSL. She swept up the red-carpeted staircase to a room where Hansonites in their Sunday best waited silently amid a lavish home-made morning tea. They lined up for her to walk around shaking their hands, like royalty. She asked for media down time.

'Go and have a rest. I'd just like to have some time with the people here so they can have an opportunity to talk with me. So can we not have the media please?'

I asked where her next stop was so we could comply, but she didn't know.

David Oldfield directed us to a radio station. We discovered the engagement had been cancelled only when the federal police advance party started pulling out. If anything, organisation had worsened since the campaign's self-proclaimed saviour had arrived. We were fuming, as usual.

Hanson spent hours at the RSL morning tea, even though all the votes there were completely sewn up, throwing her schedule into chaos. Dean, who'd now been watching Hanson through his camera lens for three weeks, said: 'She gets carried away. She gets in a group where everyone loves her and she soaks up the attention, and everything else is thrown away. She just enjoys being where people like her.' Earlier, at the saleyards, her One Nation escort had asked her, 'Do you get the feeling when you go home at night that you're suddenly lonely?'

'No,' Hanson replied curtly.

On an unscheduled walk through the Ballarat mall after her morning tea, the chicken man squawked as she strode along to an ever-increasing accompaniment of spontaneous protest. One man chanted, 'You're a racist!' Others cried, 'Go home,' and 'We don't like your kind down in our country'. A hostile crowd began following her as a Melbourne TV reporter unsuccessfully begged Hanson to answer some questions.

But at the end of the mall, no car awaited. She was stranded and I couldn't resist sending her up. 'Pauline, do you know where you're taking these people? Look behind you. You've got Ballarat following you, where are you going?' Hanson looked desperately to her escort. 'You could do a speech,' I suggested, 'A public doorstop.' Seeing a few friendly faces, she shook their hands and turned with renewed confidence to face the crowd.

'There *is* a lot of support and don't get the wrong message about what I stand for. I'm very pro-Australian and I believe in our country and I believe in a better future for all of us.' The chicken squawked at that, and a teenager in the front shook her head. 'And you can shake your head, and I don't think you realise—'

'Because you're a racist,' the young woman interrupted.

'Am I? What have I ever said that's racist?'

'Everything you say is pretty racist as far as I'm concerned.'

'No, you don't know, and that's what it is, IGNORANCE, because you have no idea of what I stand for.' She turned away. Her antagonist, seventeen-year-old Bridget Tunstall, informed us that, 'I was just here with my mother, and I really don't like her.'

Hanson led her entourage on a mad dash north to Kyneton, town of springs and abattoirs, for what was scheduled as a quiet drink at the pub. But One Nation candidate Frank Preston had spread the word, and it looked like the whole town was in the hotel or spilling riotously out into the street. Preston squeezed Hanson through the masses to the bar. When she finally got a beer a young woman called out, 'I hope you choke on it.' Another said, 'Go home, Hanson, go home to your fish and chips.'

Hanson fled the catcalls for a crowded back room and a briefing from Preston. He had to yell above loud political arguments. 'What's going to happen here, Pauline, could you speak to the people just a little bit for me? Because believe me, you have more support in this town than you could believe. Pauline, you're in real Australia.'

Hanson sighed. 'Oh, I think there's a lot of real Australia, and it's great, yeah. So what do you want to do?'

Again she tried for media down time. 'I want some space, Margo, I do not want the cameras in my face all the time.'

I refused. 'We gave you that opportunity last time and we got let down really badly, and some people lost you and some people had to speed. It's just wrong. If we can't trust David Oldfield, then we've got to stick by you.'

'This is my itinerary, Margo, right? I do not want cameras in my face.'

'Surely you can hear what I'm saying,' I replied.

She turned away to a group of meat workers who wanted her view on planned federal government changes to wages at abattoirs. She knew nothing about it, and a woman muttered darkly, 'She should have done her research before she came.' Her friend agreed. 'Yeah, know your facts before you say something.'

A Melbourne reporter desperate for some real news tried again for the elusive doorstop, but Preston rebuffed her. 'She's worn out, let her have a cup of tea, then I'm sure she'll talk to you, all right. So will you please do that?'

I snapped, 'What do you mean, you're sure she'll talk to us? Have you asked her if she'll talk to us?'

'Well, you'll not be told wrongly, so please just let her have a cup of coffee.'

'So you're guaranteeing that Ms Hanson will give a doorstop after this, are you?'

Hanson turned away from the meat workers and back to face us. 'No, I'm not doing doorstops.'

A woman wearing a Labor Party badge edged her way through the throng for Hanson's autograph. 'And I'm not demonstrating,' she said to Preston.

'I hope you're not, you promised you wouldn't,' he replied.

'I know. I'm just raising political awareness for the people of the town.'

'Well that's all Pauline's doing.'

'That's right, and she's doing a great job,' the Labor woman said with a smile. 'Never had this much political interest in Kyneton yet.'

By this time, several young women had jumped onto the bar and were dancing and chanting, 'Pauline Hanson's got to go'. Hanson hurriedly autographed Preston's One Nation T-shirt with 'Love you Frank, Pauline Hanson', and ran out the back door, leaving politics raging in the pub behind her. Later that day, she justified the lack of warmth for her in regional Victoria by blaming the youth. 'It's young school kids, that's where a lot of the protesters come from.' Her remedy? 'Don't give them school holidays.' I could no longer tell if she was joking.

My bureau chief, Mick Millett, rang for a briefing on the day's story. 'Hello, Margo, what is it today—aliens from out of space?' By now, nothing seemed unusual on the Hanson tour. Just before Mick called, Network Seven cameraman Ollie had filed footage of the photographers downing cameras and turning their backs on Hanson in mock protest at the lack of down time. He'd intended it for the end-of-year goof tape, but Seven's Canberra people actually thought it was serious and planned to run it on the news before Ollie intervened.

The only sensible observation I could make that day was that in Victoria Hanson stayed away from race. Victoria has no native title for a start, having appropriated Aboriginal land completely before Mabo, and the State is Australia's most comfortably multicultural.

In Ballarat, the One Nation candidate's wife, Lorraine Blanchard, recalled the violent One Nation meeting in the Melbourne suburb of Hawthorn the previous year. 'I was separated from my husband, I was belted around and called a racist and had a megaphone in my ear, screaming they'd kill all Pauline Hanson's supporters,' she said. Lorraine had adopted a Chinese daughter when she lived in Singapore, and was not racist. She and her husband ran a computer business, and as a Liberal voter she was disappointed with 'the banks and the multinationals—the little bloke can't get a go'.

Hanson said in a speech to a public meeting in Seymour mid-afternoon: 'We are not a racist organisation because if there was anyone who was racist in One Nation, I'd tell them where to go and I'd get them out, because that's not what I stand for.' (She still hadn't telephoned Jeff Knuth.)

Hanson was hours late for the Seymour meeting and at the last minute, after Robyn Spencer had negotiated all day, she went to the

DEAN SEWELL

Oldfield, in his element, leaves Hanson to cope alone while he joins the mayhem to yell at protesters yelling at Hanson in a Kyneton hotel.

Puckapunyal military base at dusk, comforted by an escort of soldiers in dress uniform. The media caravan was now a ragged remnant. The *Herald Sun*'s Melbourne reporter got lost early and never caught up. The Victorian police were also showing the strain, taking red lights as a matter of course and threatening to book us if we broke the rules to catch up. We started noting their breaches, just in case. Yet whenever Grant or Dean got out in front, usually by accident, the police pulled out all stops to overtake, as if their egos had been bruised. At one point Hanson offered a solution to our difficulties: 'How about if I park you all somewhere and I'll just continue going and I'll pick you up later?' Sure.

Throughout the day, my sister Gay wondered whether after all the risk and effort there'd be any story. Really, there wasn't.

'Why don't we just walk away?' she said.

'Because that's what she wants,' I replied.

By the time a military police escort accompanied her onto the Puckapunyal army base, Hanson still had not done a doorstop, and agreed reluctantly at Oldfield's request. Gay asked for her tip for the

AFL grand final. 'No,' she said, and walked away. For the last time that day, the Melbourne reporters shook their heads in disbelief.

Robyn Spencer ended her introductory speech at a small public meeting that night in the southern New South Wales city of Albury by saying that David Oldfield would be 'happy to have a few words with us before he introduces Pauline Hanson'. He didn't show.

'I'm glad I'm not the only one who loses David Oldfield,' Hanson said after a few moments of embarrassment. 'It's been a hectic day. I've been there everywhere, man,' she added, fumbling the lines of the song. She sounded relieved to have crossed the border.

For the first time in the campaign, Hanson's media turned off the TV lights and walked out of her meeting in the middle of her speech. It was no mock protest this time. We were tired, and angry at the day's pointless chaos. Oldfield looked displeased. The contingent of police, who vastly outnumbered the few peaceful protesters, were packing up as we left. Organised protest groups in all the capital cities except for Perth had dropped passionate protest—which often turned violent and thus boosted Hanson's fortunes—for studied indifference. But like their leader Jeff Kennett, Victorians—as they'd proved in Noosa at the beginning of Hanson's campaign—were up front in making it perfectly clear to Hanson exactly what they thought of her.

■

The Sydney Morning Herald writer David Marr joined the circus the next morning to interview Oldfield on race for a piece on Oldfield's contest with the Democrats' Aboriginal Senate candidate, Aden Ridgeway. Oldfield had negotiated time off for Hanson to do radio spots, but I was in no mood to accommodate either of them. David Marr was keen to see Hanson in action, and we tracked her down at River FM, where the station manager seated us behind a glass wall for a clear view of the interview.

Hanson still clung to the belief that the polls, now showing One Nation attracting only 8 percent of the vote and predicting her likely defeat in Blair, were wrong. 'When I go to the pub, when I have a drink,

DEAN SEWELL

In a hotel somewhere, Grant and Helen sleep after another long, hot, impossible day, while I just keep talking.

everyone is so supportive of you,' she told disc jockeys Peter Davies and Belinda King. (So that was her take on the Kyneton experience?)

'My kind of girl,' Peter said.

'Why don't you play "Stand By Me"?' Hanson asked, and they did.

The pair played it for human interest—Hanson had attracted significant support in regional New South Wales in the aftermath of the Queensland election result—while steering clear of her private life.

'Now, Pauline, you're on the road a lot. What won't you leave home without?' Belinda asked.

Hanson went blank. 'Oh, gee whiz, I've got to have my lippy, I suppose...' She looked at me for help. In jest I mouthed, 'the media' and pointed to my chest. 'One of the journos there is saying I won't leave home without Margo. Oh, the journos, really, they're by my side all the time. Hi Margo.' I was mortified.

Peter asked: 'How would you finish this sentence? I came, I saw, and I what?'

'And I'm not going anywhere.' She might not know it, but it certainly looked like she wouldn't be going anywhere near Parliament House again.

Hanson had told me in Western Australia that her favourite singers were Marty Robbins and Barbra Streisand, but this time she plumped for Neil Diamond, Harry Nilssen's 'Everybody's Talkin'', and Elvis Presley, especially 'Return to Sender'. 'There's some great ones from Doris Day. I know people say, "*Not* Doris Day", but—and Dean Martin,' she added. David Marr was delighted, and arranged with a River FM producer to dub the interview soundtrack to give to Hanson satirist Pauline Pantsdown for her next sampled single.

Hanson sighed. 'It's a nice change to come in and have a bit of light-hearted humour, and I can get normal occasionally.'

The police drove her to a Target store, where I found her in the shoe section. She explained she needed runners, socks and jeans to wear to the Henty Field Day; it would be wet and she hadn't packed her boots. She paused over some silky synthetic sleepwear, but decided it would be too hot for Queensland, telling Dean to get lost as he moved in for a shot.

'But it's history, Pauline,' I protested.

'It's not history, it's me doing my shopping,' she said, and moved to cosmetics. By the Yardley stand, she did a vitriolic, defensive ABC radio interview on her mobile, covering Easytax and her probable loss in Blair while testing foundation on her wrist.

At the checkout a young man confronted her. 'The way you talk about Aborigines, it's just not on. Why don't you think about your soul, what's inside?'

Hanson continued her search for jeans at a Hard Yakka seconds shop miles out on the highway. Her chief police officer barred my way in. 'She doesn't want anyone else in there, Margo.' Hmmm. Police as political minders now.

'But you can't stop me walking into a shop.'

'I'm not going to stop you, I just want to tell you.' We entered together.

The shop assistant was welcoming. 'Can I help you, Pauline? I've just heard you on radio.' But a male customer stormed out, saying loudly: 'If I'd known she was in there, I'd have blown the place up. She's got a head like a broken arsehole.' The police officer wished out loud that he could buy some jeans because they were a bargain, but you never could tell when she'd be off. I agreed, and when she emerged asked if she'd promise to wait. 'I always wait for you, Margo,' she said ironically. She modelled a pair of tight, black stretch jeans and I suggested something looser might be the look at a country show. She kept the black pair anyway, and took an hour to assemble blue jeans, a denim shirt and a red jumper. I thought she needed boots or she'd look daggy. 'No, I've already got boots back home,' she replied.

As I searched for my cigarettes, she said, 'Are you smoking all the time now?'

'Yes, and I blame you.'

'You blame me for everything,' she said with a smile. There was a certain poignancy in that remark. Hanson never did accept that as leader, the buck stopped with her.

Hanson asked the police officer what he thought of her selection. He nodded sheepishly and carried her shopping bag to the car. Dean asked Hanson to pose in front of the highway sign, 'Hard Yakka, An Australian Legend'. She agreed, after making sure it had not been 'sold off'. 'No, it's still Australian,' the assistant said.

Oldfield and the rest of the media waited anxiously at the hotel. She was hours late, but the hotel manager advised that Henty was a mud heap and Hanson gathered her media, light-heartedly snatched Dean's camera and put it over her shoulder, and led us to a discount shoe shop for a bulk purchase of gumboots. David Marr remarked that he'd done a lot of things as a journalist, but had never imagined buying rubber boots with Pauline Hanson. As we were lining up to pay, she spotted a pair of cheap black evening shoes and I helped her scour the shelves for her size. Nines. That took another ten minutes. Hanson entered another world when she went shopping.

The mood at the Henty Field Day, a showcase for the latest in agricultural technology, was all country-style good humour amid the rain and mud. Men, women and children in Akubras and Drizabones gathered politely around Hanson, as they had when National Party leader Tim Fischer, her nemesis and their local member, had visited the previous day. The New South Wales regions were the closest she'd come in her interstate tour to a relaxing day's campaigning in Blair country, and she was enjoying herself.

DEAN SEWELL

One Nation candidate David Barton at the Henty Field Day.

Hanson was jovial as we trudged through knee-deep mud. She joked to Helen about embarrassing me at River FM. 'And I'll take you to good places for shopping sometime,' she said to me. We ordered 'Bazadaise' beef burgers from Bernie O'Kane of Cobram—'the highest yielding beef of the highest quality in the world'. Hanson, the police and the media sat at a long table and Bernie crowned Hanson with a pink 'Bazadaise' cap. David Marr couldn't help himself.

'Pauline, that is not your colour,' he said.

Bernie took the pink cap for himself. 'Is that a bit poofy? Actually, I might get more money, I might get a grant now I'm a bit poofy.'

We all laughed, and Hanson agreed to a series of media scrapbook photographs of the whole party in gumboots. David Marr mused that, in her red jumper, black coat and gold 1954 halfpenny chain, she was wearing the Aboriginal colours.

For the rest of the campaign, I wore a black, big-brimmed Akubra, the Worn Out West model, bought at the suggestion of David Barton, the local candidate escorting Hanson for the day. He wore the Australian flag tie he'd worn when I'd met him in Hanson's Canberra office weeks ago, when *The Sydney Morning Herald* had taken his campaign poster photographs.

'You'll only be able to wear that hat while you're running round with me,' Hanson remarked at our next stop, a walk through Wagga Wagga, still in our gumboots. While she sat in a café eating sandwiches and chatting to David Barton, the local radio station announced: 'Apparently Pauline Hanson's in town. Well, this one's for you.' Pauline Pantsdown's 'I Don't Like It' blared out.

While onlookers might have wondered whether Hanson really loathed the media so much, relations between *The Sydney Morning Herald* and Oldfield had taken another plunge at Henty. Oldfield, after promising David Marr and Dean he'd join them in ten minutes to do an interview on race on the drive to Wagga Wagga, kept them waiting more than two hours while he stumbled through recording a free-to-air ABC television broadcast. While the other political parties prepared their own packages, One Nation's failure to do so meant the ABC's Marty and Dave had to film and produce it on the spot, following up the ABC's help in filming Hanson's Tasmanian TV commercial.

Dean, who'd kept his cool so far in the campaign, thus missed Wagga Wagga, was way past deadline to send pictures, and hit the wall. He marched up to Oldfield, pointed a finger, and let fly with some choice epithets that sent bystanders reeling. Oldfield yelled right back, until David Marr stepped up and said calmly: 'Mr Oldfield, I have to say you are a very rude person.' Oldfield crumbled and they arranged an interview back at the hotel bar in Albury.

Before the day was over, Oldfield's name was mud with the police, too. Not knowing where the evening's public meeting was, he gave a reporter the chief police officer's mobile phone number and the poor man was landed with the job of One Nation media manager. The day ended with the police and the media united in a bitch session about One Nation up the back of a tin shed at Albury show grounds which reeked of cow dung and a tang of desperation. Few turned up to hear Hanson speak in a town where hundreds had come a few months before. One Nation's surge in Tim Fischer's seat was over.

PART THREE

ANARCHY'S RULES

FOURTEEN

Wear the black boots and the brown shirt and let's just go for it

Days 22 and 23

The Mortdale Bowling Club in Sydney's west is in the seat of Banks, a Labor seat made safe by its fiery Aboriginal affairs spokesman, Daryl Melham. Banks is a stable blue-collar seat packed with housing commission flats and a high proportion of English migrants. The club's occupants at lunchtime on Thursday were white middle-aged and elderly working class, all cardigans and toupees. It was a clear, sunny day but the curtains were drawn, closing off the view of the bowling greens. Fluorescent lighting left the sides and corners of the room in shadows. One Nationites sat at tables or at the bar drinking beer and smoking cigarettes. This was the setting for One Nation's health policy launch.

David Oldfield meets Pauline Pantsdown.

Out on the street, Pauline Pantsdown wore a perfect copy of Hanson's now famous yellow top and black 'miniskirt' to await her arrival. Comedians David Mussolini Mouldfield and Paul-Ian Handsome Handpuppet, who like Pantsdown were standing for the Senate in New South Wales, joined her.

Hanson's police escort shielded her from meeting Pantsdown, but Oldfield stepped right up for combat and they faced each other, teeth bared, the perfect photo parody of a Hanson–Oldfield dust-up (and *The Sydney Morning Herald*'s picture next day).

'You keep saying that she is not a racist, Mr Oldfield, but the Australian people know that behind that is not the truth,' Pantsdown charged.

Oldfield sneered. 'Do you have a dictionary and somebody to do your make-up?'

A thin cement path between the clubhouse and the bowling greens led from the street to the club entrance. Pantsdown was there 'to be part of the very last gasp of Hansonism in Australia before it is down to the annals of history', but club officials stopped her walking down the path to Hanson's world. David Mouldfield, the wild look in his eyes nothing out of the ordinary at One Nation functions, sneaked through.

Lines of plastic seats facing a long trestle table occupied a space cleared in the centre of the room for the media. I helped Melanie open the curtains to let the light in. Pauline's People blinked and returned to their beers.

It was a strange feeling sitting there surrounded by a growing circle of Hansonites. It felt like an amphitheatre. Were we to be the sport?

Hanson walked to the table to a standing ovation. She sat down at the far left, with two men sitting between her and Oldfield on the far right.

'We're launching One Nation's health policy and it's lovely to be able to do it here today at the Mortdale Bowling Club in the seat of Banks,' she said. 'So thank you very much for coming today, and I'll hand you over to David Oldfield.'

Oldfield introduced One Nation's health spokesmen. Dr Ray Danton was a dentist and candidate for the New South Wales central coast seat of Robertson. Dr David Cunningham, a florid Scotsman of 70, was a leading light in the far right doctors' organisation, Private Doctors of Australia, which believed Medicare was an evil socialist experiment and dubbed the health minister Dr Michael Wooldridge a 'witch doctor'. So, yet another One Nation policy bought off the shelf from the extreme right.

As had become the norm since her Easytax nightmare, Hanson was the draw card, not a participant. 'The Product' sat back, fixed her eyes on a spot at the back of the room, and froze her face into an 'interested' look.

Danton, his manicured white hair and well-modulated tones adding an eerie air of conventional respectability to proceedings, announced that One Nation would abolish the universal health care system by exempting the privately insured from paying the Medicare levy and making their insurance premiums fully tax deductible. Given that the Medicare levy is progressive, with higher income earners paying a higher levy, this would starve the public health system, creating two-tier health care for rich and poor. It would also cost heaps, and Danton conceded under questioning that more than $2.5 billion would have to be found. Paradoxically, One Nation wanted a universal Medicare for dentists—government-funded annual dental examinations for all school students, and free dentistry for everyone on welfare and the aged pension. The aged would get much, much more, as would rural and regional Australians. Only one group would suffer under One Nation's health policy—Aborigines, the Australians with by far the worst health problems and, in remote communities, by far the worst health services.

'One Nation policy on Aboriginal issues is well known,' Danton said. 'We believe all Australians must be treated equally. Health services should be no different. Medical, dental and surgical services should be made available on the basis of need and not on the basis of race.' The crowd cheered. He said that currently, $131.3 million was allocated to Aboriginal and Torres Strait Islander health services, along with $17.5 million for substance abuse services. 'Removal of this dual administration of health services will generate significant savings,' he said ominously.

Oldfield: 'Questions from the ladies and gentlemen of the press?'

The event, in Oldfield's hometown—where you'd expect him to direct campaign events—had the smell of a set-up, but could we avoid it? Helen and I, jaded after all this time in Hansonville and sensing trouble, had agreed to postpone Aboriginal questions in the hope they could be eased into and pass without too much hassle. Helen opened the batting. 'Mrs Hanson, how much is this going to cost?'

Hanson: 'I'll leave it in the hands of the health person.'

Her non-existent knowledge of policy exposed yet again, I asked Danton for the cost to revenue and how it would be paid for.

Danton: 'We have full budget documentation, which will be available with all the figures as a final budget document I believe will be released in the electorate of Blair on Tuesday at the campaign opening.' This was the first indication we'd had of the date of Hanson's campaign launch.

Helen and I toyed around with general questions until the campaign-fresh, terrier-like Stephen McDonell, the Sydney ABC radio current affairs man who'd joined Hanson in Tasmania, opened the batting on race. Would the special Aboriginal health programs be abolished?

The funds would disappear into 'an overall health fund' for all Australians, Danton said.

Helen: 'Is this health policy skewed towards providing greater care for aged people and people in rural areas?'

Danton: 'The aged people are suffering and obviously the rural people are suffering too.'

'What about Aborigines—aren't they suffering?'

'Aborigines are going to be treated on the basis of need.'

'So they'll be treated equally, but rural people and older people will get treated in a special manner?'

'Not in a special manner, in a manner that they should be treated and haven't been treated in the past. They have been discriminated against.'

The audience clapped and cheered and began catcalling, 'Get back to your Resistance' and 'Wake up Australia'. When it died down, Stephen followed up Danton's straight-faced denial of discrimination against Aborigines in the same breath as his assertion that other Australians needed affirmative action to address discrimination.

'You've said there will be special treatment for rural and regional Australians—', he began, but Oldfield stood to interrupt.

'Look, once again we have a situation, I'm afraid, where the media is trying to run their agenda rather than just dealing with the facts of the policy—the fact of the policy is that all Australians will be treated equally.'

The crowd erupted into wild applause and more catcalling, and Christine Jackman yelled above the din, 'But surely you'd agree there are health problems that particularly Aborigines suffer from?'

Enter Dr Cunningham. 'Could you specify these please?'

Christine: 'Diabetes, Glaucoma. Why are they dying so much earlier than other Australians?'

Cunningham leaned forward accusingly. 'What you're actually saying then is Aboriginals are different physically and mentally than the rest of us. Is that what you're saying?'

'No,' said another reporter, 'just that they've got different and more acute health problems.'

'What health problems? So you've mentioned glaucoma, what else?'

Hepatitis and AIDS, Stephen suggested.

Cunningham retorted, 'What you've got to realise is that these Aboriginals have access to exactly the same health care as the whites.'

The special Aboriginal health programs were just tokenistic when it came to fully addressing the third-world health standard of many remote Aboriginal communities, a legacy of more than 200 years of white displacement and neglect. The one-eyed, cranky, take-from-them-and-give-to-me racism of One Nation was dangerously exposed now, and Oldfield again goaded his troops into changing the angle. To more cheers and jeers he yelled, 'I think it's a great shame that everybody in the media keeps trying to divide Australians into two groups.'

I thought I'd exhausted my anger on race on Hanson's campaign, but these blatant diversionary tactics got me going. I raised my voice above the din and asked: 'What is your estimate of the amount of money it will take to ensure that Aborigines have got the same health care and health services as other Australians?'

Someone yelled out, 'What's that got to do with it?', and the audience roared its approval. It had nothing to do with it unless you believed in equal treatment for all Australians, and this lot certainly didn't. I had to yell to make myself heard. 'How much will it cost to bring the infant mortality rates of Aboriginal people down to the level of other Australians? What is your estimate of how much that will cost?'

Danton got down to basics. 'If there is an increased mortality level in Aboriginals and the need is there for that to be looked at it, it will take whatever it takes to bring it down.' His questioning of official infant mortality statistics chilled me to the bone. It was the same sickened feeling I'd had when Hanson in Longreach, ironically given Danton's statement, had cited the 'terrible infant mortality and generally shorter life span' of Aborigines as proof that the greater number of Aborigines receiving special benefits must mean people were pretending to be black.

The Hansonites thought Danton's answer was spot on and burst into war cries again. Above the cacophony Oldfield announced an end to the press conference, but Melanie waved her arms from the back of the room and asked Oldfield if she could ask a non-Aboriginal question. 'Yes, Ms Wendt?' Oldfield said.

She asked how the health policy would affect young people, and Danton replied that young people earning $40 000–$50 000 would be much better off.

How many young people would be on that salary level, Melanie inquired.

An interjector yelled, 'Margo is', and Oldfield took up the theme. 'Well you, for example, Melanie, you for example.' The audience roared and Oldfield yelled above them, 'Everybody here that's young in the media is on at least that or more.' The audience vented its spleen all over us again, and when they calmed a local reporter asked for the estimated cost savings from the abolition of separate funding for Aborigines.

Danton waffled until Cunningham cut in. 'The actual cost, which we have outlined to you, is the equivalent of giving every Aboriginal something like $400 in their hot little hand.' Oh, those greedy, pampered Aborigines.

Helen asked for clarification of One Nation's plans on health screening of migrants only to be greeted with loud groans from an audience now at a fever pitch of angry emotion. Oldfield again called an end to proceedings, and I yelled at him above the chaos, 'David, why don't you stay here and face your questions? You never have a press conference where you don't walk out.' I walked up to Danton and demanded to know whether he would abolish women's health programs as well as Aboriginal ones, for consistency's sake. He said no as Oldfield called out to the mob, 'Well we know you'd be particularly interested in that issue.' David Mouldfield rushed to the stage and tried to hug Oldfield while bellowing, 'We're National Socialists, wear the black boots and the brown shirt and let's just go for it. Onya son, c'mon the National Socialists!' Mouldfield was dragged out, screaming, 'We love you David, we love you David,' as Oldfield asked journalists to collect the health policy documentation.

I'd been so focused on the questioning I hadn't sensed the personal hatred in the room until I turned to leave and Helen told me to be careful. A club official said, 'Don't worry, luv, I'll get you out safely.' A woman wearing a pillbox hat grabbed my arm, spun me around to face her, and put her face too close to mine.

DAVID HANCOCK

Pantsdown and Hanson's media outside the Mortdale Bowling Club. From the left, back, Grant Turner, Melanie Wendt, Stephen McDonell, Terry Miller (ABC TV soundman), Pauline Pantsdown, Marty Helmreich, Lisa Millar, Peter Doherty. Front, from left, Dave Fraser, Christine Jackman, Helen McCabe, me, Dean Sewell.

'I think you're disgusting,' she said.

'Thank you and goodbye,' I replied. I was shaken, and edged my way out through jeers.

At the other end of the cement path, Pauline Pantsdown lip-synched 'I Don't Like It' (now number twelve on the charts) as a CD player beside her blared out the tune. It looked like sanity, and Hanson's journalists gathered around her for a 'Please Explain' photograph before Mouldfield and Handpuppet did a standup comedy routine at which we laughed indiscriminately. The woman who'd grabbed me came out glaring and wrote to the *Herald* complaining about the tone of my 'Thank you and goodbye', suggesting that in my big black hat I looked like I was where I belonged with Pantsdown and the rest of the riff raff. She was referring to the 'Worn out West' Akubra that One Nation candidate David Barton wore and had recommended at the Henty Field Day.

A woman who wasn't a One Nation supporter but who had happened to be in the club approached Helen in tears, saying she was terrified at the sight of people bringing their children along with flowers to present to Hanson. 'Don't let them get to you,' Helen said. 'They're slumping in the polls, it will be all right. Most Australians don't like it and they'll prove it on polling day.'

It had come to this. One Nation had brought its people in to judge us and so they had, in much the same fashion as some extreme anti-Hanson protesters had once shouted down and threatened citizens arriving to hear Hanson speak at public meetings. Free speech when it suits, and when it doesn't, blind emotion and mob rule. And the trigger—surprise, surprise—race.

It seemed clear to me that Oldfield, having nothing else left in his armoury, was now intent on playing the anti-media card. How else could one explain him inviting the media to a press conference then goading his supporters into howling us down? A bit of chaotic, passionate uproar at a press conference was just the thing to increase support for One Nation, or so history suggested. Oldfield cemented his new strategy when he announced in an interview to the wire service AAP after the launch that from now on Hanson's itinerary would be secret because the media was so awful. He then rang journalists to give them the address of that night's public meeting.

The unanswered question was whether Oldfield was playing a double game. Was he telling Hanson that her plans were secret then telling us where she would be, or was she a party to the public illusion he was now seeking to create? (The waters muddied even further the next week when Hanson flew to Sydney for a chat with talkback radioman Stan Zemanek on 2UE. Oldfield rang around to ensure Hanson's journalists were making the trip, yet when Hanson arrived at the studio and demanded to know what the media were doing there, he launched into an anti-media tirade and unsuccessfully demanded that journalists be evicted.)

Oldfield was a crude operator who played the role of media adviser inside out. A media adviser in an election campaign was charming in public, and would clarify, correct, castigate and threaten in private. But Oldfield preached media bad faith in public and acted like nothing had happened in private, even feigning hurt that he was so misunderstood. It was a house of mirrors.

But for Oldfield to play his game we had to cooperate. My editor, Paul McGeough, backed my instinct that I shouldn't attend further press conferences where One Nation supporters were present. Seeking a guarantee that the health policy debacle would not be repeated wasn't enough, since it would have to be sought from the man who had incited the crowd.

I felt that Oldfield—knowing One Nation needed media coverage—would have had to agree to provide a safe environment for journalists to ask questions if all the Hanson journalists insisted on it, but I didn't expect they would. Still, if it happened again, I wouldn't be in the middle of his absurd games in which, judging from the personal interjections against me, I had been made a particular target. My decision was cemented when I heard that the ABC's '7.30 Report' had made the mess public, with its political anchorman Barrie Cassidy ending his campaign wrap with 'a walk on the wild side'. There I was telling Oldfield not to close down the press conference and yelling my last question to Danton and there was Helen looking appalled at Oldfield's personal comment about me.

Television is expert at stripping context from a dramatic image, and the images which appeared looked uncannily close to those of a tumultuous Canberra press gallery immigration press conference with Hanson before the election—an electoral winner for her. By night's end I'd heard that the epithet 'disgraceful' was being bandied about in the press gallery corridors about my conduct. Some in the gallery had finally found a principle they thought they could count on in analysing Hansonism—that in a public contest between the media and One Nation, the latter always won. According to them, we'd managed to snooker ourselves again. But if we didn't try to do our job of scrutiny, the foundation of our right to be there, what right had we to be there at all? I also thought there was an important difference politically in the day's debacle—that it was Oldfield, not Hanson, in the thick of the confrontation. Hanson—the woman her male fans in particular were so anxious to protect—was a mere bystander.

Helen, Grant, Dean and I took the night off after our papers agreed to send other reporters to her public meeting in John Howard's seat of Bennelong. I was depressed about the day's conflict and disgusted by One Nation's racism, and wanted time out.

A couple of Hanson journalists who did go rang to advise that Sydney had continued its brash and brutal reception to Hanson's visit. The hall was packed inside with Hansonites and outside with loud but peaceful protesters, the big crowds inside and out a rare event on the campaign. Journalists were locked out, with local officials proposing to allow only their favourite TV network, Seven, into the venue. Oldfield, after publicly announcing a media ban, got the media in when he arrived, but anti-media hysteria was now so intense that the verbal assaults came even when the media was there just to listen. A One Nation supporter walked behind a female journalist making pig noises. Another Hansonite told a reporter that One Nation had been looking into her, and knew where she worked and that she was a lesbian.

One Nation members were taking Oldfield's media hate message dangerously to heart, so Oldfield tweaked his tune a little.

> The media had a bit of a problem getting in here—some of them—tonight. Now that's wrong. We should not ever attempt to exclude the media, and I know that everyone who was involved in that probably thought they were doing the right thing, and I can understand that. Is there anyone here amongst the audience, amongst the ordinary citizens of Australia, who like the media?

Above the groans, he continued: 'I think they skipped their blue pills this morning. I will happily supply some for them tomorrow morning.'

◼

The next night Helen and I sat on a picnic table bench outside the Newcastle Entertainment Centre, while inside Hanson did her thing to a half-empty stadium. Fifty police were already starting to pack up long lines of orange barricades erected to prevent a repeat of the violent confrontation between protesters and One Nation supporters when Hanson last paid a visit to Newcastle. A few laidback, guitar-playing protesters stood companionably in the allotted protest spot.

A drunken young One Nation fan called Mitch came over with his mate. 'We saw you guys on TV last night. You must have been pissed off at what they did to you,' Mitch said.

'Yeah, we were,' I replied. They went away and came back with beers and the offer of cigarettes, which we gratefully accepted.

I was sitting in the same spot alone when Mitch wandered over again to reveal that he'd nearly come to blows with a police officer who'd tried to search him on the way into the meeting. (Body searches were compulsory that night.) 'If you don't like it, kick me out,' Mitch said he'd told the cop.

He'd got into a punch-up with protesters at the last Newcastle meeting, he said. And he'd got into a punch-up that day, too, in a shopping centre to which Hanson had failed to turn up due to security concerns. There was a big fight in the middle of the shopping centre square, he said. 'Where we were, we're all the One Nation supporters, and the opposition was on the other side yelling shit at us and that, so we were yelling shit back to them. And one of our blokes walked straight through the centre of them yelling out, 'Pauline Hanson for PM', and that sparked confrontations up. And me being the rebel that I was, I still am, being eighteen and that, I walked over and helped him out a bit, and confrontations went to confrontations, and in the end the police had to step in and help us out.'

'There's two mates from school out there in the protesters tonight,' he said, but he wouldn't say hello, 'because I'd probably punch them out first.'

'No, you've got to control that,' I said.

That would be hard, he explained affably, because he'd been in the pub since 3.30 p.m.

'Stay nice and calm then,' I replied. 'Do the freedom of speech thing. No punches, right?'

The self-proclaimed One Nation brown shirt nodded, settled in, and told me his story. 'My family is divided into three ways, the voters that are there at the moment. Mum's a notorious Liberal voter, Dad's a Labor voter, and I've only just turned eighteen this year.' He was a Newcastle boy, but had moved to Brisbane three years ago when he couldn't find work in his hometown. He'd finally got a job with Pizza Hut, but had come home five months ago after his mother's third back operation because she needed looking after. 'But there's just nothing down here, so I'm thinking I'll have to move back up to Brisbane again.'

Did he have qualifications?

'I only made it half way through year nine, I got asked to leave. I wasn't so much the fighting type then, but I was the sort of bloke who'd stand up and say what I thought, sort of like Pauline does at the moment. She talks what she believes in and not what everyone else wants to hear. And I was sort of like that in school—wanting to change the dress code and behaviour rules and that. And the way I look at it now, being eighteen, is she's saying basically along the same lines. The Asians are coming over here and taking the Australian jobs from the Australian youth. And there's just nothing left for us to take. It's like we've got to fight doubly harder, and if we take that job we've got to take the pay cut rather than taking the proper pay that we should get, because you've got the Asians coming over here and they work for next to nothing, basically. Which is really hard for a bloke like me. My Dad, he was in the hierarchy on the State Rail Authority and so was my grandfather before that, and my uncle. But for me, the railway is a dying breed, it's being run from computers.'

Mitch was the classic insecure, confused and frustrated Labor blue-collar voter turned One Nation jack boot, just going for it.

'From seeing my father's perspective, you could tell the bosses to get stuffed one day and walk into another job the next day and start again, but not any more. There's a lot more work up there in Brisbane, you've just gotta be able to undercut the Asian population. Surfers Paradise is one of the main ones—the food catering industry itself. You get the Asians coming over and, because they're marvellous in what they can do, unless you go to TAFE and do everything you can do you've basically got to be a cordon bleu chef before you can get a job. To me, I felt that was wrong and I didn't appreciate that.'

I asked if he'd tell me his full name. 'My name's Mitchell Folbigg and I'm not afraid to admit who I am.'

'Neither you should be,' I replied.

When we got back to Sydney around midnight, Dean and Grant dropped into their offices to collect super-long camera lenses. Hanson's increasing tendency to flee the media and Oldfield's media machinations meant we needed another weapon in our armoury for the last week of Pauline Hanson's election campaign, just in case.

FIFTEEN

What about stockings and G-strings?

DAYS 24 AND 25

Saturday morning on the eighth long day of Hanson's interstate tour brought us to Adelaide—proud home of the Adelaide Crows, the reigning Australian Rules champions who would defend their title in the AFL Grand Final in Melbourne that day.

The arriving One Nation contingent was in anything but a happy mood. On the plane, Dean wore his MUA T-shirt, inscribed 'Reith—Liar! Corrigan—Liar!' and threatened to write in 'Oldfield—Liar!' Oldfield marched up and down the aisle polling reporters on which was the more damaging to him, David Marr's piece on Oldfield and race in *The Sydney Morning Herald*, or Emma Tom's column in *The Weekend Australian* describing their date.

Oldfield was a true believer in the maxim that all publicity is good publicity, and most pleasingly good when it showed him in attractive female company. He'd already been filmed that week for 'The Footy Show' glorying in a spa with not one but two young women, photos of which had appeared in a women's magazine. Was he trying to impress Hansonites, or the 'elites'? He disgusted both, poor man.

Emma Tom's piece, eloquently headlined 'Violation without sex', was devastating, depicting—largely in his own words—a slavering idiot who couldn't resist putting on exaggerated Asian accents and proclaiming that feminists were 'men inside women'.

In his interview with David Marr at Albury's Country Comfort hotel bar on Wednesday, Oldfield had shown his colours on race, admitting that One Nation's pledge to abolish native title without compensation was impossible to achieve. A pipe dream. A fraud on One Nation supporters. Oldfield spent much of the trip trying to convince Helen and Melanie he was not a racist.

Hanson sat up the front looking pasty and blank. The Oldfield-inspired uproar at Thursday's health policy launch seemed to be still ringing in her ears, and the coverage had left her aggrieved. 'It was a perfectly good health policy,' she had complained to Melanie and Christine on Friday. 'But what did you write about? Pauline Pantsdown.' Melanie had protested that Nine hadn't run anything, as was their wont. 'That's right, you're ignoring me—and the rest of you wrote about Pauline Pantsdown and rubbish!' (I had detailed her Aboriginal health policy under the headline 'Aborigines: healthy, wealthy and lies'.) Hanson had also commanded Grant, her favourite photographer, to 'bugger off', saying she was sick of the print media and knew we were out to destroy her.

The first inkling that Adelaide might deliver a few surprises turned up in the person of Len Spencer, a tall, athletic man with floppy hair and by far the best tailoring sighted to date on the One Nation trail.

Spencer was the number one Senate candidate in South Australia. He was also the bloke two One Nation members had accused of carrying a handgun and threatening them with it. A 'Four Corners' program had shown an interview with Spencer denying he had a gun or a gun licence, followed by an interview with Hanson saying he had pulled a gun to ward off intruders. When confronted with a similar statement by Oldfield, Spencer had backed off, mumbling, 'When you say something in confidence, you expect it to remain in confidence, that's what relationships and trust are like.'

To a viewer, this looked disastrous for Spencer and had the whiff of an Oldfield attempt to force Spencer out. Later, Spencer 'clarified' that he did have a gun licence because a previous employer who often carried large sums of cash 'required me to carry a gun'. But Spencer was evidently a survivor, and whatever bad blood remained between the two was a mystery as Spencer ushered Oldfield into his sparkling new white Mercedes sedan at Adelaide airport.

Spencer jockeyed hard with Dean for the plum spot behind Hanson's car as the One Nation-police-media convoy zoomed from one half-empty shopping centre to another on the morning of Grand Final day. Dean, who had bowed to my pleas and changed into a Midnight Oil 'head injuries' T-shirt, played at squeezing Spencer out as I amused myself snapping rolls of black and white film of Spencer and Oldfield when Dean passed them. The ABC car drew level with Hanson's car while Marty leaned out of the car window to film her. Hanson's campaign had become a raw battle of wills. The day was grindingly pointless, and everyone light-headed.

While Dean and I were waiting outside a shopping centre on Adelaide's outskirts for Spencer's Mercedes to catch up, I knocked on Hanson's car window and handed her Emma Tom's piece.

Spencer soon appeared, without Oldfield, and escorted Hanson on her walk. Her chin jutting out, she marched past utterly uninterested shoppers—it was Grand Final day after all—getting it over with. A One Nationite raced up with the news that Hanson's supporters were waiting to cheer her at another entrance. 'Oh well, never mind,' said Spencer, and kept walking.

A local TV reporter asked Hanson on the run if she was backing the Crows in today's big match and she nodded. She was wearing the Adelaide team's red, navy and gold scarf, thoughtfully provided by Spencer.

'You actually know a bit about the team, then?' the reporter asked as the cameras rolled.

'No, I don't know a lot about it at all,' she replied.

'You're not actually a supporter of the team?'

'No.'

Hanson had proved amazingly successful at drifting above the chaos and extremism in her party, her rag-tag collection of Queensland MPs, and her inability to articulate policy. Somehow, many voters still believed in her, and her political impact and unusual persona had lifted her to a level of media celebrity that rolled on regardless of her failings on substance. But her once unshakeable belief in herself was showing signs of severe strain, and she was finding it increasingly difficult to 'perform'. One Nation had now managed to pick the worst possible time and place for her to recover her balance and feed off the public adoration she so needed to restore her confidence: Adelaide on Grand Final day.

It was 45 minutes to kick-off. Hanson seemed to be the only person in town, including the police and journalists trailing her, who was not transfixed by this fact. Impatient with the stupidity of it all, I joined her on her dogged shopping centre march and said the only way she could hope to get on the TVs was to watch the Grand Final. She needed to watch it in a pub with some of her supporters, let the camera people take some shots, and then she could relax—all the media would go away. 'No, it won't get on TV, nothing positive gets on TV,' she said. I gave up, went to a music shop playing 'I Don't Like It', and bought a copy.

Hanson's car carried her off from another entrance, losing most of the media. Her police driver led *The Sydney Morning Herald*, News Limited and ABC cars on a dodgem-car spin through the car park, until—at 30 minutes to kick-off—Hanson brought things to an abrupt stop. She climbed out and spoke intently to her police and Spencer. Hanson was not happy; she was sick of shopping centres, and she was cancelling the rest on the list.

Right on kick-off, Hanson's car and Spencer's Mercedes pulled up outside his luxurious bluestone home with tennis court and swimming pool in the prestige suburb of St Peters. One Nation in Adelaide was obviously a special brand; led by a rich man who, at first glance, had absolutely nothing in common with any battler I could think of, apart from a liking for guns. Dean, Grant and Marty prowled down the path of the house next door to photograph Hanson and Spencer if they ventured out to Spencer's backyard.

Helen, a South Australian, was bitter about missing the match. She turned on the car radio and stared at it. 'She needs her bloody visit to Adelaide recorded and that's it. They'll be doing colour stories galore about what's happening around town today and she'd get a run, of course she would. It's insane. She should have stayed home if she wasn't going to watch the game.'

Hanson and her team chose that moment to dash out to Spencer's local, the Hackney Hotel, and ask for lunch. The publican said no. Lunch was finished, and he and his customers were trying to watch the football, if they didn't mind. Hanson, Spencer and her security men closeted themselves in a darkened room without a television set, declared it a private function, and left one police officer on the door. The lucky cop bought crisps and watched the game with Helen, Stephen McDonell and me.

At half-time the Crows were down and seemingly out and the Hanson party fled again. We left Grant and Dean, still filing pictures from their computers on the bar floor, and Helen took the wheel to give chase. Her heart wasn't in it. When the police car and Spencer ran a red light, she turned off to Elder Park by the river, where we could sit on the grass and watch the football on a big screen. If Hanson had a brain, that's where she'd go now, Helen reasoned. And if she didn't have a brain, too bad.

Dean and Grant had got there by the time Hanson arrived at the park, only minutes before full-time. The Crows had staged a magnificent comeback, and thousands of Adelaide fans were beside themselves with joy at their impending victory. 'Get lost!' they shouted at Hanson's approach. She did. The TVs missed her, having been told by Oldfield that she wouldn't appear.

Hanson was in the Stanford Plaza Hotel foyer, ready to spring, when Oldfield walked in. She strode over to give him a tongue-lashing. 'Have you seen that article about you? It's not very complimentary.' He agreed. 'Why do you go out with those feminists?' He mumbled excuses. 'Well you're getting the worst reputation, David.'

The pair joined Spencer for a drink in the cocktail lounge. Across the room, Helen and I were toasting the Crows and looking forward to a night free from One Nation at Don's Table, the restaurant owned by

DEAN SEWELL

South Australia's lead Senate candidate, the amazing Lennie Spencer, had fun throughout Hanson's dreadful Adelaide tour. Dean took this picture before the crowd watching the Adelaide Crows grand final win told Hanson to 'get lost'. Spencer polled well, but was snookered by the other parties preferencing the Democrats.

the late former South Australian Labor Premier, Don Dunstan. Hanson wanted her dinner function to be private, which sounded great to us.

Within minutes of the trio leaving, Spencer returned and pulled up a chair. Just call me Lennie, he said. He said his wife was a doctor but would reveal nothing of what he did for a living, except that he'd worked as a barman at the Playboy Club seventeen years ago, and had once served Don Dunstan in his heyday. We asked how he and Oldfield were getting along. All was well, he said. They had fought it out in a three-hour phone call after the 'Four Corners' program went to air, and he was still dealing with police inquiries on the gun matter. The affair had caused him grief. In fact, they hadn't spoken again until today. Spencer then proceeded to shred Oldfield. He was supposed to give Oldfield a lift to the dinner, but 'if his make-up's not on, he'll just have to be left behind'. Oldfield was obsessed with sex. Were Hanson and Oldfield having an affair, Helen asked. 'Oh no. Pauline doesn't like sluts.'

At that point Oldfield appeared, looking flustered. 'You left this,' he said, holding Lennie's navy jacket. Lennie allowed that he had. 'Have you been looking for it?' Lennie had not. 'I was worried you might have been worried about losing it,' Oldfield said. 'Oh no. I knew you'd look after it,' replied Lennie. Oldfield was dismissed.

Oldfield's fluttering and Lennie's bitching made for a strange scene. Clearly, in the tussle between One Nation's two smoothies, Lennie was intent on taking the upper hand. He now said he thought he wouldn't take Oldfield to the dinner after all. He wanted to take us instead, and maybe we'd also join him later at the gay venue, the Mars Bar, as well? We reminded him that Hanson wanted a private function. No worries, he said, he was the host and he would decide. We went in his Mercedes to the best-heeled do I'd seen on the campaign trail. The TVs were outside the venue to film Hanson going in and Lennie then offered to set up a special media table for all of us. We declined. 'You don't want to be here, do you?' he said wistfully. He seemed so disappointed, I agreed that he could join us later.

Over dinner and drinks at Don's Table the assembled reporters traded tips. Melanie said Lennie and Oldfield were planning to hit the gay clubs. Without Hanson along, no one was interested. Marty had his camera and Grant and Dean wore their mini-cameras round their necks, just in case Hanson showed up and decided to dance. I rang Lennie and he had interesting news—Hanson was on her way.

When their car pulled up, Hanson got out, but jumped straight back in at the sight of us inside. Spencer and Oldfield appeared to have set up their own leader! They wheeled her into coming inside, into what came to feel alarmingly like a scene from *Cabaret*. Everyone was pretty drunk. Oldfield was dressed completely in black; Lennie, pulling the strings, was smiling broadly as if delivering to us a trophy. Hanson, in a deep red suit with black cuffs, wore the heaviest make-up I'd seen on her. She looked almost like a parody in drag.

By reflex I began talking to her about Aboriginal policy, but Lennie loomed over us. 'Can't we talk about something, anything, other than policy? What about stockings and G-strings?' Hanson looked up, startled. She'd lost the plot, but who hadn't?

Over more drinks, Lennie insisted Hanson had to see the Mars Bar and she finally agreed. He put Dean and me in his car, shut the door on Oldfield when he tried to join us, and sped off. Unsurprisingly, Hanson's police escort vetoed the Mars Bar as too dangerous for her, so Lennie drove on and dropped us at another club, where hundreds of ecstatic revellers in a Grand Final frenzy were lined up to enter. We were left stranded in an unknown place surrounded by drunken football fans and no taxis. Adelaide was on fire, and so were we.

We found Lennie back at the hotel cocktail lounge sitting with Hanson and Oldfield smoking a cigar. I took his cigar, crushed it and threw it back at him. Dean did his block in the same blunt style he'd used to blast Oldfield at Henty. Hanson stood up, grabbed my arm, and marched me into the dark, empty hotel disco. She explained that they had pulled up at the second club, but again the police had felt that any club scene on Grand Final night could turn ugly for her. Lennie came in to make amends. I told him to get lost.

Why was any of this happening? Politics is a hidden game, an image game. On Hanson's campaign, they splattered themselves all over us and we ended up splattered, too. While Hanson was calming me down, Stephen and Lisa were in the bar comforting Lennie. In tones of wonder, Stephen later described Lennie, curled up like a boy, moaning, 'Is Margo going to talk to me again? Have I upset Margo? Is this the end of my relationship with Margo?' Lisa told him not to worry. 'She'll like you tomorrow.'

Oldfield started massaging Lennie's neck, telling how he'd swung a week's holiday at Bedarra, the rich people's resort on the Great Barrier Reef.

When Hanson and I returned, events took another turn. She accepted an elderly man's offer to dance to Neil Diamond, and Oldfield pulled his blonde date for the night onto the floor beside her. Grant and Dean each shot off a frame and Hanson froze. 'You don't understand,' she said plaintively to Grant. 'People only understand what you print, what you make out as my life—what my life is and what I do.' I asked her to stay for a drink with her journalists to get things back on the rails. She looked at me and, after a long pause, said with feeling: 'I trusted my husbands and look what happened.' She retired for the evening.

One Nation's industrial relations policy launch was scheduled for the next morning, and I was relieved that I didn't attend One Nation press conferences any more. While I slept off a hangover, One Nation people surrounded the media outside the Mitsubishi car factory and again intimidated questioners.

The battleground this time was sex discrimination. One Nation wanted to bring back the old Men and Boys, Women and Girls employment ads. Hanson had often spoken publicly about how she had wanted to hire only women in her shop. Told she couldn't, she'd replied: 'Can I ask for someone with boobs?' That, of course, would breach the *Sex Discrimination Act*, but Oldfield repeatedly denied the obvious, called Stephen 'nefarious', and again incited the crowd to attack. Someone called Lisa 'an educated, intelligent bitch', as Lennie's doctor wife stood open-mouthed. Hanson stood under a tree, with her back to the melee, signing autographs.

That afternoon we lifted off to return to Queensland. In moments, Hanson's home team, the Brisbane Broncos, would kick off in the Australian Rugby League Grand Final. The queen of the working man had broken every golden rule of the politics of football—like knowing the teams in the grand finals, giving tips, and attending the games. She'd always said she was not a politician, and she was right.

SIXTEEN

Telling the truth, laughing

DAY 26

Monday at 11.45 a.m. was the electric moment in this defamation case when, in the presence of the person aggrieved, the court asks to be apprised of the material in question. This time the tension was even more charged than usual. The complainant, a self-proclaimed champion of free speech, was asking Queensland's highest court to curtail it in the desperate last week of her election campaign.

The ABC was in the dock today. Its youth radio network Triple J had played Pauline Pantsdown's first single, 'I'm a Back Door Man', in August 1997 until Hanson got an injunction from the Queensland Supreme Court pending a defamation trial. (Despite the limited airplay, listeners voted it number five in Triple J's annual Hot 100 that year.) The ABC had appealed, and Hanson had waited twelve months to lodge a statement of claim detailing the alleged defamation against her. She had already had the ABC's appeal adjourned.

In Queensland's most stately courtroom, oozing solemnity with its wood panels and high ceiling, the president of the Court of Appeal, Chief Justice Paul de Jersey, flanked by Justices Margaret McMurdo and Bruce McPherson, asked to hear 'I'm a Back Door Man'.

Brisbane's court reporters sat in media boxes to the right and left of the judges. Hanson's journalists, fresh from Lennie Spencer's high-camp heaven in Adelaide, sat in the well of the court, craning for a view of the person aggrieved. Pauline Hanson, flanked by Peter James, sat at the back. A gaggle of curious lawyers—in the Supreme Court on other business—sat in.

To a dance beat based on the soundtrack of the 1930s movie, *The Perils of Pauline*, Hanson belted out from sampled Hanson-speak:

I'm a back door man; I'm very proud of it,
I'm a back door man; I'm homosexual,
I'm a back door man—yes I am—I'm very proud of it,
I'm a back door man; I'm homosexual...
I'm very proud that I'm not straight,
I'm very proud that I'm not natural.
I'm a back door man for the Ku Klux Klan with very horrendous plans.
I'm a very caring potato...

Justices de Jersey and McPherson looked straight ahead, stiff and deadpan. Justice McMurdo permitted herself a brief smile which she tried to hide by looking down. Just about everyone else in court smiled too. Hanson, wearing a deep blue two-piece suit with brass buttons, shook her head. She dabbed her nose and her cheek with a handkerchief and cried.

The ABC's barrister was Brisbane Queens Counsel Robert Mulholland. He'd earned his stripes as a criminal lawyer partly by successfully defending Queensland police officers accused of corruption in the 1970s and early 1980s. As a reporter in Queensland before leaving my home State more than ten years ago, I'd seen him become one of the most effective legal inquisitors of endemic police and political corruption during the Fitzgerald Royal Commission in the late 1980s. Mulholland had appeared as counsel for the ABC, which had forced an inquiry after Sydney journalist Chris Masters' 'Four Corners' investigative piece, 'The Moonlight State'.

The Fitzgerald Royal Commission's revelations had triggered the demise of National Party Premier Sir Joh Bjelke-Petersen, the man who'd terrorised conservatives with his Joh for PM campaign. His government had passed a law banning Aborigines from buying pastoral leases on the open market, and he was duly outraged when the High Court held the laws invalid as a breach of the Commonwealth *Racial Discrimination Act*. The same government had so little regard for free speech that it had banned street marches. It had also banned as obscene movies, books and records the rest of Australia took for granted. Like Hanson, his successor as terrorist of the conservative establishment, Sir Joh was a big free-speech man. During the recent Queensland State election Sir Joh, the politician Hanson said she most admired, had officially endorsed her on television.

Still, Brisbane did seem a bigger, brasher, more sophisticated and cosmopolitan city than the one I'd left all those years ago. Had it really grown up? I had my doubts. Pauline Pantsdown's second single, 'I Don't Like It', was racing up the charts and was all the rage in Sydney dance clubs. Yet at the trendy Brisbane club 'City Rowers', situated on the Brisbane River amid the flash new hotels and restaurants, the track was banned because, 'We don't want to offend anyone'.

Pauline Hanson claimed that 'I'm a Back Door Man' suggested she was homosexual, a transvestite, a prostitute, and engaged in child sex. As proof, she produced an affidavit by her son Adam, which said he'd been ragged about the song at his boarding school.

Bob Mulholland's case was simple. The song was incapable of being defamatory as alleged because 'no reasonable listener would believe that it represents the respondent's actual views'. Triple J played to 'a rainbow audience of young listeners', he said, making it even more obvious that the literal words were not to be taken seriously. Just to be sure, a disclaimer asserting the song's satirical purpose appeared at its beginning.

Pauline Pantsdown was Simon Hunt, a media studies lecturer in Sydney and a declared homosexual. His song proclaimed a stereotypically homophobic view of male homosexuality as a device to send up Hanson's racism. If anything, a literal mind might assume the song was alleging that Hanson was homophobic. Would even one listener believe that the song was alleging that the twice-married, multiple-liaisoned heterosexual mother of four was really a rampaging male homosexual intolerant of straights?

The glaring, telling omission in Hanson's case was that she did not counter the actual defamatory imputations in the song—that she was homophobic and racist. She hadn't seen fit to sue over Pantsdown's second song, 'I Don't Like It', which conveyed the same message as 'I'm a Back Door Man' more directly. 'I don't like it when railway lines aren't white/I don't like it when day becomes night/Why can't my blood be coloured white?/Coloured blood is just not right.'

As for homophobia, Hanson personally didn't seem into that, although there was plenty of homophobic material on One Nation's Web site. She frequented gay bars. She had gay friends. She had removed an anti-homosexual reference from her draft maiden speech written by John Pasquerelli. She had a policy of extending property rights to gay partners—a highly unusual example of consistency with her 'equality for all Australians' rhetoric. (After the election, her Queensland MPs refused to support a State Labor Government Bill implementing her 'policy', and David Oldfield voted against a similar measure after his election to the New South Wales Upper House.)

With Hanson, however, you couldn't rule out the possibility that she didn't in fact pick up the accusations of homophobia and racism in the song. The court might validly find there were certain minds in Queensland who could not see the meaning of 'I'm a Back Door Man', but would they believe its literal assertions? Some people might find 'I'm a Back Door Man' obscene. But obscenity was not the issue before the Court, or was it, beneath the gloss of the new Brisbane?

Because Hanson had not alleged imputations of racism or homophobia, the ABC could not plead the defence of 'discussion of public affairs' or 'truth'. It was left with the stark argument that the literal meaning of the words was so absurd anyone could see the joke. But would the judges see the joke, and if they didn't find it funny would they allow others the chance to laugh?

Veteran Sydney QC David Rofe appeared for Hanson. Here we had 'a very controversial politician' alleging in her own voice not only that she was homosexual, but that she was 'proud of it'. (Presumably a declaration of shame would have ameliorated the horror of it all.) Without a shred of supporting evidence, Rofe 'revealed' to the judges and everyone else in the court that 'potato' meant a receiver of anal sex. Rofe said the fact that Triple J had a young audience bolstered his case, not Mulholland's, because more mature people might not realise the true meaning of 'potato'. They certainly might not—'potato' is a gay slang term for Caucasian gay men, as distinct from 'rice', slang for Asian gay men. A 'potato queen' is a gay man who likes Caucasian men. At least Hanson wasn't facing the appalling imputation that she was into Asians.

'She's saying, "I'm a man", and we know she's a woman,' Rofe said. Indeed, so what on earth was the problem? According to Rofe, if the injunction was lifted, Triple J would play the song 'day in and day out' until polling day, and 'the damage to this particular respondent in her particular role would be enormous.' Was he seriously suggesting that Triple J listeners would not vote for Pauline Hanson because they thought she was a male homosexual with off-the-wall sexual habits? And wouldn't the mainstream publicity of the song's lyrics created by her court appearance disseminate the knowledge of these dastardly allegations to many more voters than a few spins of the Triple J turntable?

Rofe's points didn't seem to lead anywhere, and Justice McPherson suggested another line of argument. Was the ABC really suggesting, he asked, that 'Ms Hanson and her reputation is so beneath the contempt of the ordinary person' that you could ridicule her at will? Yes, said a grateful Rofe, and 'that's not the message that this Court should give to the people of Australia.' The damsel in distress at the back of the court nodded approvingly.

The court adjourned to consider the matter at 12.25 p.m.

Hanson need not have come to court for the appeal hearing. She had chosen to come. It is a dangerous political ploy to confront your satirist in a public forum, let alone mention her name when it's Pantsdown, because that step publicises the satirist's message and invariably ends up making the subject look ridiculous. But Hanson specialised in smashing established political wisdom, and she did need to get on TV in the campaign's last week.

Oldfield had confided to journalists that Hanson's legal advisers had been pessimistic about getting the initial injunction, and did not rate highly the chances of keeping it on appeal. This gelled with the confidence of the ABC's lawyers that the appeal was almost certain to succeed, so therefore Oldfield must have factored in a possible loss when calculating the electoral gains Hanson could make from making the court case Hanson's election story of the day.

A loss would add grist for the ever more strident mill of One Nation allegations that every establishment institution was against them, and remind the redneck element of her vote what nasty things all those poofta-ridden Sydney trendies thought they could say about their Pauline. A win would vindicate her with the same redneck reminder, but see her honour protected by one of the very institutions to which One Nation was so antagonistic. After all, Hanson proposed a panel of citizens to sack judges with whom they disagreed on sentencing. Hanson wanted to abolish the Family Court, and indeed family law itself, in favour of people's tribunals, and routinely lambasted the courts and lawyers over native title. And David Oldfield, we'd learned from David Marr's article, respected the law only when he believed it 'correct'. Still, a win would be one in the eye for one One Nation bogey, the media, even if another, the legal system, poked it.

The credibility problem for Hanson as far as the travelling media were concerned lay in her rank hypocrisy on the matter. Ever since Sydney she had berated the media in private and at public meetings for giving attention to Pantsdown at her expense. Yet here was Pantsdown now the centre of attention due to Hanson's own decision to come to court.

Oldfield's usual bungling added another problem. When ringing around journalists the previous night advising of Hanson's attendance in court, he could not say when the hearing would be held. The case did not appear in *The Courier-Mail*'s court list for the day, so I rang Pantsdown's lawyer, Owen Trembath. He wondered at my interest, since Hanson wouldn't be there—only the lawyers attended appeals. She'd be there anyway, I replied. Trembath hung up to organise a Pantsdown dash from Sydney airport.

Tears lost their power, I thought, when the crier chose to display them in a public place. As Hanson cried in court, I thought of one of the many anecdotes I'd heard amid an upsurge in racism since One Nation's success at the Queensland State election. An Australian couple had adopted a baby from the Philippines 21 years ago, and the young woman, now working in a restaurant to pay her way through university, suffered the humiliation of two groups of diners requesting that she not serve them. Unlike Hanson, she'd cried at home.

To me, Hanson's calculated presence in the court meant her tears were a political stunt. Helen disagreed, saying she thought that Hanson, whatever Oldfield's intentions, had come to court for vindication, not publicity, and that her tears were genuine. She had a hard time convincing her Sydney editors that this was the case.

But as a journalist on Hanson's campaign, it was always hard to make a judgment on her because of the complication that she seemed to be fighting Oldfield's plans. He had asked journalists to gather at the front entrance of the court where Hanson would make a brief comment before going in, but Hanson's car drove into the court car park around the back and she avoided the media. We were thus in the bizarre position where the star turn didn't seem to want to cooperate with her own party's 'strategy' to resuscitate her campaign.

Pauline Pantsdown landed in Brisbane five minutes before the court adjourned. On the plane she'd done her own make-up, for the first time. Pantsdown in court as spectator would have added more than one delicious flavour to proceedings, because Simon Hunt was the son of David Hunt, recently retired from the New South Wales Supreme Court as the nation's most distinguished defamation judge.

The eminent Queensland justices filed back into court at 12.40 p.m. Chief Justice de Jersey cited Justice Hunt at length on the law then got down to it. Hanson's views had seen her become a well-known and controversial public figure, he said. 'I'm a Back Door Man' was 'a mindless effort of cheap denigration' and no 'reasonable' jury would find against Hanson at a defamation trial. The injunction would stay. Queensland's judiciary did not get the joke.

DEAN SEWELL

A win at last. Hanson emerges from Court with Peter James and her QC David Rofe (directly behind her). She made a statement then left by the back door only minutes before Pauline Pantsdown's arrival. They were destined not to meet during the campaign.

Hanson slumped back into her chair and breathed out.

It was a military operation to ensure we had a picture of Hanson even if she tried to flee. After the adjournment Helen and I manoeuvred her into walking close to the glass windows as she made her way along the corridor back into the courtroom, so the photographers could shoot her from the courtyard below. When she got into the lift to depart, I relayed to Dean the movement of the lift lights in case he had to run around the back to shoot her exit. Hanson did a brief doorstop in the court entrance.

'I'm so delighted to see the appeal was rejected,' she said in faltering tones. Was she upset when the song was played? 'Yes I was. I was just very upset by it. I'm just so pleased. What the meaning is that freedom of speech does not extend by allowing people the right to defame others and to tell lies.' She walked back into the court and again exited by the back door.

Pantsdown arrived two minutes after Hanson's departure. The men in wigs milling in the courtyard scurried away for fear of being seen on TV with her, as reporters surrounded her for a doorstop.

'What this does for the rights of satirists in this country is quite unimaginable,' she said. 'My piece is based on the strategy of the late Weimar satirists in the way they used to satirise Adolph Hitler.' Hitler had proved too difficult to satirise on race and nationalism because his own statements were already extreme, Pantsdown said, so the Weimar satirists parodied his method of argument and use of the German language. 'The song "I'm a Back Door Man" was a satire of Ms Hanson's views on race. Rather than take her own already extreme views on race, I took a few of her statements on homosexuality and used the same method of argument that she had used in order to satirise her views.'

Did she regret hurting Hanson's feelings, Helen asked?

'I regret the grief she has caused to the many thousands of Australian people who she has divided with her views. I regret that Mrs Hanson has caused unimaginable pain to the Aboriginal people, who were so close to finding some sense of justice. It is a satire. If people are hurt by satire, then they should get out of the political game and leave it to people who can actually justify their actions and their words and their policies. My song is trivial.'

We asked about her set-to with Oldfield at the Mortdale Bowling Club. 'Mr Oldfield criticised my make-up the other day and I think what I wanted to do today was make it a little bit worse.'

She didn't find Mr Oldfield sexy?

'No, not at all.'

'He'd hate you for that,' I said.

'He has actually called me a fringe dweller, so I don't think he finds me attractive either.'

Pantsdown later took a walk down Brisbane's Queen Street Mall in the CBD, and was mobbed by young fans seeking her autograph.

Helen thought Hanson had had a good day because the song would appear lewd and offensive to the majority of Queenslanders. I couldn't see that it would gain her any votes, though it might shore up the votes of people already intending to vote for her. The risk for her, in my view, was that the news stories would be novelty items, and that's what she'd look like too. That's certainly what Hanson's campaign had become to our readers—a series of off-the-wall yarns merging soap opera, farce, incompetence, ludicrous policy prescriptions, and now courtroom melo-drama. Then again, our readers were not, in general, attracted to One Nation.

All the TVs ran reports featuring the lyrics of the song, Hanson's statement and Pantsdown's response. Our story was headlined, 'Court shirtfronts back-door man', and noted Hanson's entrance and exit from the back.

That night, *The Sydney Morning Herald*'s lawyer toned down the suggestion in my piece that the ABC would be up for substantial dam-ages, saying the judgment sounded like a typical banana-bender aberration and he couldn't think of a jury which would award any dam-ages. I argued he was thinking of a Sydney rather than a Brisbane jury, but he said the ABC would appeal the day's findings to the High Court on principle. (In June 1999, the High Court refused the ABC leave to appeal.)

After the judgment a posse of Sydney defamation lawyers and aca-demics lampooned its reasoning. The most telling critique came from Tony Fitzgerald, a recent refugee from Queensland and now a New South Wales Supreme Court judge. In a speech in Sydney soon after the election, called 'Telling the truth, laughing', Fitzgerald opined that 'the saturation coverage of political activities and disputes would be unen-durable if there was nothing to alleviate the hypocrisy and boredom except the gaffes and posturing of politicians and aspirants to that role.'

As a homegrown, inherently conservative Queenslander, Fitzgerald's romantic notions of Queensland life had been rudely destroyed by the success of his Royal Commission, a post he had accepted reluctantly. His success in exposing Queensland's dark underbelly and triggering the fall of the National Party Government after decades in power had—due to National Party detestation—cost him his chance as Queensland's most brilliant lawyer to join the High Court.

There was deeply felt conviction in the reminder in his speech that Voltaire—the man who would defend to the death the right of others to say what they liked regardless of how strongly he disagreed with them—was beaten, imprisoned and exiled for his satires directed at authoritarian rule.

'Many of today's right-wing reactionaries probably dwell nostalgically upon such effective methods of dissuasion in their yearnings for the recent past as they imagine it existed,' he said.

'To those slightly more liberal (and intelligent), the importance of satirical commentary which causes a society to examine itself and confront its deficiencies is self-evident.'

Hanson had created a new curb on the free speech she once so gloried in at other's expense. Welcome to Queensland, again.

SEVENTEEN

Today is the beginning of the real campaign

DAY 27

The Gatton One Nation branch had been asked on Sunday to organise One Nation's campaign launch for Tuesday, just four days out from Election Day. Dot Cornwell, the branch secretary with the dying husband who we'd met in such unfortunate circumstances, led a team of residents who bedecked the Gatton senior citizens' hall with flowers and blue and yellow balloons, brought in a swing band from Ipswich, and arranged refreshments.

By lunchtime on Tuesday, Mary Van Ansem, a weather-beaten, softly spoken country matron, had been working in the hall since 7 a.m. She looked stoic rather than enthusiastic as she told me she was on the Gatton One Nation fundraising committee, 'and a member, a proud member sad to say'. The short notice hadn't surprised her. 'As Pauline said, "I'm going to leave this launch until the very last so as not to give the politicians any chance to latch onto it".'

Gatton: scene of Hanson's revelation that she saw herself as the mother of the nation, scene of her flight after her disastrous family policy launch, scene of the pub crawl where an old rogue called Col had asked if she used rat bait to attract journalists. Gatton was Hanson's town.

It was a mild sunny day, and after the travails of Hanson's interstate odyssey it felt good to be back in the country town I'd begun to know. We were relaxing over lunch at a low-slung, shady old hotel when my bureau chief, Mick Millett, rang with my editor-in-chief's first campaign request. Greg Hywood wanted a vertical wide-angle shot of Hanson speaking at the launch for page one and a story on how she'd got to this moment in her campaign. That's what all the media groups planned, a set-piece campaign launch story. *The Australian* even had a team in their Brisbane and Sydney offices ready to fill two pages with One Nation's policies and costings.

Back at the hall the band played 'The Road to Gundagai' and a happy country crowd clapped along. I felt relieved that this looked like one One Nation function that wasn't going to disintegrate.

Scott Balson, a digital camera around his neck ready to record the launch for his One Nation online propaganda 'newspaper', said hello. Balson and *The Sydney Morning Herald* had skirmished during the campaign after his 'newspaper', a money-making venture based on subscriptions, featured a story of mine on One Nation preferences. I'd advised *Herald* lawyer Mark Polden, who on cruising the Web site was startled to find that just about every story in our newspaper was listed. It appeared a blatant and extensive breach of our copyright, although in typical One Nation style, Balson had claimed it was all a mistake. Balson had retaliated the next week after the *Herald*'s election Web site ran a column by Catharine Lumby on the politician–journalist relationship. She'd begun her piece with the anecdote of a private photo of Hanson, *The Daily Telegraph*'s Canberra political correspondent Malcolm Farr and me on Queensland election night appearing in the One Nation 'newspaper'. Balson ran Catharine's piece in his 'newspaper' and retrieved the photo he had removed at my request and put it back online. Then, after the *Herald* article in which Jeff Knuth had stated his views on Aboriginal policy, Balson had suggested in his 'newspaper' the ludicrous theory that Fairfax had run the article in revenge for the breach of our copyright.

Balson was a slight, pale, polite and clever man who looked like a typical computer nerd. He owned a successful Web site building business as well as idolising Hanson and running One Nation's online propaganda operation. I mentioned that the *Herald* had had to write a few letters to him recently. He laughed it off. 'It's all part of the fun, isn't it?'

The first speaker was a spruiking inventor who urged the audience to contact the media to get publicity for a washing machine—patent pending—that could wash and dry clothes in twenty minutes.

Heather Hill introduced Hanson with the claim that the campaign had seen 'probably the most intense vilification of a person that I believe we will ever witness in history.'

Pauline Hanson had lifted somewhat, but she sounded like it was a big effort.

> Today is the beginning of the real campaign. Today the others find out we have not yet begun to fight. This Saturday, Australians will decide if it is the elite of the media, of academia, and those others who set themselves above ordinary Australians who dictate our future, or whether it will be the people themselves who decide our fate.

She said nothing new and at the end described her vision as, 'Our own flag, our own people, our own language, our own future. Our own Nation.' The crowd applauded with gusto and sung an enthusiastic rendition of the national anthem.

Oldfield then announced that, 'as far as the press is concerned, Peter James is waiting for you outside with the various policy documentation.' Out we went, straight into a trap. Lo and behold, after all the promises over all the weeks that full costings of One Nation's billions in promised new spending and details of how they'd fund it would be available at the launch, there was nothing. Where was the costings document? 'I'll get them to you by five,' Peter James mumbled. That meant after the deadline for one television station, even if anyone was inclined to believe him. After our campaign experiences no one was. James also announced that the campaign launch was Hanson's last media event—the rest of her campaign was 'media free'.

The ploy was brazenly simple—delay the release of the costings document, announce a media blackout, and thus avoid any questioning of Hanson on costings before Election Day. Opt out of accountability through deceit. It was breathtaking. 'I'm sorry, we were promised the costings at this launch, Peter, at every single [other] launch we've been to so far,' I protested. 'Could you please explain?' Silence. We decided to go back inside and tackle Oldfield.

'We're waiting for the costings, David,' I said.

'Speak to Peter James about that,' he replied.

'He said no comment,' Helen countered. Oldfield raised his voice and began speaking more to the crowd than to us. 'Those costings will be announced later today. Now I'm not going to go on with any more of this. You can see quite clearly the way the media treat the people of Australia. You can see that they have absolutely no couth whatsoever [and] we've made it very, very clear that we want the media to leave. This launch is complete—we would ask you to leave.'

Stephen asked why the costings weren't there.

'You are on private property, I would ask you to leave. There is no point continuing on this sham—'

I interjected, 'It certainly is a sham', and amid a torrent of questions Oldfield upped the ante.

'Ladies and gentlemen, I am going to have to call upon security to start removing you if that is necessary.'

'Call them,' Stephen McDonell said.

'That's what's about to happen now,' Oldfield replied.

Oldfield strode off to the right side of the hall. Stephen, Helen, Christine Jackman, Leisa Scott, Mark Strong from *The Queensland Times*, Network Seven's Colleen Daly and I sat together on the left side of the room and waited. Melanie Wendt, Lisa Millar and most other TV reporters left the hall. They could afford to keep themselves nice and still get the story, since their cameramen remained inside to record whatever it was that would happen next.

Oldfield used the microphone to allege that once again the media were trying to get 'something' to use against One Nation. 'Those members of the media who are not wanting to be involved in this particular situation and are decent enough to leave, please do so. Those of you who are not decent enough to leave, bear in mind we have just called the police and we will have you ejected.'

The police? He'd called the police without any warning, and he'd done that rather than explain what was going on? With that threat on the table I felt we couldn't possibly leave. It would be accepting that a political party could, on a whim, successfully use the threat of state force to stop the media asking questions. Oldfield, a nihilist to the core, was deliberately seeking to create institutional conflict, and we'd just have to wait and see how the police handled his self-created drama.

Stephen rang his office for legal advice on whether he should leave the hall if the police so requested. Mark Strong was the firmest of all on staying put, because Hanson's armed Australian Protective Service guard had on Peter James' orders escorted a *Queensland Times* journalist from a press conference after the Queensland election. The federal Justice Minister Amanda Vanstone had, just the week before the incident, told One Nation not to use government security officers for such purposes, after Oldfield had ordered one to escort Hanson's biographer, Helen Dodd, from Hanson's office. Hanson said she would not allow *The Queensland Times* to attend any press conference because of their story reporting damaging statements made by Heather Hill during the Queensland election campaign. The other journalists present had done nothing to counter this challenge to freedom of the press, and had continued the press conference after the eviction. But the disturbing incident had triggered a formal resolution by the Queensland parliamentary press gallery to walk out if a politician tried the same thing again. Hanson had blackballed *The Queensland Times* since the eviction. Vanstone again wrote to One Nation, warning that the security officers were 'not provided as bouncers'.

In what was starting to feel like Act 2 of the play without script begun at the Mortdale Bowling Club, Oldfield calmed rumblings from more aggressive elements in the crowd with, 'Relax and wait for the police to arrive and arrest those people.' On the other side of the hall, curious One Nation members began interviewing us.

Why weren't the costings here, someone asked.

We didn't know.

'It doesn't look as though you're going to get it though, does it?'

'No, we're going to get arrested instead,' Helen replied. 'It's very important that we make the point that we have to scrutinise them on behalf of our readership and ask them how they pay for their promises. You cannot lie like that, policy launch after policy launch, just blatant lies.'

Another bloke took the opportunity to explain why Easytax was great as Scott Balson alleged we were deliberately disrupting the launch to harm One Nation.

'Blame us if you like,' I said. 'If we're promised something and we don't get it, it's not our fault.'

A reporter from ABC's Radio National, fresh to the Hanson campaign, asked for an interview. I thought I may as well go for it, because Oldfield calling the police had made us the story and that meant scrutiny of our actions too.

'I think we've got a duty to push as hard as we can on behalf of Australian voters to find out how they'll pay for their policies,' I said.

Should we leave once asked?

'In the circumstances no, because we're here on a false premise. We've been told constantly that if we come today we will get the costings, we will get how they will fund their promises. Since we've been lied to, since this is public space, I'm willing to wait it out in the hope that they will finally deliver what they promised.'

Behind us, about eight police officers entered the hall. Oldfield crossed the Rubicon, waved his arms towards us and demanded our arrest. The crowd cheered him as the Radio National man threw in a tough one. 'Margo, you don't think you've become too close to this whole campaign and this whole issue of Pauline Hanson?'

Gulp. I didn't say yes or no, and instead focused on my output rather than on the tortured process of getting there. 'It's really important that the media scrutinises Pauline Hanson as a very important player in this election, and I've taken it seriously and I've tried my best to give balanced coverage, and I'm happy with my coverage.'

The police did not comply with Oldfield's demand and moved to the back of the hall. Oldfield walked back to the right to cover up the rejection with some crowd stirring.

Stephen called out: 'Do you have some policy costings yet David, to give us as you've promised?'

Helen: 'David, do you have any explanation as to why they're not available now?'

Oldfield whipped up a section of the crowd, including Dot Cornwell, who had greeted me warmly an hour before, to begin clapping and foot stomping to 'Out, Out, Out'.

Hanson stood in a corner with her back to the melee signing autographs, oblivious to the commotion. She hadn't just opted out of accountability; she'd opted out of her own campaign. The tableau exposed the final, shocking split between Hanson the phenomenon and the political party she had spawned. And we'd acknowledged the continuing power of the phenomenon amid the ruins of One Nation by approaching not the leader, but the apparatchik, for answers.

The room was in stalemate, and Leisa Scott said with beautiful understatement, 'I really think that we're starting to become the story here, I think we should go.' As we edged our way out through the crowd some old men jostled us, and I heard a photographer yell out, 'Get your hands off me' just as someone else shirtfronted me.

'Is this the way you carry on with other parties?' he demanded to know.

If they tried a stunt like this, yes, I replied.

'We are not treated like this by any other party,' Helen said.

Up strode Jack Paff, an ex-cop I'd met during the Queensland election campaign who was now one of One Nation's most accident-prone State MPs. Even Paff could work out, if Oldfield couldn't, that One Nation assaults on journalists might be counterproductive to the cause.

'G'day, Jack, how are you going?' I said.

'What's the problem?' he asked.

'Oh, just the usual.'

'What they want to try and do now is have an afternoon tea,' he said. A bloke started pushing me and Paff told him to back off.

By the time I got outside Oldfield was already there finishing an interview with the Radio National man on how dreadful the media was. Now he wanted to answer questions after all, and had abandoned the 'private meeting' which he'd supposedly called in the police to secure.

'The media are basically anarchists who are looking for fights and looking for problems, and those people are largely led by Margo Kingston from *The Sydney Morning Herald*, who I'm sure is larger than life to the media. That unfortunately is causing a problem for everyone else.'

What about today's launch, which was to have been Hanson's big day? 'We were always prepared for the fact that it was never going to be a big day for Pauline based on the media never giving her a fair go, as they usually don't. This is just another example of the Sydney media leading an assault on democracy, the Sydney media deciding that they are going to dictate what takes place in this country, and the Sydney media trying to tell the Australian people what to do and that they're in charge and that [the people] will do what they've been told.'

Mark Strong interrupted the interview with, 'As a representative of the Ipswich media, I believed there were going to be costings—'

Oldfield cut in: 'We've been through that.'

Oldfield always referred to the 'Sydney media' and the 'Canberra press gallery' in his anti-media remarks, in order to press the anti-Southerner button in Queensland and the anti-'elite' button everywhere else in Hansonville. After so expertly venting his spleen he tried to return inside, but the doors were locked and he banged on them for entry, whereupon he popped his head out and invited Mark Strong to join him. Now the local media were exempted from the lockout and invited to witness the 'private meeting' cum 'afternoon tea'. What a moment for the blackballed *Queensland Times* to be asked back into the fold! Mark refused, in solidarity with his colleagues.

Oldfield wanted to get Hanson's face onto local television screens in Blair to score voter sympathy. 'Oldfield attacks the media' didn't have anywhere near the potency as 'Media attacks Hanson', and, from the consistent antagonism towards Oldfield displayed by grassroots One Nation members, might actually be counterproductive. A reporter from one local television station obliged him, scoring what her newsreader breathlessly described as an 'exclusive' interview with Hanson. It comprised the immortal words, 'I have not had a fair go.' Hanson avoided serious questions by yet again exiting through the back door.

We drove to Vacy Hall in Toowoomba, where we'd stayed up late all those weeks ago worrying about our role in the Hanson–Kennett meeting, ironically enough the most successful political moment of her campaign. Calls from radio stations around the country poured in requesting interviews, and I realised I was in deep trouble.

I did wall-to-wall radio interviews for an hour, putting the case for the defence, before tackling my news story. How do you write a story when the party you're reporting on has personally attacked your role in it? I wrote a tortuously chronological account stripped of any interpretation and included the criticisms of the *Herald* and the Sydney media. Then Oldfield called to say he was returning my call. I hadn't called him for two weeks and I certainly hadn't started now. He offered to fax me the costings. Although I already had them via other reporters, I said sure and hung up.

No wonder One Nation had gone to such elaborate lengths to avoid questions. The costings document was one page headed, 'Pauline Hanson's One Nation Federal Budget'. It was a bald summary of promises and their cost that bore no relation to the promises made in the campaign. The funding cuts comprised mainly the abolition of 'multicultural funding', grossly overestimated at $1.5 billion, and the abolition of foreign aid ($1.8 billion). The 'budget' was rubbish.

Paul McGeough rang to read over the story he'd tweaked in the light of my deadpan presentation. He chided me on my lead paragraph, that Hanson had imposed a media blackout after refusing to release her costings. 'Surely you mean "attempted" media blackout?' I hadn't even thought about tomorrow. He also suggested that since I seemed to be appearing on television regularly these days, my mother might not approve of the constant chewing. Well, she would, because I was chewing nicotine gum in a losing battle to stay off the fags I'd given up for nine months before Hanson's campaign. Stop chewing anyway, McGeough said.

It was a wired experience watching the television news as participant rather than reporter. The compliant local news network excelled itself not only with the Hanson 'exclusive' but the false and damaging statement that we'd been arrested. It was reassuring, in a warped way, to see that such bad reporting occurred even when the media reported on itself.

Laurie Oakes' report was the killer. He led the Nine Network's bulletin with the story of Oldfield calling the police, with the introduction that the media had played into One Nation's hands. I knew his interpretation of the event's effect would be the accepted wisdom in the Canberra press gallery. My paper ran the story on page one, as did *The Age*, forced to run AAP wire copy because it hadn't bothered to turn up. The Murdoch broadsheet papers seemed more political in their judgment. *The Courier-Mail* editor, Chris Mitchell, reprimanded Christine Jackman in strong terms for remaining in the hall, and ran a short story on page eleven (Oldfield's lines denying an affair with Hanson had made it onto page one of this 'broadsheet' paper.) *The Australian* ran a colour piece, rather than a news story, on page nine. To me, that looked like downplaying the yarn because the editors thought it could help One Nation. If, as most media people thought, the media on the ground had played into One Nation's hands, then so be it. It was not the media's job to cover up our role in Hanson's campaign. Let the people decide.

I got a taste of the criticism to come on Radio National's Late Night Live, where Phillip Adams found the whole thing a bit of a hoot. 'It is my great pleasure to welcome back to the program what's left of Margo Kingston on the campaign trail with Ms Hanson. I hear you got arrested today, Margo.'

Thank you, Phillip.

'Are you getting to the point where you perhaps don't entirely trust David Oldfield?'

'Oh, there's absolutely no trust. He is the strangest media adviser I've ever met. I think that he actually specialises in lying to the media so that we do get angry—'

'Well if that's the strategy, Margo, you fall for it every time.' Bullseye.

'Well, I don't think so at all.'

'Did David Oldfield have a charge in mind? Was it trespass or recalcitrance?'

'All of a sudden, we were told that this was actually a private afternoon tea, that it wasn't a policy launch at all.'

'He's talking about arresting the woman who's given up both footy grand finals for democracy. What are they going to think at Fairfax when they discover you're an anarchist?'

I took a deep breath. 'Hang on, do you remember the first program we did my first week on the trail, and I was carrying on about how horrible it was to go through a red light? God knows that was just small bikkies compared to what's happened since. Since the very start of the campaign [we've] been asking for basic rules of engagement. I am literally a force for order on this campaign, Phillip. I am after claiming an institutional role for the media in election campaigns. As it's gone on, not only haven't [One Nation] sought to accommodate us, but they've actually sought to close down our official space, to the extent where they surround press conferences on their policies with One Nation supporters who howl us down when we ask questions. So I have tried the whole campaign to conduct myself in the institutional role of the media—'

'With the daintiness we've come to expect from you, over the years.'

'Well, it's just hard to know what to do at this stage. What do you do when you're set up to such an extreme extent? Do you protest, do you say that the Australian people have a right to know what [the party's] policies will cost and how they should be paid for, or do you say okay we'll leave? And to my mind this is a party whose preferences will decide this election. And if we don't assert our role here, then we're headed for mob rule, and I just think that the media had to stand its ground, and we did.'

'You've been listening to the voice of Australia's leading anarchist, the woman who is leading the campaign against Pauline Hanson whilst pretending to simply be reporting on it for *The Sydney Morning Herald*.'

'Thanks a lot for that, Phillip, and it's not true.'

'Of course it isn't, of course it isn't.'

Crikey, with friends like that enemies weren't required. If I were out to destroy Hanson, I certainly wouldn't have handed a loaded gun to David Oldfield. To recover my composure I watched the ABC's 'Lateline' program, appropriately enough on the theme of the chronic lack of trust in politicians. *The Sydney Morning Herald*'s political correspondent and my boss, Laura Tingle, went toe-to-toe with federal Liberal MP Tony Abbott, the man who'd employed David Oldfield before his defection to Hanson. Abbott said the media was too tough on the pollies, Laura that we were there to ensure politicians were accountable, that they didn't mislead or deceive voters. It was the same argument, in much more refined terms, that we'd had throughout the campaign with One Nation. The interviewer, Maxine McKew, asked Laura what she thought of the media's behaviour that day. I felt that Laura was looking straight at me when she said the media had allowed itself to become the story.

That hit me harder than anything else so far on the campaign, and I worried all night about whether I'd done the right thing. I just couldn't accept that we should have walked away. If the media became that defensive about its reputation in the face of its unpopularity, it had lost the game anyway. The media had to be aggressive in asserting its institutional rights, otherwise it would lose them. If the public wanted no explanations then that was their right, but at least they'd know that's what they were choosing. And at least journalists' judgment on the ground was about our job, not our politics. It was about substance, not appearances.

The campaign had become personal precisely because One Nation couldn't or wouldn't play by standard rules of engagement between politicians and the media. True, the rules have been corrupted, allowing the major parties to stage-manage political journalism. But they do at least serve to keep the personalities largely separate from the roles they play as politician and reporter, roles that are intrinsic to the democratic process.

The next day, Oldfield took to the airwaves to describe us as 'a pack of dogs', and later 'a pack of burglars'. Not once until the end of the campaign would he or anyone else in One Nation answer any questions on One Nation's 'federal budget'. His reason: no questions were necessary because 'the figures are perfectly correct'. He added the police to the list of institutions out to get One Nation: 'I don't know why they bothered to come if they weren't going to do anything. The press has even got the police scared.' He officially buried One Nation's tattered commitment to free speech and freedom of the press. 'What comes with freedom of speech and freedom of the press is honesty on behalf of the press, and I think the Australian people are fairly sure they're not getting that. So if they're not going to get the truth from the press, they're better off getting nothing from the press.' Except, of course, that David Oldfield as de facto leader of One Nation was on tap to be interviewed by the media he claimed was so unfair about how unfair the media was.

Scott Balson wrote an incensed article in One Nation's online 'newspaper' headlined, 'The day the media snapped', with mug shots of the journalists he blamed and a detailed conspiracy theory on how we sabotaged the launch. By week's end, some media commentators had savaged us too. There was no protest at the fascist undertones of Oldfield's 'arrest the media' demand, apart from a strong *Sydney Morning Herald* editorial for which Hanson's media contingent was pathetically grateful. 'Adolph Hitler used to insist that the propaganda war in politics was won by parties and leaders who discarded the accepted forms of debate and unashamedly trumpeted the Big Lie,' it read. 'Disaffected groups, he argued, were more prepared to accept the Big Lie than the little truths of political reality. By attacking the media as an un-Australian institution, by banning it from any further coverage of the One Nation campaign and by refusing to answer legitimate questions about the costing of promises, a series of anti-democratic decisions clothed in the mantra of 'democracy', One Nation has perpetrated the Great Lie of the federal election campaign. What we have with One Nation is not a party but a vehicle for the cult of Ms Hanson and her delusions of grandeur. Cults become vulnerable when the facts about them are exposed.' Beside the editorial, a Moir cartoon depicted One Nation as a cockroach scurrying under a fridge when exposed by torchlight.

But *The Courier-Mail* political columnist, Dennis Atkins, opined: 'For the past week the media has turned One Nation events into open warfare, culminating in the us-and-them stand-off at Gatton on Tuesday. If there is one thing One Nation's voter base distrusts and dislikes more than the political establishment, it's the media. Those journalists who led the belligerent attack on One Nation at Gatton should consider their actions when the party picks up between six and eight seats.'

It looked like the Queensland media establishment—so terribly twitchy about One Nation since its meteoric rise during the Queensland election campaign—had found its scapegoat if One Nation did well again.

The Courier-Mail columnist Terry Sweetman threw his weight behind the theme. 'So, One Nation goaded "the dogs" into an ill-judged sit-in with the Grey brigade jeering from the sidelines. The spin doctor's potion was made even more potent by the fact that the media is one of the very institutions that One Nation fans neither understand nor trust and now love to hate.' For all this supposed big effect our actions had had on One Nation's election prospects, it was passing strange that *The Courier-Mail* readers would have struggled to find the news story of our dreadful behaviour. If the event threatened such a dramatic switch in One Nation's fortunes, why hadn't it been on page one?

The Sydney Morning Herald commentator Gerard Henderson critiqued the event on Radio National, saying we'd lost our professional objectivity. Journalists could not afford to get 'too close' to their subjects, he said, and should have been swapped during the campaign. But that was easy when the campaign process was so settled and stale. On Hanson's trail, it would take most of a week to work out what on earth was going on. And isn't the journalist's job to get as close as possible, in an effort to see what is actually happening? If you can get up close enough to see, should you turn away because it's difficult to remain 'objective' up that close?

Gerard wrote to me after the election expanding on his critique. 'The media's role is to behave professionally and to report and analyse facts. It is not to become personally involved—not to cheer and not to boo. In other words—to be a reporter of the political debate not an activist in it,' he wrote. It was a classic statement of official media theory—the reporter's role is as observer. It sounds so good on paper—and is so totally unreal in practice. If the political journalist's job is to uncover the truth and deconstruct political platitudes designed to mislead voters, then sometimes, and perhaps more often than we did generally, we had to fight hard to get it. And that's what I'd done on this campaign. It hadn't come out predigested and prearranged like the major campaigns. It came out rough and raw, and so did I.

'I didn't realise I was playing such high stakes,' I said to Helen. 'I was just trying to do my job and didn't realise my bloody career was on the line. If they do well and she wins her seat we'll get the blame.' 'If she wins we're in deep strife,' Helen replied. Grant and Dean replaced our visions of the press gallery killing its own with visions of us liberated to write stories on country flower shows. We might as well wallow in paranoia while we had the chance, because early next morning we had to prove to Hanson that she could not celebrate the beginning of her 'real campaign' with a media blackout.

EIGHTEEN

We're all poor lean people and we're bangin' on your gate

DAYS 28, 29 AND 30

We stood on the footpath of the deserted main street of the tiny town of Yarraman in Blair waiting for Pauline Hanson. It had taken a 500-kilometre criss-cross of Blair to find her. In the mid-afternoon heat and dust we waited like a posse of outlaws for our prey. The two federal police who followed her everywhere in her home State wandered out of the haberdashery shop first, saw us, and smiled.

Pauline Hanson followed. She wore blue jeans and a long-sleeved white shirt buttoned to the neck. Her face was stripped of colour and her eyes had taken on the wild, unfocused look I'd seen on many of her members throughout the campaign. Her expression did not change when she saw us. She walked to her car looking straight ahead and said nothing as we gathered around her asking questions on her cost-

The Herald *headlined the story 'Hunted Hanson remains silent'. The caption to this picture: 'Far from the madding crowd...Pauline Hanson campaigned in the almost deserted streets of Yarraman in Queensland yesterday.'*

ings. The leader of One Nation was mute. The toughness, the once-more-unto-the-breach bravado of the 'little redhead from Ipswich' had disappeared. Hanson was a beaten, fractured woman, retreating to the Blair haven in the bush where her vote was solid. She was far, far away from the voters she needed on the edges of Ipswich, the Labor town she had stormed in the 1996 election but who, according to the polls, had now had second thoughts and were bringing her down.

Hanson often reminisced at her public meetings about her introduction to politics, how she'd put up her hand to stand for the safe Labor seat of Oxley, the only Liberal to do so, then been disendorsed after standing by her anti-Aboriginal comments. 'It was a wake-up. It was a shock,' she'd say. 'It was like being told 'Hey, listen, you know nothing, we know everything, you shut up and we'll tell you what to do.' That's not why I was going into politics. I wanted to have a voice.' Now it was gone. And so was she.

She drove for an hour along thinning gravel roads to an isolated property. As Hanson's car disappeared up the long winding path to a sanctuary hidden from view, a woman from One Nation parked her car across the cattle grid to bar our entry.

As Dean drove back to Brisbane, I played the tape of One Nation's jingle, 'Poor Lean People', produced just in time for the campaign launch. Dot Cornwell had talked me into buying the tape for $10. A North Queensland fan sang it in the broad-accented, traditional Australian ballad style.

You've all had it pretty good for the last 200 years—
You crushed us at Eureka and you never saw our tears,
You robbed us with your rum trade and we fought in all your wars,
We paid in blood and bodies and no one kept the scores.
Now you've taken all our guns away to protect us from ourselves,
And you gave our jobs to strangers and you sent us all to hell.
Now we're standing in the dole queues while we contemplate our fate,
And if we're over 50 then for us it's all too late.

Now we're poor lean people who can no longer wait,
We're all poor lean people and we're bangin' on your gate.

You took away our dignity and you messed with all our lives,
But come the next election and we'll see who holds the knives.
To ATSIC you gave millions and you wonder where it went,
But in your heart right from the start you know how it was spent.
You're all bitten by the travel bug and we pay for all your trips,
You stay in all the best hotels and you tax the waiter's tips.

We're all poor lean people and you made us all this way,
We're all poor lean people and that's how we're gunna stay.
Poor lean people with our backs against the wall—
Look out little Johnny 'cause you're riding for a fall.

You sold off all our assets and you taxed us to the floor,
Then you hit us with a GST and screwed us all some more.
You taxed us on our incomes and you tax us when we die,
Why don't you tax the air we breathe, c'mon now don't be shy.

We're just poor lean people and we're rednecks so you say,
We're just poor lean people tryin' to find another way.

Now we're poor lean people, we can no longer wait,
We're all poor lean people and we're bangin' on your gate.

Class war, the taboo aspect of Hansonism, set to music, with knives. Pauline's People were rural poor and fringe city poor clinging to old cultural values they insisted were still central to Australia's identity, because otherwise they felt like white trash. And white trash kicks Aborigines because it makes them feel better.

All the little Blair towns the search party—the ABC, Network Seven, *The Sydney Morning Herald*, News Limited and Tokyo TBS television— had torn through during the day were bereft of mobile service, which died within minutes of Ipswich. Town after town had no bank, and public phones were invariably out of order. The jobs had gone and the youth dragged down the main streets each night until the police told them to call it quits. The events of their communities marking the passage of each year were petering out as young people left for the capital cities. It was hard not to feel in the eerie devastation of it all that the system had decided that these people and their culture were expendable, and they had been left alone to whither away in silence.

At the centre of One Nation, the hardcore 5 percent was mad and dangerous. The city carpetbaggers who had built the party around 'the product', David Oldfield and David Ettridge, had hitched a ride. Squeezed between the mad and the cynical were desperate Australians who'd flirted with their very own cargo cult heroine as their means to scream. But now Pauline Hanson, the lady with the lamp to her followers, leading the self-pitying and the forgotten from the darkness to the light, had gone to ground.

Yet Hanson had put on a federal election campaign which could not be beaten for its sweep of Australia, its spontaneous political debates between grassroots Australians, and the homemade, heartfelt protests against her racist excesses by citizens on the street. Her campaign could not be beaten for guts either. Neither John Howard nor Kim Beazley had held one public meeting during the campaign. She'd held more than 20 unvetted public meetings, walking into unknowable questions and hostilities, backing herself to come through. She'd left us, the media she professed to despise yet needed so much, to package her frenetic days for public consumption.

She had managed to engage thousands of Australians in political debate who had, before luck and timing threw her onto centre stage, been a part of the ever-growing band of citizens rendered sullen and disgusted by the people who governed them. While the dwindling numbers of grassroots members in the slick professional major party machines made it almost impossible for them to staff their polling booths on election day, Hanson's only asset was that she had grassroots members to burn.

Some of them had rejected the grand visions of Paul Keating for the 'comfortable and relaxed' soothings of John Howard, but found there was little difference—except that Howard screwed down the victims of his economic number crunching more than Keating had. Howard's cloak for his unforgiving, sink or swim economics in the 1996 election had been his dangerous flirtation with scapegoating, making 'minorities' a term of abuse in Coalition advertising and pledging to govern 'for all of us'. Hanson had thrown that back in his face by making the message explicit and extreme. Kick the chosen scapegoats please, don't just fiddle around with them. There had to be some lessons in all of this. There just had to be.

At the end of the journey she'd begun at the 1996 election, Hanson's voice and her people's screams had been heard so loudly she'd become the most famous Australian politician in the world. Hanson had begun to unravel the seemingly seamless nature of our transition from White Australia Policy racism and our crushing indifference to the plight of indigenous Australians towards tolerance and reconciliation. She had also opened a fault line in the apparent completeness of the ideological victory of economic rationalism, with its refusal to value anything that could not be measured in cash.

In the beginning, Hanson was demonised and her supporters derided as fools. Yet were she, and they, really to blame? John Ralston Saul's definition of 'the élite' in *The Doubter's Companion* (Penguin Books Australia, 1995) kept running through my mind.

Every society has an élite. No society has ever been without one. The thing élites most easily forget is that they make no sense as a group unless they have a healthy and productive relationship with the rest of the citizenry. Questions of nationalism, ideology, and the filling of pockets aside, the principal function of an élite is to serve the interests of the whole. They may prosper far more than the average citizen in the process. They may have all sorts of advantages. These perks won't matter so long as the greater interests are also served. From their point of view, this is not a bad bargain. So it really is curious just how easily they forget and set about serving only themselves, even if it means that they or the society will self-destruct.

There is no reason to believe that large parts of any population wish to reject learning or those who are learned. People want the best for society and themselves. The extent to which a populace falls back on superstition or violence can be traced to the ignorance in which their élites have managed to keep them, the ill-treatment they have suffered and the despair into which a combination of ignorance and suffering have driven them.

Now easygoing, 'egalitarian' Australia had experienced its unique brand of far-right populism feeding off disgust with our elites. In our version, we had a female leader and a political amateur, which had made her both easier to pull apart and much harder, since Pauline's People, despite everything, admired her refusal to abide by the rules and her dogged insistence on coming back for more. Surely it was the duty of the elites to solve the causes of Hansonism, because Hanson was only the symptom, not the disease. After all the anger and pain of Hansonism, that was the lesson I felt I'd learnt from covering her campaign. Pauline's People felt they no longer understood their society and what it was for, and many of them felt they were being told they no longer belonged in it. They couldn't make head or tail of the political discourse, and no one could explain it to them or even wanted to, let alone help them join the brave new world their elites insisted was inevitable.

I remembered a scene in an Adelaide coffee shop when a woman had burst in demanding the right, as a mother of two children, to hear

Hanson's vision. A dog-tired Hanson threw her head back and said like a mantra:

> I'm offering more for this country than what the previous major parties have done for this country for a long, long time. We've seen this country being sold out, we've seen our kids have no future of ever possibly getting a job in this country, we've seen our industries and manufacturing sold out, we've seen our land sold out from underneath us, and we don't even know whether where we're Australians or not. That's my vision for Australia, to rebuild all these things again so that we have pride within ourselves and our nation and a future for our children.

Apart from the culturally loaded comment, the Democrats would have endorsed every sentiment. Democrats leader Meg Lees' election speech for radio said:

> The Democrats stand between those who see everything as numbers on a balance sheet, and ordinary Australians who depend on public services. We stand between those who pursue competition policy and the lives of small businesses and rural communities being destroyed in the process. We stand between those who want to sell everything our parents and grandparents have worked and paid for, and the rest of us, who want a secure future for our children.

What Hanson had that the Democrats didn't was a common language with the disenfranchised. They could understand what she was talking about. It was the standard 'commonsense' of the ignorant unencumbered by rigorous analysis, yet there was often a nagging grain of truth in Hanson's half-baked simplicities. And maybe if the powerful, including the media, had engaged with the scream rather than returning it, the monster of One Nation might not have grown to terrorise us all. But the powerful either played a devious game of footsie, as had Howard in the beginning, or tried to deride her into oblivion.

The federal National Party leader of the 1970s and early 80s, Doug Anthony, put the issue so simply. 'I mean this economic rationalism is one thing, but you've got to realise that Australia wants to be decentralised and there are people's concerns to look after and they need to think about that.' And if 'they' didn't, and just kept getting richer and fatter, maybe one day they'd lose the stability in Australian society that allowed them to keep doing it.

■

According to the media commentators, the media's outrageous behaviour had resurrected One Nation's campaign. According to Hanson we'd destroyed it. Now Hanson the naive was beginning to see fault in her guru, too. After we'd found her in Blair, she flew to Sydney with Oldfield for her pre-booked two-hour appearance on Stan Zemanek's radio show. She'd then told her federal police officers she was changing her return flight to an earlier time and that Oldfield was not to be informed. A deeply embarrassed Oldfield, followed by the media who'd made the trip down with them, arrived at Brisbane airport alone. I learnt later that she'd taken the afternoon off from what was supposed to be an intensive last few days of campaigning in Blair to visit her father—the man she'd told us was famous for his homemade chicken rolls—in a Gold Coast nursing home. She'd often told her fans that when she'd told her father she wanted to be in politics he'd told her not to be silly, it would make no difference. After she'd won the seat of Oxley, she'd told him she wanted to start a new party, and he'd said don't be silly, it will make no difference. When she'd launched One Nation he'd been in the front row clapping, and was now her biggest ally, she'd say. She returned to see him now. Perhaps he was the only person she trusted any more.

The Faustian pact between Oldfield and Hanson had fallen apart. She needed him for substance, but had chosen a man whose narcissism and contempt for her and her supporters had helped tarnish her extraordinary appeal to Pauline's People, and constantly threatened to tear the grassroots party apart. And here he was; now de facto leader of One Nation, the public face of the party in the final days of a campaign she looked like she'd lose. He'd played a dangerous hand when he'd played the media card.

Hanson's media weren't committed to finding Hanson any more. There was no point. She'd refused to reveal the whereabouts of her last public meeting on Thursday night, even to the local media she needed to report her final speech to the voters of Blair. She'd instructed Oldfield not to say when and where she'd be voting on Saturday for the standard happy snap of the leader at the polling booth, and she'd issued a ban on the media attending her election night bash. That meant no communication from Hanson to her people on election night, whatever the result—no live crosses to the TV election night specials, no anything. Melanie had been desperately concerned that her head office would not understand such an unprecedented step, and tell her to fix it somehow, but that hadn't happened either. No worries, Laurie Oakes had said. Too bad. We'd have to be there, of course, standing outside, and the Nine Network and some other media were considering employing security guards in case there was trouble.

On Thursday night we gathered at our hotel restaurant for a premature post-campaign dinner. A *Los Angeles Times* journalist who'd contacted me for an entrée to see Hanson—and whom I'd advised would be better off doing it solo—called in. He'd walked into Hanson's office to be greeted by Oldfield as a long-lost friend. He'd scored a long interview with Oldfield and had sat around the office all afternoon until Oldfield gave him a lift to the public meeting, held in her dead spot, Ipswich. The same David Oldfield who had refused to answer questions from the foreign media at the Easytax launch at the campaign's beginning was now escorting the foreign media to One Nation functions. His compulsive need for a media audience had come to this. The *Los Angeles Times* witnessed exclusively Pauline Hanson's final public speech of One Nation's first federal election campaign.

My sister Gay from *The Age* joined us on Friday and we drove to Hanson's Ipswich office in case she showed her face. Paul McGeough wanted to finish *The Sydney Morning Herald* news coverage of Hanson's campaign with the story of her muteness in Yarraman, and that seemed to me an appropriate time to call it quits. So while Helen, Gay and Christine Jackman endured consecutive rambling interviews with Oldfield in the office, Grant and I had coffee at the Globe Café across the street discussing when to get to Hanson's house the next morning to follow her and ensure we got voting shots. A woman at the next table said she lived near Hanson, and suggested we watch Hanson's house from her place over coffee. Grant gave her his mobile number on the back of my card and she agreed to ring if she saw Hanson leave her house. Still feeling squeezed between the antipathy of One Nation on one side and denunciation by media critics on the other, I thanked her for thinking we were okay. 'Of course you are, she's the one that's not,' she replied.

The Electoral Commission office was in the same building as Hanson's office, and the parties were camped outside handing out how-to-vote cards to locals who needed to vote before Saturday. I struck up a conversation with an elderly woman knitting contentedly behind the National Party table. The National Party was bleeding to death in Blair, a natural National Party seat, and a dearth of volunteers in the district had seen her bussed in from Brisbane to keep the flag flying. What did she think of Pauline Hanson? 'She's the best thing that happened to politics because those other two parties just wandered on. I know I'm National, but it needed this one to come in and give them a serve. We're all at sixes and sevens up here, you have no idea, no one knows which way it's going. But at the moment she's a good frightener.'

Gay came out of Hanson's office after her first interview with Oldfield shaking her head. 'He's obsessed with the media, that's all he cares about. He actually loves it that Pauline's away and the media are around him,' she said, disconcerted. 'I asked him at the end if there was anything else he wanted to stress, and he said, "Just that I'm a really nice guy".' Helen had ended her two-hour stint in the office watching Oldfield pack and make phone calls with, 'The best advice I can give you is to employ someone to take that step back and tell you where you're going wrong, like you say you do for Pauline.'

Oldfield did the final campaign doorstop, One Nation's last plea for votes. Unlike David Ettridge and sundry other One Nation officials who'd predicted winning a swag of Lower House and Senate seats, Oldfield was at least a realist. 'If Pauline Hanson is re-elected, just that will be successful from our point of view. If we win anything beyond Pauline's re-election, then that is very successful, considering what we've had thrust against us.'

He was preparing his supporters for a bad result?

'No, our supporters are incredibly confident, all of our candidates are incredibly confident. I'm the only pessimist in this party.'

'Do you feel responsible at all for the breakdown in the relationship with the media?' Lisa Millar asked.

'Not at all, because I understand that the media dislike me and they like Pauline. If I've got that situation, then I'm doing the right job, because the important thing is to have a person between the candidate and the media. So if the media don't like me and they like Pauline, then I'm doing my job.'

Throughout the campaign I'd veered between seeing Oldfield as a genius or a fool, and now I had my answer. He was boasting about his success as her media adviser when One Nation's sole vote-winner was absent on the final day she could appeal to voters for support. It didn't matter whether we liked Pauline Hanson or not. She wasn't there. Instead of her down-home charm, viewers saw his big-city cynicism on the last night of the election campaign. He wasn't standing between the candidate and the media; he'd replaced the candidate. At the end of it all, as we walked away, he said it had been nice working with us.

'It's been a nightmare working with you, David,' I replied.

Oldfield rang around journalists very late that night to say Hanson had now agreed to vote at Ipswich primary school at 2 p.m., but that we were still banned from her election night function. I didn't trust him, and after his campaign launch set-up I wasn't going to risk another one. I rang him for the first time in weeks and told him I wanted personal assurances from Hanson that she'd be there, otherwise we'd follow her from her home. He wanted to discuss an unflattering *Herald* feature on him in the paper that morning. When I said I hadn't read it, he said: 'I don't care if you track her.'

'I know you don't, David, but do you care about whether she'd like to be tracked tomorrow? The issue is not whether you care, the issue is whether she cares.'

The only thing we had going for us to restore cordial relations with Hanson on the last day of our mutual odyssey was that Oldfield was flying to Canberra early next morning to appear as an election commentator for the Nine Network.

NINETEEN

She's lost it

DAY 31

I rang Pauline just before Dean and I reached her home at 7.30 a.m. on Election Day. It was the first time we'd spoken since she'd dragged me into the hotel disco in Adelaide a week before. Her voice was so faded I could hardly hear her. 'How did you get my number?'

'I stayed at your house, Pauline.'

'Oh, and you kept it did you?'

'Yes, but I've never used it before.'

She took the point. I said I didn't trust David Oldfield but would accept her word on voting. 'Well, I will be there at 2 p.m.'

'Okay, we'll turn around and have some breakfast.'

Helen had once wondered aloud whether Pauline or I would crack up first—I'd won, just. I was worn out and emotional and absolutely determined that somehow, some way, Pauline Hanson and the media would end the campaign in a civil fashion.

Hanson contemplates the possibility of political defeat. A One Nation supporter appears surprised that she's discussing it with me.

'I do trust her, I think everyone on the campaign does. She's all there is left to trust—that stupid woman,' I said on the drive back to Brisbane. 'After the campaign launch I said to McGeough, "I'm not going to be able to get an interview with her on Sunday." He said, "Oh well, you've always delivered in the end, haven't you?" I thought, "Fuck, how do I get her back onside after this?"'

'That's one of my problems in this campaign. I don't understand her and she doesn't understand me in the way we think. We don't connect. The only time we get along is things like shopping for jeans; apart from that we're like different species. But I quite like her personally, do you?'

'I've never really got that close to her,' Dean said.

'You've got so close it's a joke. You've been looking at her face non-stop for four weeks—how close is that? You probably know her better than her ex-husbands know her. You know every single mood. What do you think?'

'I just haven't thought of it in that way.'

'You do it in pictures, I do it in words. That's the only difference. I've been looking at that stupid woman for four fucking weeks, no wonder I'm nearly mad. Do you like her as a person?'

'Personally, yes. I don't dislike her.'

After breakfast Dean drove to Rosewood so Gay could do an Election Day colour story for the early edition *Sunday Age*. Gay and I even got nostalgic for Queensland for a moment seeing the big old rambling Queenslander homes on the main street. As we approached the Rosewood State School, we saw a poster of the Liberal candidate, Cameron Thompson, on display on the front lawn of a neat weather-board home.

His ears had been cut off and replaced with plastic ears. His eyes were whited out. His nose was painted half-brown and half-white. A scraggly black moustache and goatee beard had been drawn on his face. Half his teeth were white, the other half black. A metal element had been screwed into his head. On the poster's other side his lips were painted red and blue fangs hung out of his mouth. He wore dripping blue glasses, and had a red slash across his forehead. There was a Nazi sign on his left cheek and a dagger through his head. It was the best imaginable incentive to vote for Cameron Thompson.

But Gay said she hoped Hanson won Blair. 'I actually wouldn't mind the rednecks represented in the Parliament by a couple of people, just to defuse it. They've got no power now, so what happens to those feelings of resentment and alienation if she loses? Why not absorb them—let them have a couple of people in Parliament? You don't think she's a horrendous redneck either. She might be a good representative for them; she's not like the people who made that poster.'

'I agree that this alienation is a dangerous thing, and the asset she's got is that she's not evil, she's ignorant,' I replied. 'If she goes down and the establishment thinks she's the problem not the symptom, the next stage could be a clever leader, a much tougher nut to crack and much more dangerous. But she won't take responsibility for her party. She's just a figurehead legitimising its evil policies, trying to split her image from its reality. I used to think she mightn't be racist intentionally, just through ignorance, but who cares when every policy is racist? It just doesn't matter. So I hope she loses.'

We arrived at the primary school where Hanson would vote early, and the man on the One Nation table struck up a conversation. Tony Price was a pig farmer and the president of One Nation's Ipswich branch. He raised the issue of the campaign launch, for which he'd organised the swing band.

'Calling the police was not necessary,' he said. 'Oldfield either did it on purpose or it's part of his normal character. The thing is Australia's got an aggressive media. Remember Frank Sinatra? (Sinatra was black-banned by unions on a 1974 Australian tour for calling female journalists 'buck-and-a-half hookers', and forced to apologise.)

'I don't like Oldfield at all. People in the party are afraid of him actually. I'm not, because I'm just a volunteer—I'm not seeking anything. The most important thing is for people to be happy, and there's things that are unhappy in the Party. I'm not a very aggressive person and I didn't like that launch.

'Do you know about the Solzenitsyn thesis—that you have to experience things to understand them?'

After the drubbing by my colleagues over the campaign launch I could relate to that all right.

'I was speaking to someone this morning [about the launch], and he said, "You shouldn't be criticising the party." And I said, "I'm not criticising, I'm telling you what happened, and I was there." That was a nice function of country people and they weren't used to that level of conflict. The launch went beautifully until then. It's a pity, but these things happen and that's how it is. The most important thing is there are positive people that don't want that and I'm one of these people. You're welcome to come along to the show ground tonight.'

One Nation certainly kept its surprises coming, even on the last day. I showed Tony the two photographs I'd brought to remind Pauline that despite the paranoia on both sides by the campaign's end, we were all just human. One was of her with her arms around Dean and Grant at the Linville races. The other was her surrounded by the 'Please Explain' journalists in front of the lighthouse in Tasmania.

'I'm here because I like Pauline Hanson and I believe in what she's doing,' Tony said. 'The most important thing is that it will be orderly tonight, and we haven't got any problem with you coming in.'

Tony was incensed at the major parties' decisions to put One Nation last on their how-to-vote cards. 'Take the ready-mixed concrete industry. Say there's two firms in a town, and if another firm comes in they collude to put it out of business. That's basically what the Liberal and Labor and National parties have done—collude together to keep a new party out. If you were a concrete manufacturer, you could go along to the competition commission.

'One Nation is a nationalist party. It certainly isn't necessarily racial stuff, it's a matter of putting your own people first before everybody else. I used to live in Wales and they had a Welsh nationalist party there, which was similar to One Nation. They were concerned about their own language and culture, and also protecting industries. They didn't have the problem of being called racist. I'd prefer Australia to be a predominantly white culture, so would most of our members. It means that you want to maintain the culture and the racial balance. That doesn't mean you're prejudiced, it's simply the way things are. The most important thing is that in these areas she represents, she articulates a view. It's a view that's going to carry on because they've suddenly found someone who's going to listen to them. They haven't had anyone listen to them for decades.'

Melanie Wendt and I had planned to try to give Hanson lots of space when she arrived to vote, to keep her calm and cooperative. But the national media contingent had swelled to almost three times its usual size, and when Ollie walked straight up to her car on her arrival all the cameras followed suit. As she voted a crush of media filled the window outside taking pictures. She did the unprecedented again by showing her completed ballot paper to the cameras, revealing she had given her second preference to her main rival, Cameron Thompson, the same man a Hanson supporter had defiled in his front yard. Pauline Hanson was still a Liberal at heart. The Hanson tour reporters stood back and looked on.

She came out glowing, an amazing transformation from her recent cardboard cut-out persona. She looked like she had at the Linville races. She was floating on the relief of ending the campaign and her blind faith that her people would lift her to victory. If she fell over, she'd fall hard.

But she was being crowded, and began to look frazzled. Lisa Millar asked if she'd mind stopping for a few moments for a quick doorstop. I directed her to the spot we'd chosen under a tree. 'Pauline, we actually thought we'd get in the shade, so you look—'

Pauline: 'Relaxed and comfortable.' She giggled as at least 50 media representatives encircled her, pushing in ever closer.

Melanie and I stood facing Pauline at a decent distance at the front of the pack and held our ground. Melanie ended up on her knees, pushing people back, yelling, 'We need to leave some space, for Christ's sake.'

I said, 'Is everyone ready, are you ready Pauline?'

'I'm relaxed Margo, I'm relaxed,' she said, laughing.

She made the amazing prediction that One Nation would win twelve to fifteen seats and six Senate spots. In her days off from the media she'd talked herself into believing in miracles, aided and abetted by doe-eyed male officials like Peter James and Scott Balson, who wanted her happy even by delusion. She wouldn't predict who'd win the election, confessing that she hadn't read the polls in the newspapers (with One Nation steady on 8 percent) because, 'I had some housework to do'.

Peter Doherty: 'This is the most relaxed we've seen you in a few days. What's the secret?'

Hanson: 'I got rid of the media.'

Margo: 'Here we are, Pauline.'

Pauline: 'I'm back!'

Melanie: 'What can we expect at the show ground tonight—a bloody big party?'

Pauline: 'Oh yeah.'

Margo: 'Can we come please?'

Pauline: 'All of you?'

Margo: 'Yes.'

Pauline: 'Are you going to leave the mikes and the cameras behind?'

Melanie: 'Sometimes. Are you happy to do live crosses tonight?'

Pauline: 'Do you mean all you guys would like to party with us, One Nation?'

All: 'Yes.'

Pauline: 'You know you could get a reputation?'

Margo: 'We already have.'

Melanie: 'What's your message to John Howard tonight—to be very, very scared?'

Pauline: 'I think they all need to be. I want to walk into that House, I want to walk back in with One Nation members around me and say "I'm back". I told them I would be.

'I think you got enough out of me,' she said, and walked away chatting to Stephen McDonell about the mood in the polling booths.

'Will you be buying us drinks tonight?' Melanie asked.

Pauline paused. 'No, bring your own.'

We were in.

Walking back to her car, Hanson turned and saw Gay beside me. She smiled. 'How did you end up here?' she asked.

'I just arrived a couple of days ago. At the high point,' Gay replied with a laugh.

'And did you calm this one down?'

'I've had no success at that at all, Pauline.'

'Now you know how I've been feeling,' she said, laughing.

■

The early buzz at the Ipswich show ground hall, among the blue and yellow balloons and wall-to-wall posters of Pauline Hanson wrapped in the flag, was excited and expectant. On very early figures, One Nation was polling well across four States, and with 3 percent of the vote counted in Blair Hanson had 49 percent of the primary vote. The Nine Network's computer was calling Blair for Hanson and radio commentators began talking about that notorious hidden voter support for One Nation. A bright-eyed Scott Balson predicted that One Nation would hold the balance of power in the House of Representatives, before introducing me to his young son, Alex.

'Your father persecutes me,' I said.

'Call it tit for tat,' Balson said with a smile.

The ubiquitous woman from Rosewood and her daughter Alice approached. 'I don't care what happens, I just want her to get in. I want to kick them up the backside. You hate her, don't you?'

'No, I don't hate her, I hate her policies. I like her,' I replied.

By 8.10 p.m., One Nation was polling 9 percent across Australia and 16 percent in Queensland. Nearly one million Australians had cast their vote for One Nation. Hanson was falling away a little, although the commentators' consensus was that she'd scrape in.

Geoff Barker from *The Australian Financial Review* Canberra bureau was incredulous. 'Their campaign veers between farce and soap opera, their polices are lunacy, this woman is bizarre and they're STILL getting all these votes!'

'I'd say you'd be tempted if you lived in a seat like Blair,' I replied.

A crestfallen David Anning arrived to reveal that the early Blair figures were coming in from small outlying country booths, and that only 20 percent of voters in one Ipswich booth had plumped for Hanson. 'It's a real worry,' he said, ten minutes before Oldfield said on TV that the later booths would favour Hanson. Just before Hanson arrived she was down to 37 percent on primaries—the result predicted by *The Sydney Morning Herald* poll two weeks before—and looking shaky. Analysts said she needed at least 42 percent to get over the line with second preferences. The Treasurer, Peter Costello, called her gone on the Nine Network but no one else was game to give her away just yet.

At 8.15 p.m. Pauline Hanson arrived in a multi-layered shimmery purple and red taffeta dress, looking like she was going to a ball. Her face was almost ecstatic, and I thought she must have had some good news from her scrutineers on the leakage of second preferences to her. A horde of media enveloped her and I interviewed her amid the scrum. 'How are you feeling?'

'Good.'

'Do you reckon you've got a good show in Blair?'

'I think so.'

'Do you reckon you can do it?'

'What's the figures?'

She'd come to her election party without a clue what was going on! I put a gloss on her position, now looking dire, to keep her calm. 'Well you're polling around 37, 38 but your scrutineers report significant leakage (of preferences). So it's a little bit lower than you hoped, but no one's prepared to call you down and out except some Victorian called Peter Costello. What do you say?'

'No, I'm very confident. Yep.'

A while later she came across to Network Seven's Peter Doherty for her first live cross and asked Helen for a briefing on how One Nation was going.

Badly—it had a chance to win only Blair.

She asked who her competition was in Blair.

Cameron Thompson, the Liberal to whom she had given her personal preferences.

Scott Balson, who'd set up a computer to see the Electoral Commission results direct and was supposedly her results adviser, called out, 'I love those earrings, Pauline. They're beautiful.'

Hansonites began asking me how she could lose Blair when she was so far ahead on primary votes. They didn't understand preferential voting, and it was just dawning on them that the other parties putting her last was a big problem. They looked so shell-shocked I realised that the One Nation grassroots really had believed they'd scoop the pools just like they had at the Queensland election.

An old man, almost in tears, said he'd ridden his pushbike all around Ipswich putting stuff in letterboxes, and had ridden all the way out to Coleyville to put a personal message in her letter box: 'Best of luck for the third of October, Pauline.'

The woman from Rosewood was crying, and she pleaded with me to make it all right. 'Whatever happens, One Nation has done all right. Can we just get Pauline, just Pauline?'

Balson's wife joined us. 'Have you media people all got closer together chasing her around the countryside for the last few weeks?'

'Well we've got to operate together because no one ever knows where she is. We'll be friends for life.'

'So is there a Liberal media team and a Labor one?'

'People usually take turns, come in for a week and go for a week, but because One Nation is so unpredictable you need to have one person on all the time to start to understand how One Nation does things.'

'But why are there so many?'

'Pauline Hanson, because she's had such success and Sydney and Melbourne and Canberra are confused about what One Nation means, has almost equivalent media to the national leaders. While Meg Lees is not trailed around by the media, Pauline Hanson is, and it's actually a compliment to One Nation that that's happening.'

'Granted it's coverage, but what I would argue about is the bias,' she said.

We decided not to argue about that and had a beer instead.

The mood was turning against the media as the devastation of picking up no Lower House seats and Hanson's probable loss in Blair became clear. The cameras, especially from national current affairs programs, were giving her no space at a time when she was looking like falling apart.

'There's talk they'll send us out before she gives her speech. The cameras are crowding her out,' Melanie said.

At 9.20 p.m. Lisa Millar stood with Pauline awaiting a live cross to the ABC. Lisa hadn't picked up the latest results and asked Helen and me for an update. 'She's lost it,' Helen said. Hanson stared at us with the same shocked look I'd seen in the eyes of the supporters to whom I'd just explained the preferential voting system. No one in her party had told her the bad news.

With 76 percent of the vote counted, Hanson was stuck on 37 percent of primaries, and One Nation's only victory was the election of Heather Hill to the Senate at the expense of the National Party. Pauline Hanson had resisted all pressure to stand for the Senate instead of Blair on the grounds that she had to give her other candidates hope. And she'd resist all pressure to take Heather Hill's place, too. 'Let the people judge me,' she'd said so often, and so they had.

In his last piece of crackpot political advice, Peter James advised Hanson to throw the media out before her speech, a move which would mean that the million odd voters who'd put their faith in her would not get to see her thank them. As he issued the demand for our departure at the microphone, Hanson was at the bar signing autographs, and I asked her to autograph the back of my T-shirt. I'd worn the one she'd lent me when I'd stayed over. She signed and dated it. 'I'm not going to get that back, am I?' she said. 'No,' I replied. Grant had got her to autograph his Henty Field Day gumboots a week before; this was my souvenir of the most disturbing experience of my journalistic career.

DEAN SEWELL

Peter James says no to filming Hanson. She was almost in tears. He later ordered the media out, but no one obeyed until Hanson's campaign journalists led the way.

I asked her what she'd do now, and she murmured that she'd get on with 'the next stage of my life'.

A young woman I'd seen on the One Nation table outside Pauline's office on Friday told me she'd been spat on at a polling booth. 'I had a lot of people abuse me today. I was in the sun all day from seven in the morning until six tonight, and people ripped up my ballot papers and threw bits of paper in my face. They took the number plate of my car. For the first time I was angry.' She began to cry.

Scott Balson asked me if Hanson really had lost. 'My feeling about this whole bloody election is that it's a great tragedy. No one wants the two-party system and we've got it again,' he said.

I thanked him for One Nation's decision to let the media in. 'Any campaign is always a shitfight between the media and the politicians. There's nothing new in this stuff except One Nation doesn't know any rules at all, so we get a bit hysterical. If at the end of a campaign the warring parties can't shake hands and have a drink together then it's not Australia any more.'

'With the Internet, it's going to be very interesting in three years' time to see how that election is fought,' Balson said. 'What I've been doing is just a taste.'

We were evicted as the TVs confirmed a Coalition win. Hanson had gone down after winning 48 percent of the vote on a two-party preferred basis. Cameron Thompson, with just over half of Hanson's primary vote, had edged her out, and now she was crying. David Anning came outside and I asked why One Nation had left it to journalists to break to her the news of her defeat.

'She never knows. It's not up to me. I kept saying, 'You're dreadful communicators.' It's a bit of a sad story really because her heart is definitely in the right place. She's been betrayed by so many people around her that she doesn't know who to trust any more. Pauline believes in people and is a bit naive. Different people talk to Pauline and she doesn't know who to believe.'

Pauline Hanson had proclaimed for two years that she would have a voice no matter what. Her voice—despite its lack of clarity and outright refusal to adjust to the demands of Australia's political and media institutions—had reverberated around the nation and the world. She'd forced policy change, created fear and insecurity, triggered doubts about our national identity, fractured the National Party, scared the hell out of the Coalition and Labor, and triggered thousands of heated debates on politics and values among Australians who had previously either ignored or disdained such matters. She'd become a cultural icon and an unlikely celebrity who'd forced the big cities to consider the regions, an engagement between the haves and have nots, and a confrontation of the new culture by the old. Just when racism had largely become socially unacceptable, she'd given racists the courage to hurt and humiliate their fellow citizens. And she'd done it all with only a strange and crude former foot soldier of the Liberal Party as her political brain, without funds, and despite the total lack of professionalism which had become part of her appeal. One Nation had let maniacs and fruit loops walk off the street and get preselected in the name of an ill-educated, narrow-minded, hard-working, proud small businesswoman who'd proved a charismatic communicator with Pauline's People.

Now, at a hall on a hill in Ipswich, there were more media looking in through the glass louvres than there were people to look at. The media on the outside were watching the death of a phenomenon within.

We could not hear her concession speech, and I found a half-open louvre to put my tape recorder through. A young woman on the inside walked over glaring and shut it, but had second thoughts and returned to open it again.

Pauline congratulated Heather Hill, reassured her people that she was still president of One Nation, and said thank you to Peter James and her staff. She blamed no one and did not mention David Oldfield. 'But anyway, there's been a lot of work and effort and I thank every one of you for manning the booths in Blair. Let's just continue working together.'

She asked her children, Adam and Lee, to the podium, and held Lee's hand. With a rueful half-smile to let her audience know she was sending up her most famous campaign comment, she said: 'It's her fifteenth birthday today and I've had her working on the polling booths. What sort of a mother would do that to her daughter?' She hugged Lee as Pauline's People sang 'Happy Birthday', said 'Thank you very much, I love you all', and left the stage in tears.

Outside in the dark, a TV set blared out the final campaign speeches of our national leaders. Kim Beazley said: 'We must as a people constantly turn *to* each other and not on each other and against each other. We must as a people, and I believe we do, operate in a way that gets the very best out of the multicultural and multi-racial society that we are.'

John Howard said: 'I also want to commit myself very genuinely to the cause of true reconciliation with the Aboriginal people by the centenary of Federation.' A Howard promise made post-election, after both parties had shut down the race debate during it. Strange, that Pauline Hanson had forced on John Howard a Wik settlement more favourable to Aboriginal interests, and had now forced him to take responsibility for an issue he had always seen as being of secondary importance.

The major parties had closed ranks and swapped preferences to solve the problem of One Nation's challenge to their power, but now they had to try to address the problem of why so many Australians were prepared to vote for it.

Declaring victory over One Nation, National Party leader Tim Fischer said: 'The National Party has stood up and repulsed this full-frontal assault from One Nation. This is one of the finest hours for the National

DEAN SEWELL

Hanson's children offer comfort after the crowd has sung 'Happy Birthday' to her daughter Lee.

Party in its contribution to the body politic, the political fabric, of Australia.' His job had just begun, as had that of all the parties and all our democratic institutions, including the media.

The last picture Dean took on the campaign was a long shot of an old woman slumped in a chair, staring at nothing in an empty hall papered with Pauline Hanson posters.

■

On Sunday morning I decided not to camp outside her home. It would feel like chasing a bird with a broken wing. I didn't think there was a chance she'd talk because she wouldn't have anything to say yet, on her future or that of the Party. She had a lot of thinking to do, and that was after the crying was over. But my competition, News Limited, was out there, so I steeled myself and called.

A thin voice answered the phone. She didn't want to talk so I suggested we have a drink in a few weeks. 'No. You're flying back to Canberra. I'm staying here in Ipswich. Our paths will never cross again.'

INDEX

Page numbers in *italics* refer to photographs.